IMAGES
of America

FOLLY BEACH

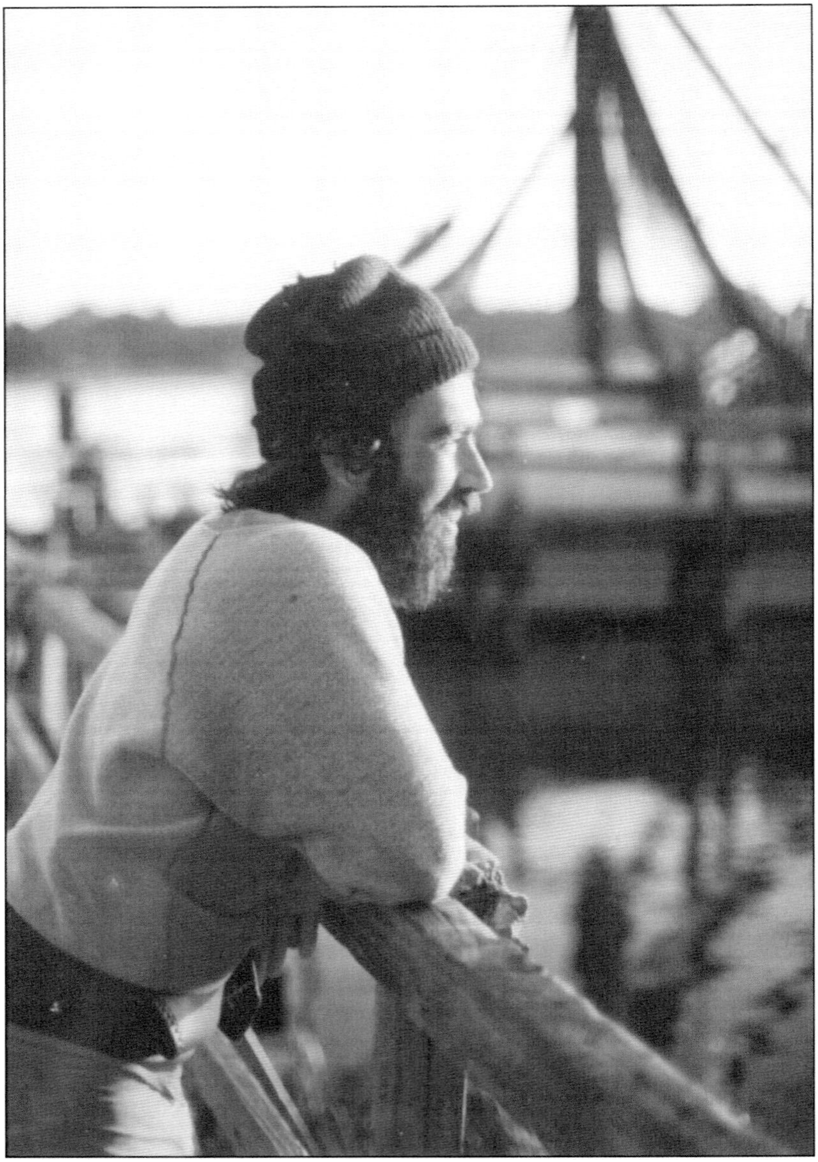

Folly's past and future are shaped by the sea. Ancient sand dunes now provide a haven for cottages and million-dollar homes, side by side. Sands on the beach are constantly shifting with the tide, crumbling buildings like sandcastles whenever a hurricane passes over. The people who cling to this fragile barrier island have historically lived close to the land and drawn sustenance from the water, including Bill Perry, seen here, who made a good living as a commercial crabber. Shrimp, fish, oysters, and crabs do not get any fresher than on Folly Beach. (Courtesy of Bill Perry.)

On the Cover: Built in 1876 to replace the original Morris Island Lighthouse destroyed during the Civil War, the iconic brick beacon emerging from the ocean at Folly's eastern tip has evoked feelings of wonder and pride in generations of visitors and residents. Built nearly a quarter-mile from the water's edge, erosion has left the structure stranded in the surf. Recent efforts by the Save the Light organization have helped assure that the lighthouse will stand for generations to come, beckoning people home to Folly Beach. (Courtesy of Daniel Timmons.)

IMAGES
of America

FOLLY BEACH

Stratton Lawrence

ARCADIA
PUBLISHING

ISBN 978-0-7385-9859-8

Published by Arcadia Publishing
Charleston, South Carolina

Printed in the United States of America

Library of Congress Control Number: 2012946549

For all general information, please contact Arcadia Publishing:
Telephone 843-853-2070
Fax 843-853-0044
E-mail sales@arcadiapublishing.com
For customer service and orders:
Toll-Free 1-888-313-2665

Visit us on the Internet at www.arcadiapublishing.com

This book is dedicated to the people who call Folly Beach home—some for a season, some for a century.

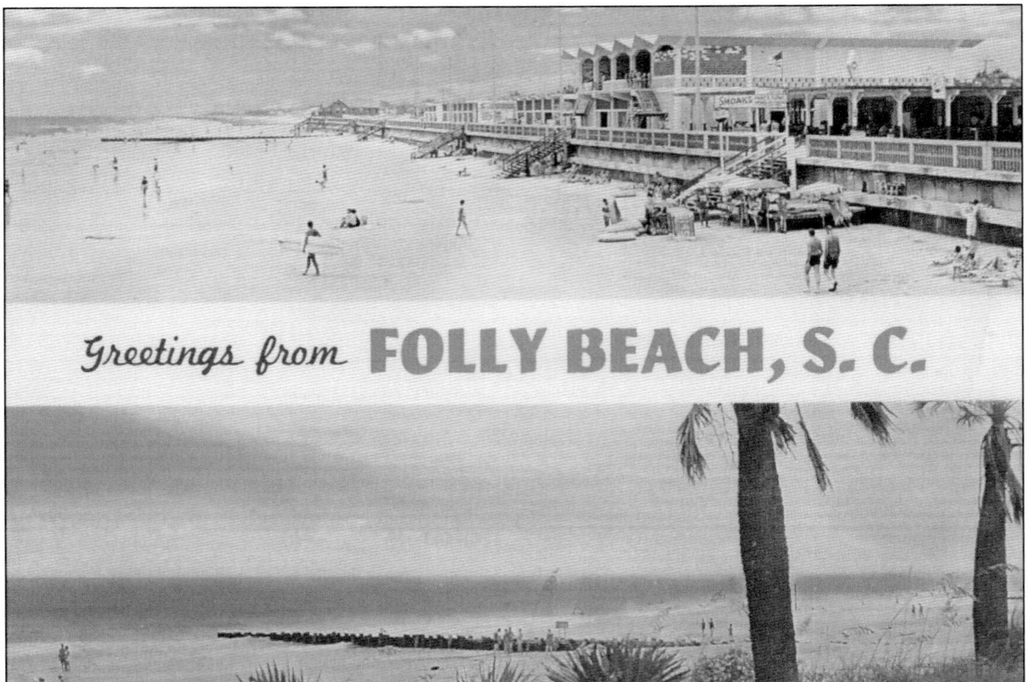

No matter where you live and how old you are, no place will ever be the same as it is in the moment you love it best. Fortunately, those moments still occur daily on Folly Beach. (Postcard photographs by Jack Wilbanks, courtesy of Maebelle Barnett Bazzel.)

Contents

ACKNOWLEDGMENTS

This place is different from any place I've seen or lived in before. It's been hard for me to work here, as the wild waves, playing the role of siren, beckon me every time I get stuck, which is often. And I, like a weak sailor, turn to them, causing many hours to be knocked into a thousand useless bits.

—George Gershwin, on trying to work from home on Folly Beach

My immense gratitude goes out to Maebelle Barnett Bazzel, whose efforts to preserve the photographs of the "old Folly Beach" were invaluable to this book. Wallace Benson, Greta Anderson, Robert and LaNelle Barber, Betty and Henry Schultz, Cliff and Martha Harvey, and Bill Perry and Betty Sue Cowsert each opened their homes and their family treasures to me during my research, demonstrating incredible patience, trust, and genuine Folly Beach hospitality. Sincere thanks go out to Patricia "Cookie" Jamison Wilbanks Bragg, Cheryl Fennell, Marlene Estridge, Andie Weathers, Lynn Pierotti, Robert Bohrn, LaJuan Kennedy, Carol McLendon Porter, Vivian Browning, McKevlin's Surf Shop, Omar Colon, Susan Breslin, Cramer Gallimore, Lish Thompson, Jared Booth, Teresa Parrish, Andy Lassiter, Caroline Richardson, Richard Brendel, Bob and Lynn Lawrence, Cal and Billie McRae, and my editor, Maggie Bullwinkel, for their contributions and help with this project. This is not the first book about Folly Beach. No Folly-lover's library would be complete without copies of *Folly Beach: A Brief History*, by Gretchen Stringer-Robinson, and James Hagy's *Edge of America: Folly Beach*. The efforts of these predecessors provided insight and clarification to my own research on many occasions. Recognition is also due to Capt. Jack Sheppard, who restored in me the belief that pirates do still exist on Folly Beach.

Most of all, I would like to thank both Goose the dog and my beautiful fiancé—and perhaps by the time you read this, wife—Hunter McRae, for tolerating me during the frenzied month-long push to complete this project as my deadline loomed. Sometimes we all need a reminder to relax and slow down. It's Folly.

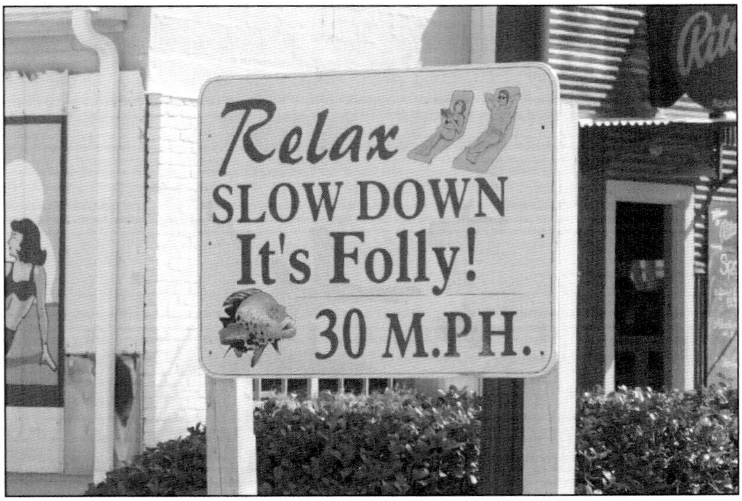

INTRODUCTION

When I was a freshman at Davidson College in 1999, a photograph taped to the wall of a friend's dorm room caught my eye. In the image, two boys are wading through waist-deep water at the base of the most incredible lighthouse I had ever seen. "Where is this?" I asked, imagining some faraway place. "It's in Charleston, where I'm from," said my new friend, Daniel Timmons.

That same photograph appears on the cover of this book.

I made my first trip to Folly Beach soon thereafter. Although I had attended Camp St. Christopher on Seabrook Island as a child and made several trips to Charleston with my family from our home in Darlington, South Carolina, we had never made it to Folly.

Occasionally, over the four years of college, I would convince a friend or two—usually late at night—that we should make the three-and-a-half-hour trek down for a day at the beach. Arriving at 4:00 a.m., my go-to plan was always to drive out to the north end of Folly Beach and fall asleep in the dunes, waking up with a sunburn—but in the precise place I wanted to be, more than anywhere else in the world.

I moved to Charleston in 2003, and to Folly Beach in 2007. By 2010, I was offered a position as the editor of the *Folly Current*, a short-lived local newspaper on the island. Attending council meetings and interacting with citizens on a daily basis, my fascination grew from a love for the natural beauty of this barrier island into a profound appreciation for the people who have spent their lives on this occasionally brutal, but always endearing, wild sliver of land. It is because of these people that this book exists.

If you want to build a community with genuine character, put it at the end of a dead-end road. Folly Beach draws the occasional comparison to Key West, and not just because Jimmy Buffett likes to hang out here. Like the Conch Republic, there is only one way on and off of Folly Beach. Whether you are running from something or just out exploring, when you reach the end of the line, you either have to turn around or put a stake in the ground and settle down.

For the first families that chose to stay put, living on Folly Beach was not easy. Mosquitoes, brackish wells, and sticky humidity are far less bearable without the comfort of electric fans and filtered tap water. Even then, most locals grew accustomed to sweating through summer nights, and the bugs were just another animal in the yard, accompanying the pigs, goats, and horses that were once plentiful on the island.

What is it that binds us to a place so brutally fickle? Folly Beach does its best to hold on to its sliver of geography, but the sea is forever its master. It's that feeling of truly living on the "Edge of America" that holds people here, despite the perpetual threat of the ocean lashing out and taking their homes and livelihoods with it.

The truth is, once someone visits Folly Beach, they dream of the island for the rest of their life. There is magic in the sand and water here that is unparalleled along the Atlantic seaboard. Perhaps it is the island's dark history. During the colonial era, Folly was called Coffin Land—where people sick from an ocean transit would be left to recover, or more likely, to perish.

During the Civil War, Folly Beach served as a Union military camp, integral to the Yankees' plan to take Charleston via Morris Island. The first "city of Folly Beach" began when as many as 13,000 Union soldiers labored in the island's woods and along its shores.

Folly's sole historical marker commemorates the 55th Massachusetts Volunteer Infantry, the African American regiment that laid down their lives on these shores. Beneath today's friendly sands and gentle waves, Folly Beach harbors a dark history, hidden from the eyes and minds of today's revelers, who are content to smile in the sun.

Beginning in the early 1900s, an island once cursed by soldiers for its harsh conditions was quickly transformed into a subtropical paradise, where busy city dwellers went for respite. With a paved road to the beach came a bowling alley, a Ferris wheel, a bustling Center Street economy, and national notoriety. George Gershwin is among our most famous early tourists, renting a bungalow in 1934 while he wrote *Porgy and Bess.*

Center Street remains the hub of Folly Beach, hosting festivals that draw crowds from around the state several times a year, including the Sea and Sand Festival, Folly Gras, and A Taste of Folly. These street parties often attract old-timers who recall the days when Folly Beach was a constant celebration each weekend, from nights spent shagging on the pier to long days playing in the surf.

Although Folly's economy has shifted to being almost entirely tourism-based, a few fishermen and oystermen still make their living plying these waters, most setting out from Crosby's Seafood, Bowen's Island, and Backman's Seafood on Sol Legare Road. These timeless workers tell the continuing story of an island shaped by its proximity to the sea, tucked between the unforgiving Atlantic and a tranquil expanse of salt marsh.

Hurricanes have brought great change to Folly Beach, including in 1940, 1959, 1979, and Hugo in 1989. The devastation wrought by each opened the door for new waves of development, dramatically altering the landscape of the island as an influx of visitors and new residents took advantage of affordable real estate.

In 2011, Folly Beach experienced heavy erosion due to the offshore swell of Hurricane Irene, underlying its fragile nature and the risk homeowners take buying property on an ever-changing barrier island.

For those who have spent their life here, the alterations over the last 80 years have been dramatic. On a stretch of sand where the ocean tides rule, change is a natural constant. Today, those who call Folly home love their six-and-a-quarter miles of paradise more than ever.

Politics have always been entertaining—and frustrating—on Folly Beach, generally because of the passion that residents put into their island. "Folly politics boil beneath the surface," reads one August 1951 headline in the *News and Courier.* Those same words have rung true in each decade since, as each generation fears that change will alter their island forever, from the nine-story Holiday Inn built in the 1980s to the drinking ban on the beach in 2012.

Police chiefs still get fired and leave in disgrace. Mayors occasionally resign in a huff. From the formation of the township commission to govern the island (1936) to the establishment of Folly Beach as a town (1951) to its incorporation into a city (1973), each step of making Folly "official" has been met with a stubborn, independent spirit by islanders. But the magic of Folly Beach perseveres.

Countless postcards sent from Folly cite its "excellent year-round climate" and "tempered ocean breezes," lauding the island as "one of the finest bathing beaches in America." "Restful and bewitching," states another.

One postcard discovered in the research for this book reads, "In addition to these scenic and climatic wonders, the island abounds in numerous enchanting legends."

Those legends continue to grow. Turn the page to discover their roots.

One

A Wild Sliver of Land

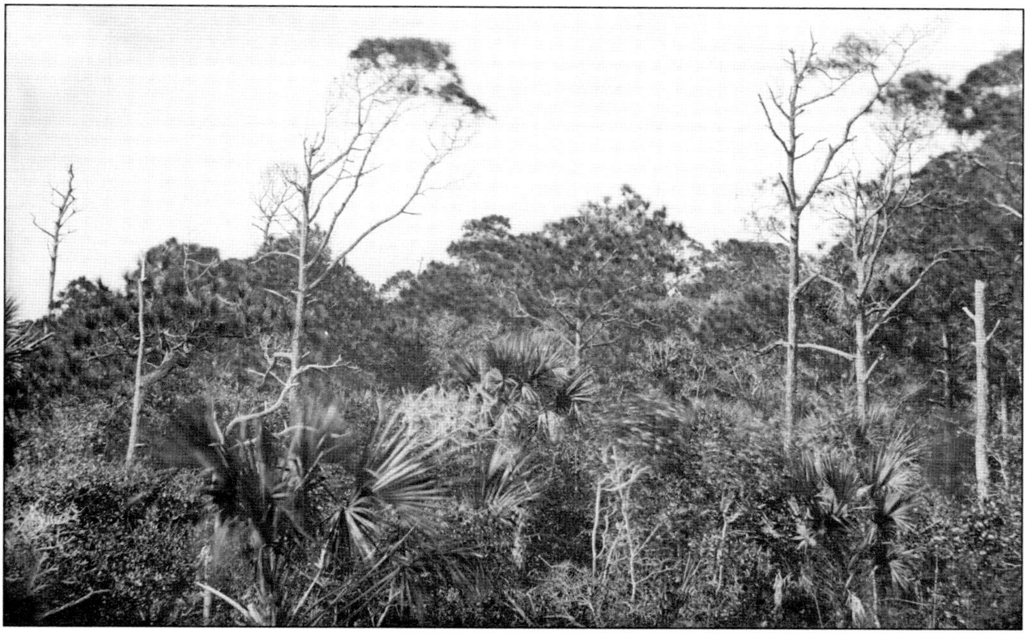

Scoop up a handful of sand on Folly Beach, and you are literally holding the mountains in your hands. Over millions of years, the ancient Appalachian range eroded, depositing sediment downstream and into the ocean. Currents and waves shaped that sand as the ocean level receded, eventually leaving behind barrier islands like Folly Beach, a rugged pile of sand boldly protecting the salt marsh and the rest of South Carolina behind it. Folly's maritime forest was particularly developed among coastal islands, with pine, oak, magnolia, and palmetto trees. The first English settlers used the Old English term "Folly" to label islands with dense foliage. Only on present-day Folly Beach did the name stick, a fitting moniker for a wild island that still retains its natural character 300 years later. (Courtesy of the Library of Congress.)

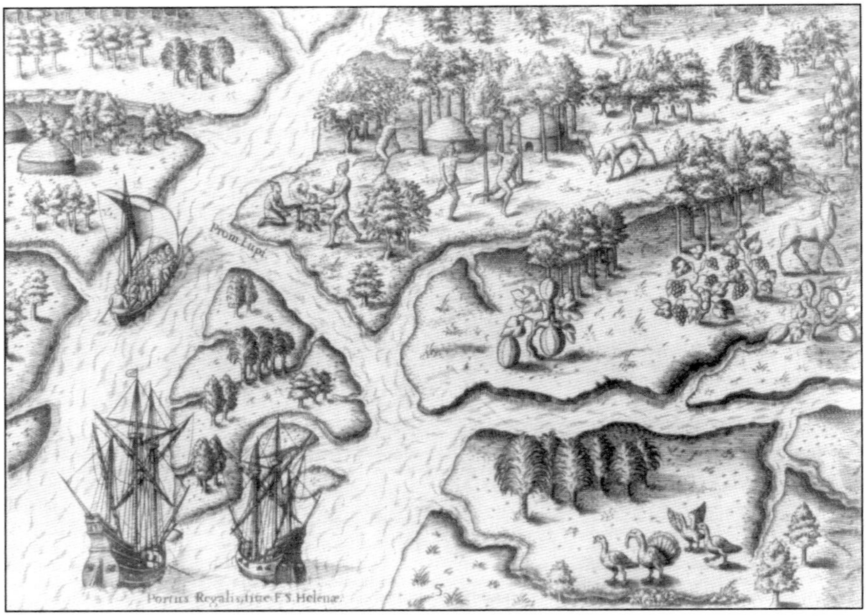

By the time the English established Charles Towne in 1670, the Native Americans living in the Lowcountry had been rendered nearly extinct by a century of interaction with Spanish and French explorers. The Bohicket tribe, a subgroup of the Cusabo, is the most likely to have utilized Folly as a summer hunting and fishing ground. This 1591 engraving by Theodor de Bry depicts a French expedition to the Port Royal area, near Beaufort. (Courtesy of the Library of Congress.)

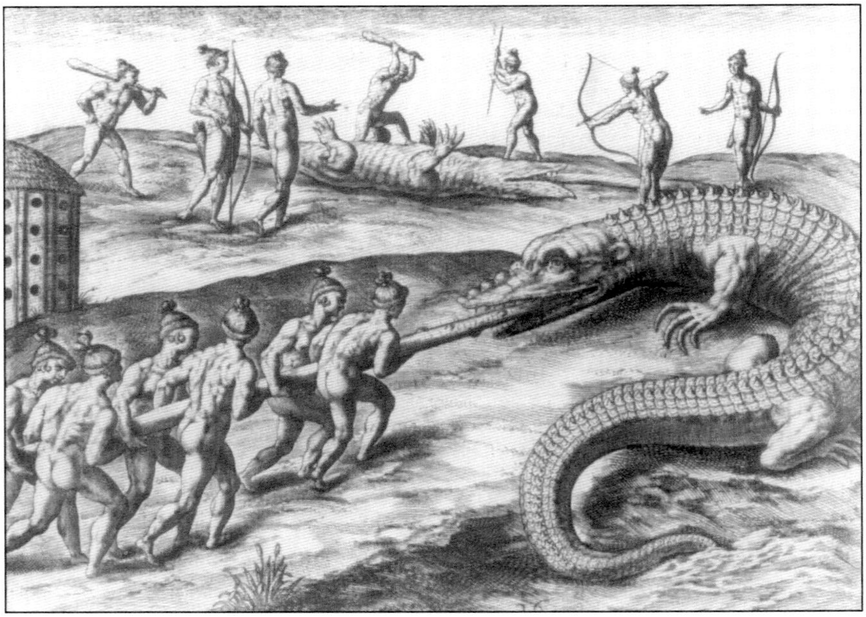

"There remains now . . . nothing of them but their names, within 300 miles of our sea coast," wrote South Carolina lieutenant governor William Bull Jr. in 1770 of the state's natives, demonstrating why, nearly 250 years later, we know very little about the early inhabitants of our sea islands. De Bry's engravings, derived from watercolors by explorer Jacques Le Moyne, offer our best glimpse of what life along the coast must have entailed. An alligator was killed by shoving a pole down its throat, followed by an attack with clubs and arrows. (Courtesy of the Library of Congress.)

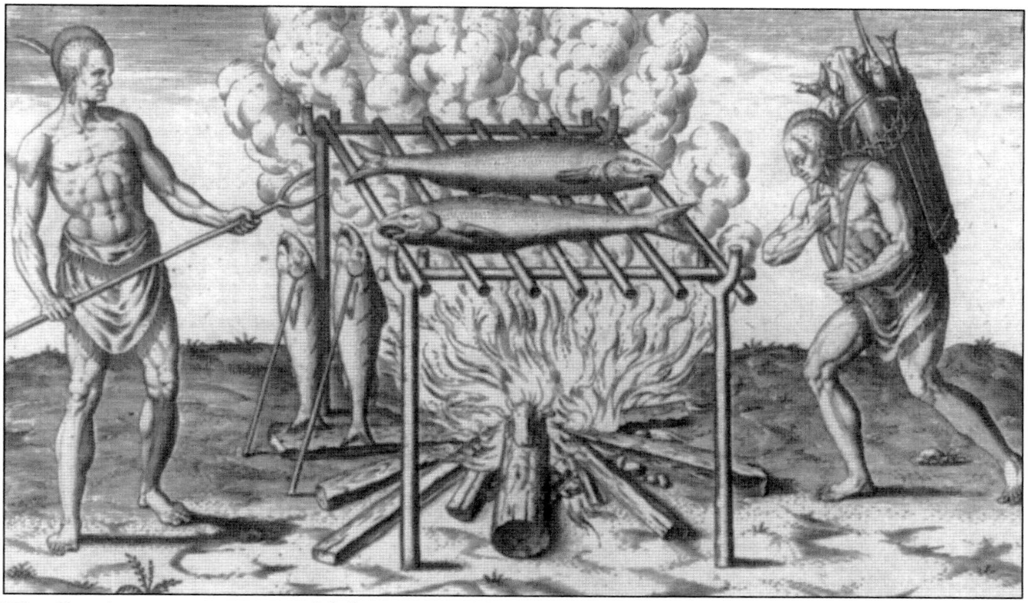

The Cusabo natives were avid fishermen and hunters of deer, turkey, bear, and elk, supplemented by farming corn, squash, beans, melons, and even peach and plum trees. It is possible that today's practice of smoking a pig has its roots in the native method of barbecuing meat over tree-limb grates and an open fire, as seen here. Estimates place the Cusabo population around Charleston at 3,200 in 1600, a population diminished to 535 by the year 1715, after many natives were shipped to the West Indies as slaves. By 1750, all remaining Cusabo had integrated into tribes further inland. (Courtesy of the Library of Congress.)

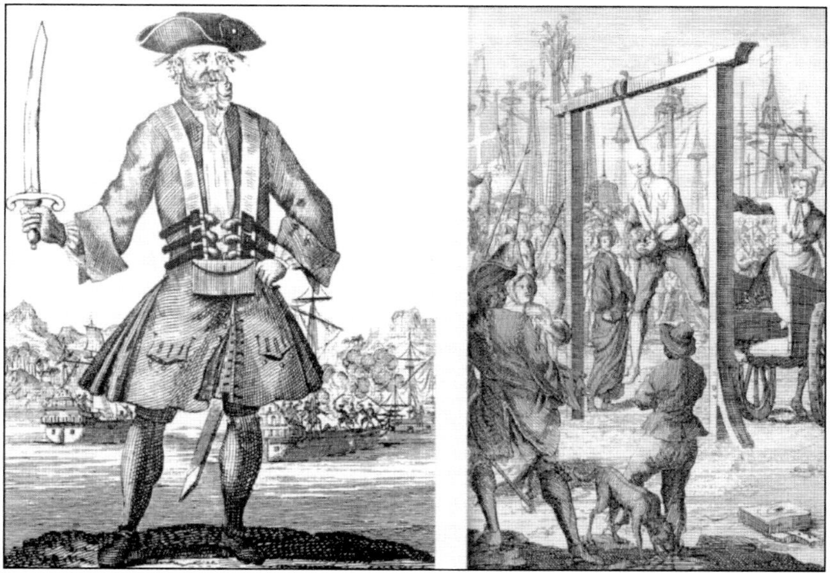

The first Europeans to regularly overnight on Folly Beach were likely pirates, including Edward "Blackbeard" Teach (left) and Stede Bonnet (right), known as the Gentleman Pirate, who preyed on merchant ships sailing past the island in 1717 and 1718. Bonnet was hanged on the Battery in downtown Charleston in December 1718. Stories of pirate treasure persisted in the Union's camps on Folly during the Civil War, when ghost stories and rumors of hidden treasure were common among the soldiers. (Courtesy of the Library of Congress.)

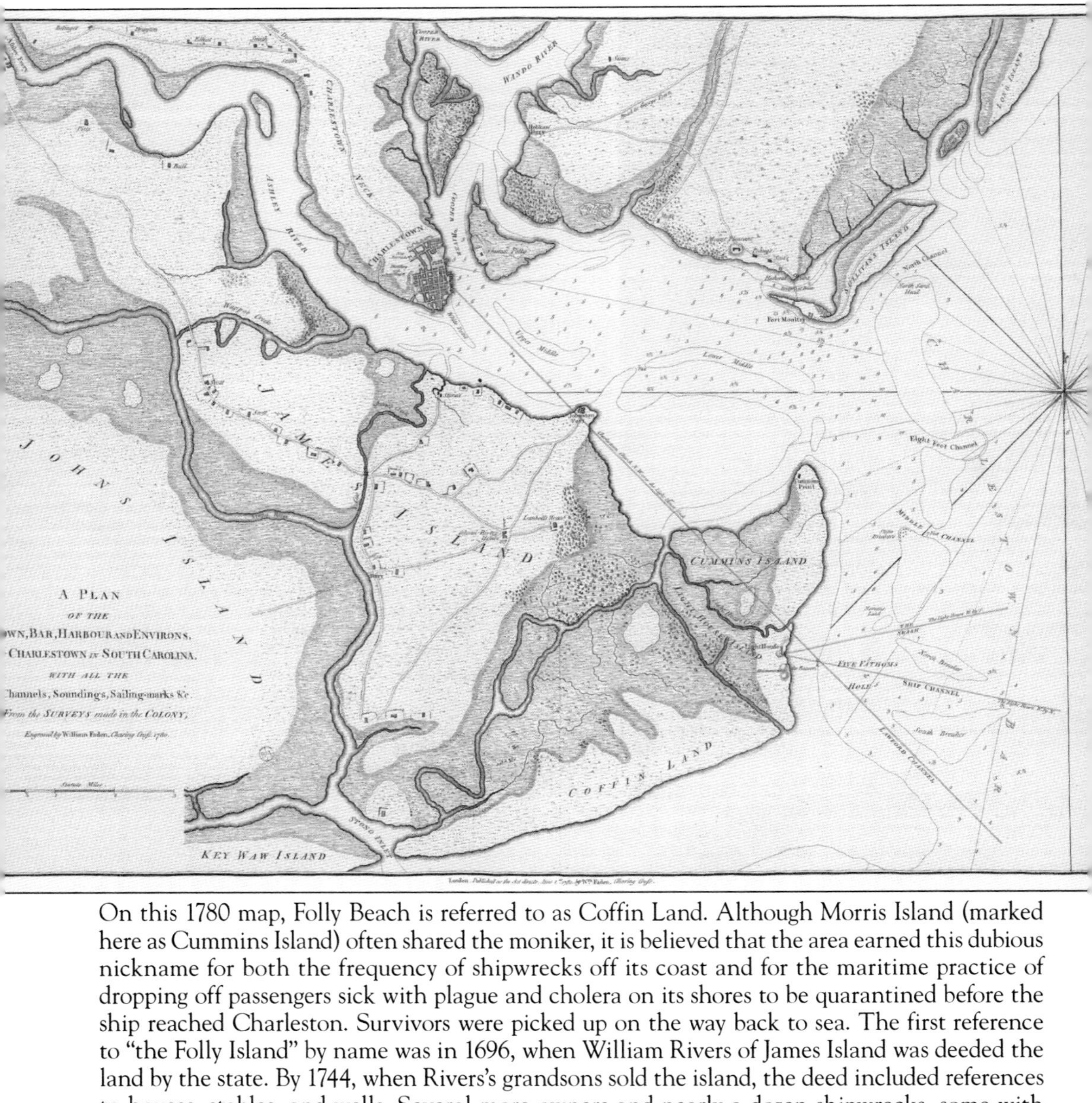

On this 1780 map, Folly Beach is referred to as Coffin Land. Although Morris Island (marked here as Cummins Island) often shared the moniker, it is believed that the area earned this dubious nickname for both the frequency of shipwrecks off its coast and for the maritime practice of dropping off passengers sick with plague and cholera on its shores to be quarantined before the ship reached Charleston. Survivors were picked up on the way back to sea. The first reference to "the Folly Island" by name was in 1696, when William Rivers of James Island was deeded the land by the state. By 1744, when Rivers's grandsons sold the island, the deed included references to houses, stables, and wells. Several more owners and nearly a dozen shipwrecks, some with fatalities, passed through Folly during the 18th century. In 1822, Folly Island's 2,640 acres sold at public auction on Charleston's courthouse steps for $11,000 to Andrew Milne. It was under his ownership that Folly Island first made news, after the ship *Amelia*, bound from New York to New Orleans, wrecked on its shores, resulting in a cholera outbreak. Charleston's city leaders scrambled to prevent an epidemic, sending members of the city guard to Folly to prevent passengers from escaping the island. Of the 120 passengers, 20 perished while marooned on Folly. Soon thereafter, Milne sold the island to Peter Campbell, who built the first known plantation house on the island, most likely growing Sea Island cotton. (Courtesy of Thomson Park Revolutionary War Battle Site.)

Two

Blood in the Sand

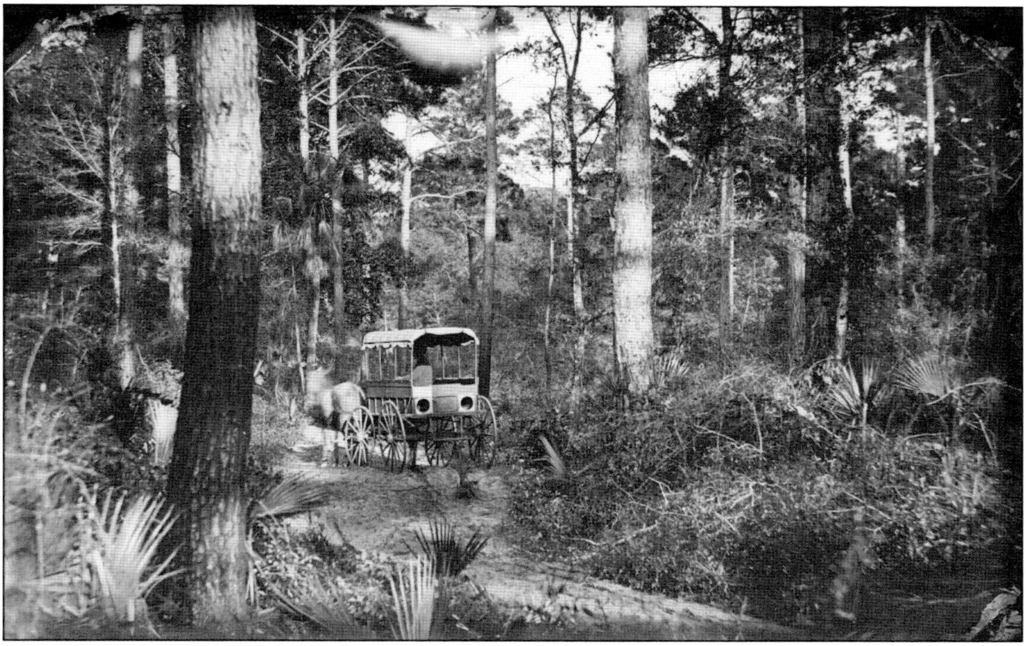

The first roads on Folly Island were cut by Union troops who camped there during the Civil War. Thanks to the barrier island's thick foliage and high canopy, the North was able to move troops and artillery throughout the island without tipping off the Confederate troops on Morris Island to the scale of their presence. "It was so well covered that Confederate pickets and spies did not realize that a tremendous battery armed with 47 guns was being constructed at the east end of the island until the morning when these guns opened up and drove the Confederate forces away from the west end of Morris Island," wrote James Allen in a May 31, 1925, article in the *News and Courier*. "It shows how completely screened this old military road was from hostile observation." Those roads, cut by the thousands of Union troops stationed on Folly Island in 1863 and 1864, are now traversed by bicyclists and golf carts. (Photograph by Haas & Peale, courtesy of the Library of Congress.)

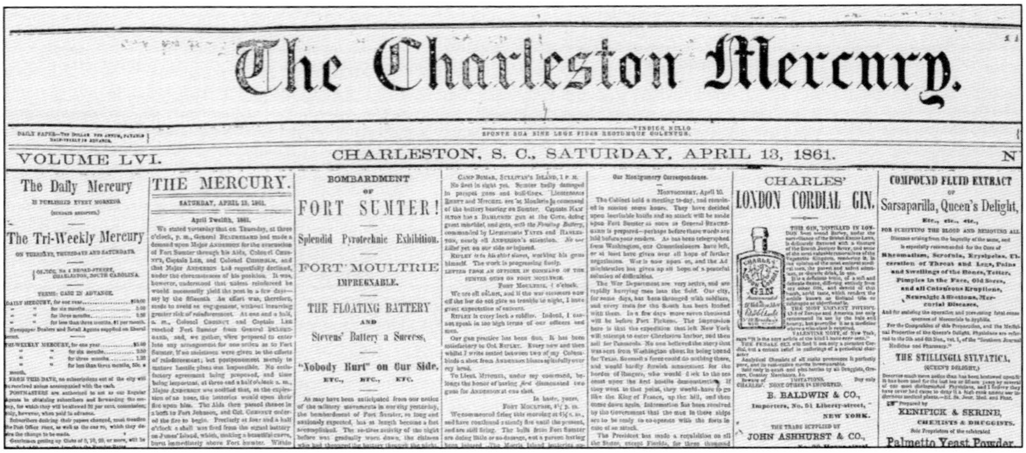

The Charleston Mercury.

VOLUME LVI. CHARLESTON, S. C., SATURDAY, APRIL 13, 1861.

The Daily Mercury

The Tri-Weekly Mercury

TERMS: CASH IN ADVANCE.

THE MERCURY.

SATURDAY, APRIL 13, 1861.

April Twelfth, 1861.

BOMBARDMENT OF FORT SUMTER!

Splendid Pyrotechnic Exhibition.

FORT MOULTRIE IMPREGNABLE.

THE FLOATING BATTERY AND Stevens' Battery a Success,

"Nobody Hurt" on Our Side,

ETC., ETC., ETC.

Our Montgomery Correspondence.

CHARLES' LONDON CORDIAL GIN.

B. BALDWIN & CO.,

Importers, No. 51 Liberty-street,

NEW YORK.

THE TRADE SUPPLIED BY JOHN ASHHURST & CO.,

COMPOUND FLUID EXTRACT OF Sarsaparilla, Queen's Delight,

Etc., etc., etc.,

THE STILLINGIA SYLVATICA,

(QUEEN'S DELIGHT.)

KENIFICK & SKRINE,

CHEMISTS & DRUGGISTS.

Palmetto Yeast Powder

The first combat shots of the Civil War occurred within earshot of Folly Island. When the Confederate batteries around Charleston, including on Morris and James Islands, began their assault on the Federal soldiers at Fort Sumter on April 12, 1861, residents sat along the Battery and toasted on their balconies. The following day's headlines in the *Charleston Mercury* were celebratory, touting the "splendid pyrotechnic exhibition" that began with one 10-inch mortar soaring across the harbor "like a firefly." With the headline " 'Nobody hurt' on our side," few could have predicted that the four-year war that began that day would claim more than half a million American lives. (Courtesy of the *Charleston Mercury*.)

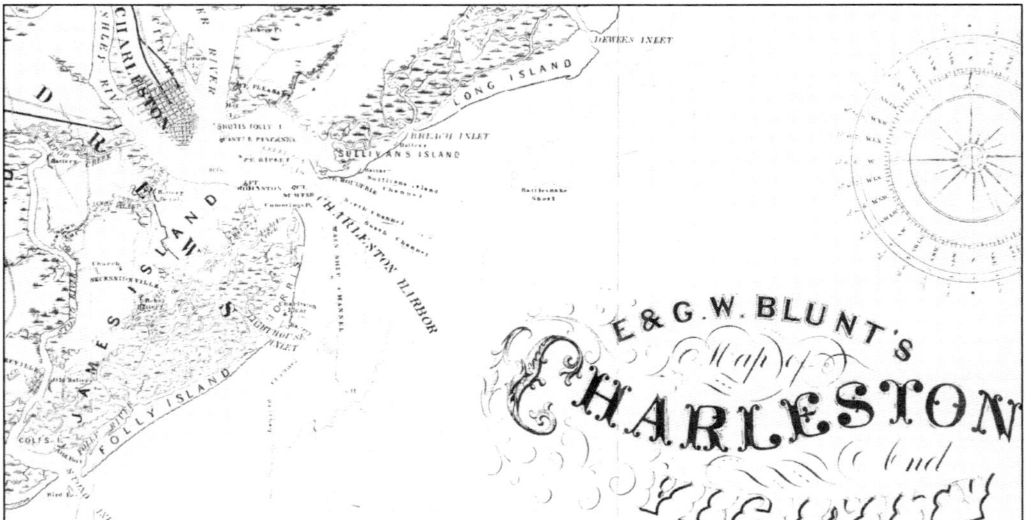

Soon after this map was created in 1862, Union forces began to utilize Folly Island as a major camp and staging ground. Beginning in March 1863, thousands of troops arrived to an island of dense woods and seasonal ponds that harbored alligators, snakes, and a relentless mosquito population. The North controlled the Stono Inlet, moving soldiers to Coles Island before transferring them to Folly. Notice the placement on the map of the original Morris Island Lighthouse, as well as the identification of the small island housing Castle Pinckney in Charleston Harbor as Shutes Folly. Big Folly (the west end) and Little Folly (the east end) were effectively split by the present-day Washout, crossable only at low tide. (Courtesy of Charleston County Library.)

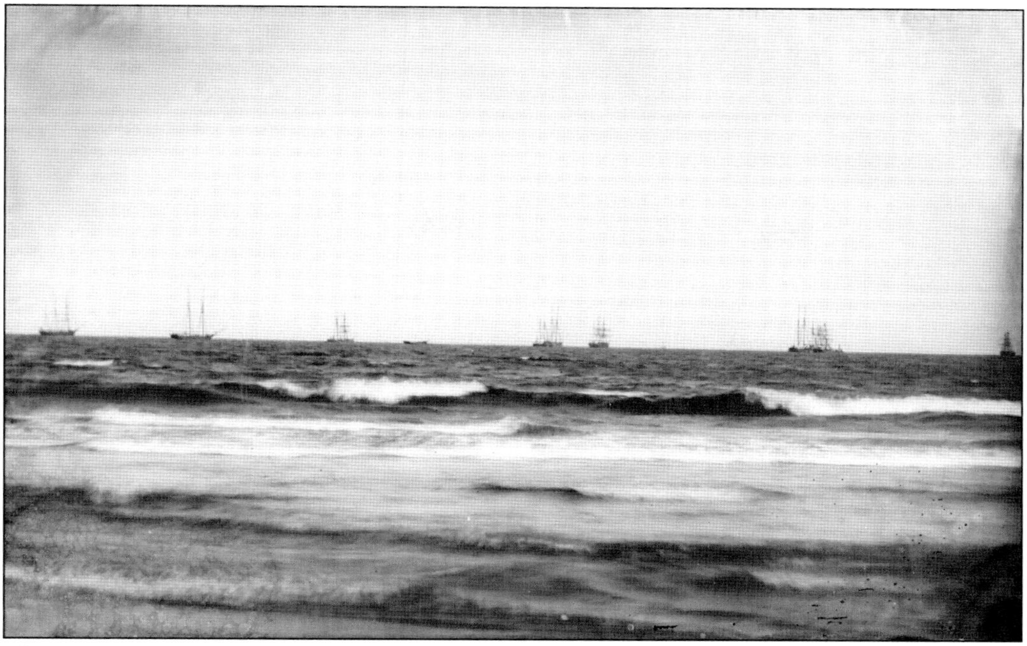

The Union's blockade of Charleston Harbor must have been a comforting site to Northern soldiers hunkered down on Folly Island in the summer of 1863. The Confederates never surrendered Fort Sumter and the Union failed to take it, forcing an offshore standoff that persisted until Union general William T. Sherman's march through the south in February 1865. The barren waves and blockading ships dotting the horizon off Folly's coast have since been replaced with shrimp boats and surfers. (Photograph by Haas & Peale, courtesy of the Library of Congress.)

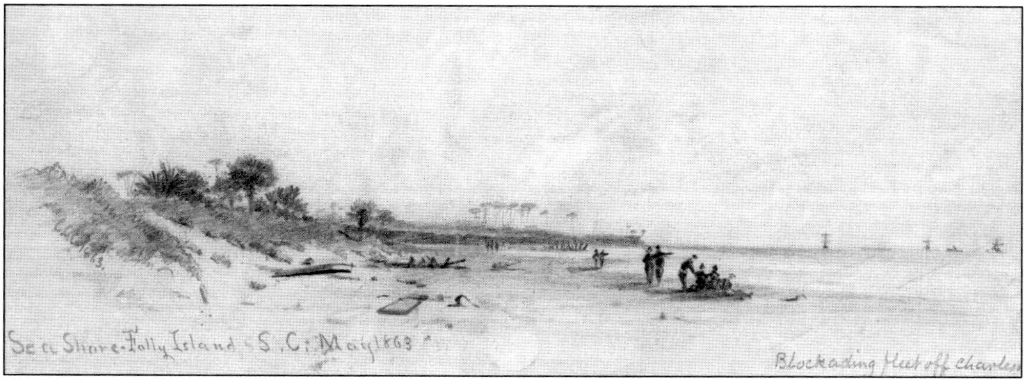

This panoramic pencil drawing by artist Alfred Waud illustrates the wild and sizeable dunes on Folly as well as Union soldiers pointing toward the sea and the ships forming the blockade. Drawn in May 1863, the coming summer would prove to be the most eventful in Folly's history. The island served as the staging ground for Union general Quincy A. Gillmore's plan to take Charleston via an attack on Morris Island. At the peak of Union occupation in 1863, as many as 13,000 troops were based on Folly, forming a tent city with far more residents than the island has ever supported in the 150 years since. (Courtesy of the Library of Congress.)

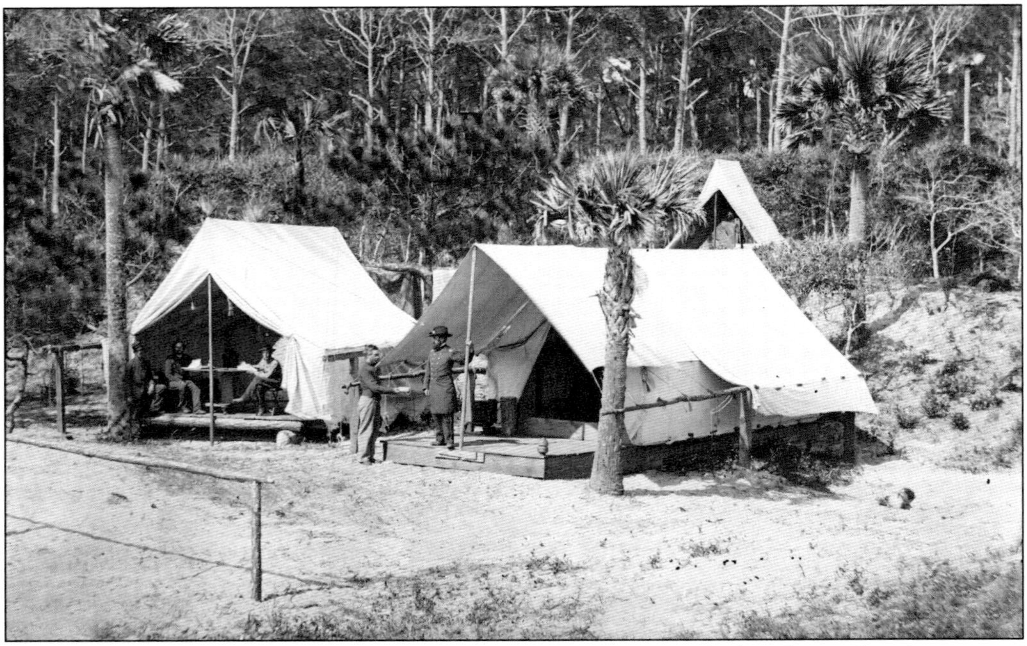

In the summertime, soldiers made camp in front of the dunes on the beach to take advantage of the mosquito-clearing sea breeze. In winter, they retreated into the interior to escape no-see-ums. Here, General Gillmore consults with a soldier outside of his tent. Notice the high dunes and dense woods behind their camp. (Photograph by Haas & Peale, courtesy of the Library of Congress.)

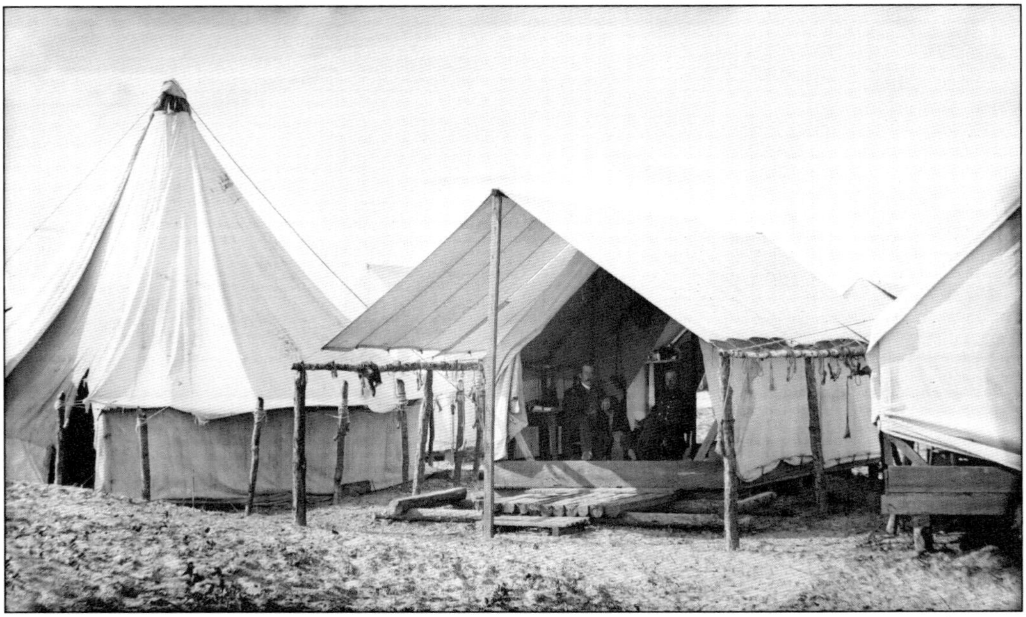

Passing the day in the shade underneath an open-sided tent on Folly Beach is now considered a pleasurable activity. For the Union soldiers awaiting battle on the island's shores, however, moments of leisure were likely fraught with anxiety and the constant threat of disease. Water quality on the island was poor. Wells produced muddy, smelly water, leaving most soldiers to drink from shallow holes lined with a wooden barrel, dug just a few feet deep to reach brackish water. (Photograph by Haas & Peale, courtesy of the Library of Congress.)

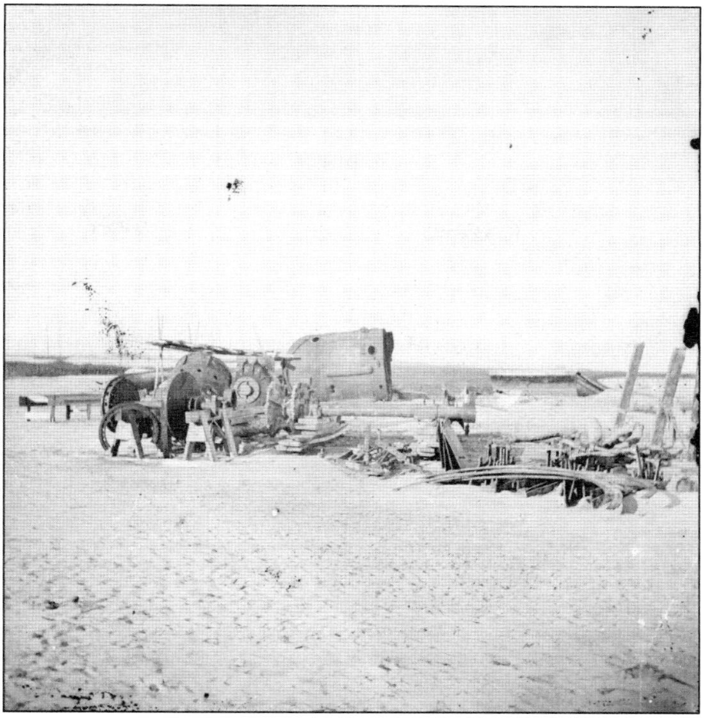

British-built and designed and reinforced to take fire and slip through the Union blockade of the harbor, the Confederate ship *Ruby* found an even more formidable foe in the sandbars of Lighthouse Inlet on Folly's northern end. Running aground on June 11, 1863, the wreck took fire from Confederate-held Morris Island and Union-held Folly as both sides made alternating attempts to salvage the supplies onboard. This photograph was taken near the war's conclusion in February 1865. (Courtesy of the Library of Congress.)

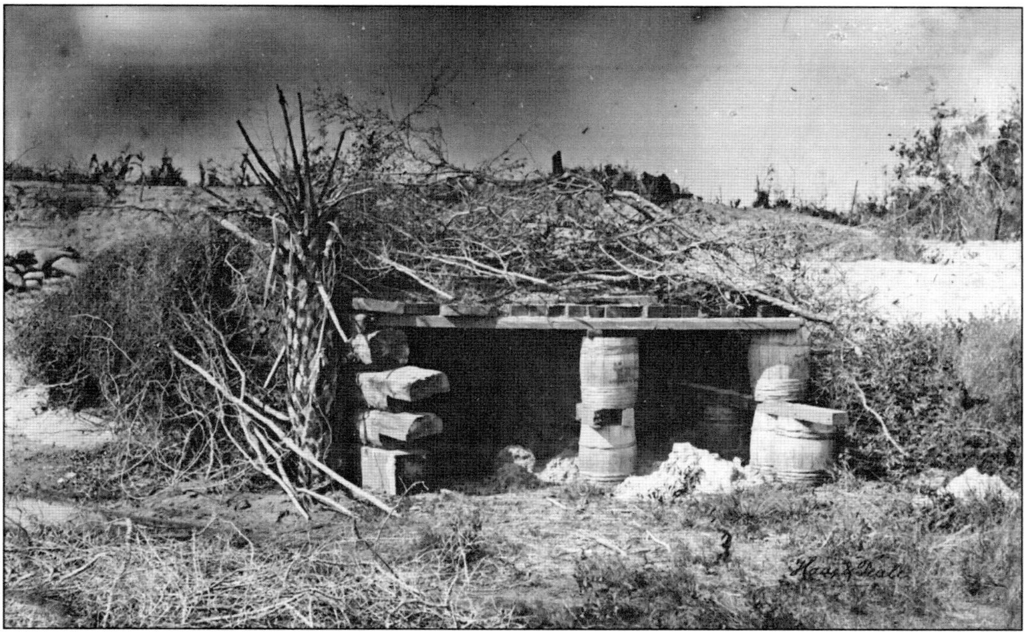

The north end of Folly was dotted with "splinterproofs," designed to provide a safe haven from the incessant shelling that the Confederates on Morris Island launched across Lighthouse Inlet. Men stationed at the island's north end spent much of the day crouched in these makeshift bomb shelters. Folly's only true "combat" occurred on May 10, 1863, when a force of 120 Confederate soldiers attacked the Union troops stationed on Little Folly. Due to their efforts to conceal the substantial size of their forces gathering on Folly, the Union soldiers were not allowed to return fire. (Courtesy of the Library of Congress.)

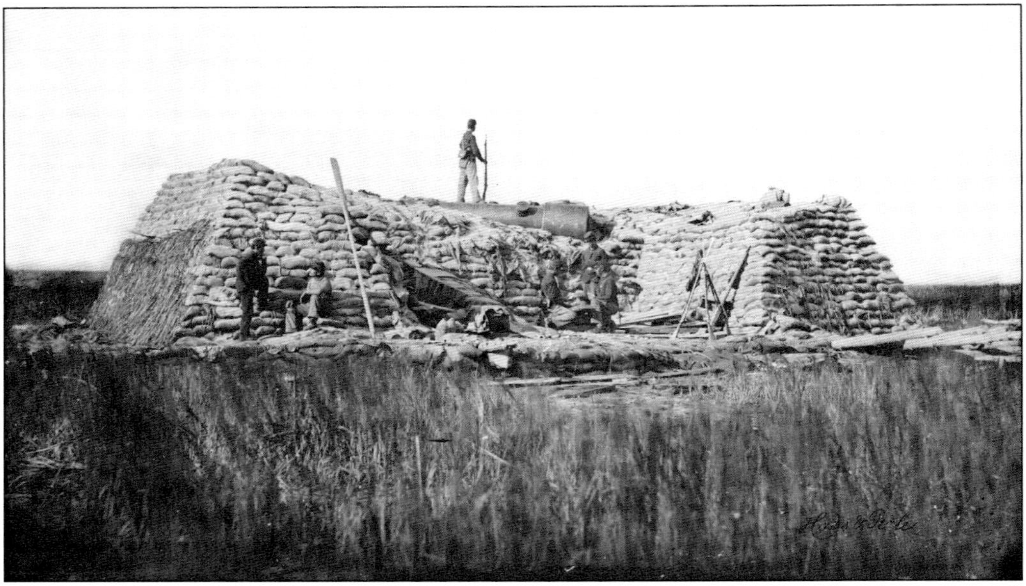

Built atop a manmade earthwork of sandbags on a marsh battery between Folly and James Island, the Swamp Angel housed a 16,500-pound rifled Parrott cannon whose shells could reach downtown Charleston. With its target the steeple of St. Michael's Church, the August 22, 1863, shelling forced the evacuation of the city south of Broad Street. Capturing Charleston, "the cradle of the Secession," served as both a strategic and symbolic goal for the Union. (Photograph by Haas & Peale, courtesy of the Library of Congress.)

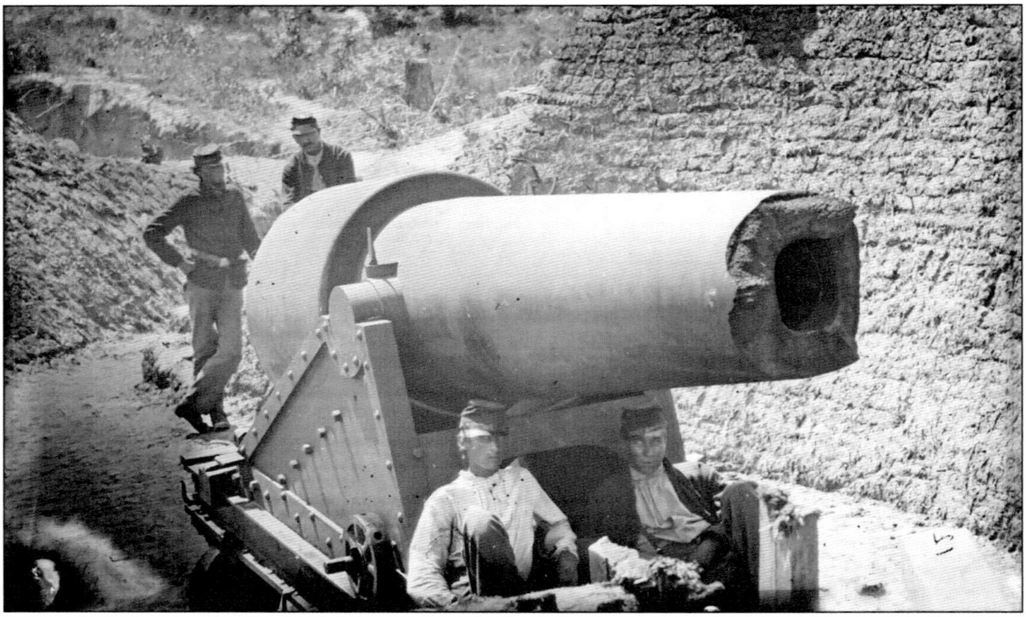

After firing 36 rounds into Charleston, the Swamp Angel's cannon burst, much like the broken muzzle on the cannon seen here on Morris Island. The explosion temporarily ended the bombardment of the city by Union troops from Folly's marsh. Confederate troops, however, continued to fire on the marsh battery, with Union soldiers occasionally appearing atop the deserted outpost to maintain the illusion that the battery was still functional. (Photograph by Haas & Peale, courtesy of the Library of Congress.)

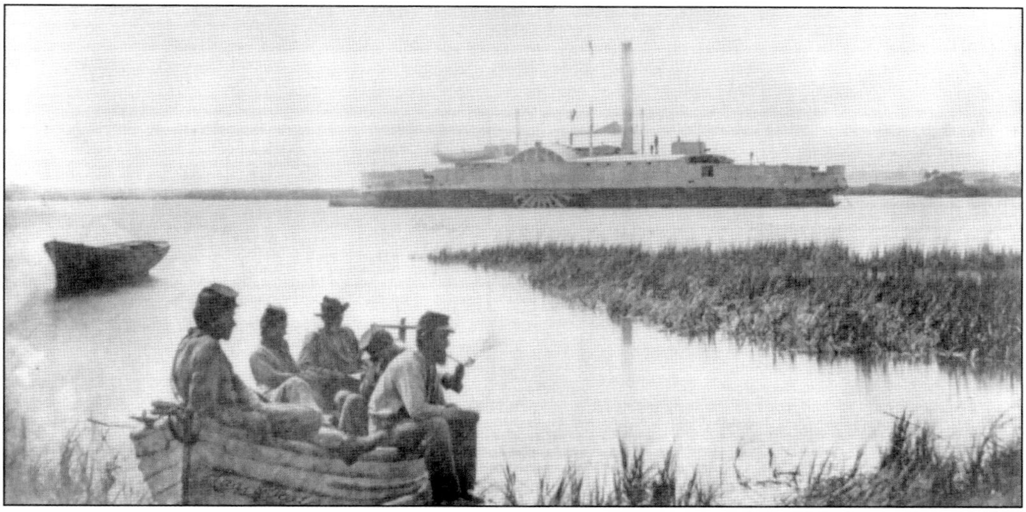

Union soldiers relax in a rowboat with the USS *Commodore McDonough* in the background. A ferryboat by design, the flat-bottomed *McDonough* proved useful in the Lowcountry for its ability to navigate shallow creeks that were impassable for other ships. The Union utilized the *McDonough* throughout the war to transport troops and bombard Confederate batteries across the Charleston area. (Photograph by Haas & Peale, courtesy of the Library of Congress.)

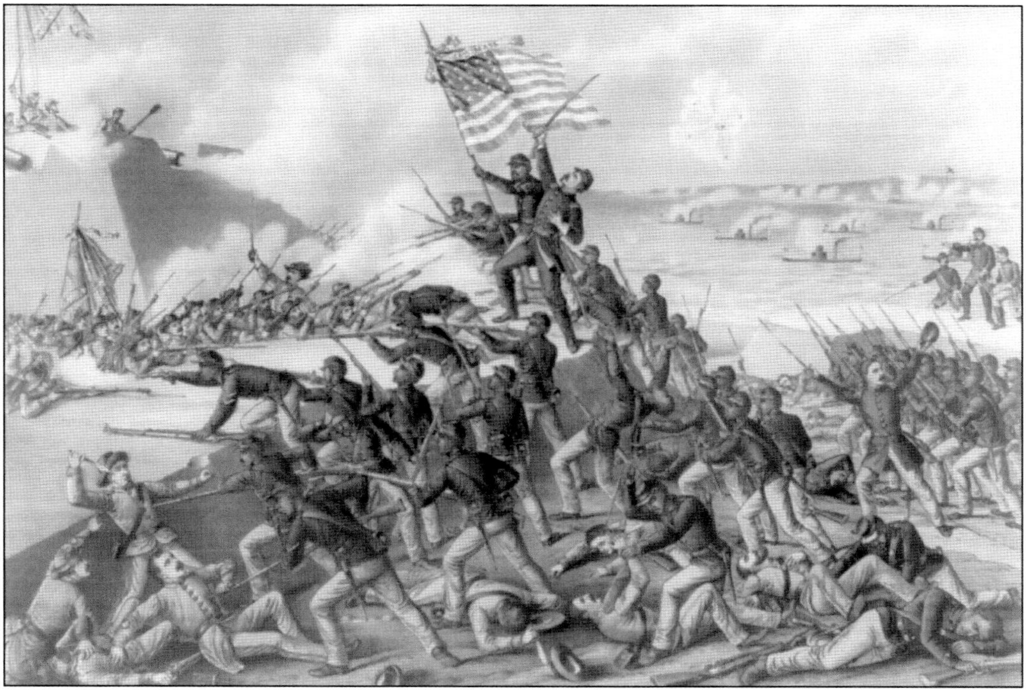

On July 10, 1863, the Union launched its attack on Morris Island with a two-to-one advantage, handily capturing the south end of Morris. In their assault on Fort Wagner the following day, however, the Union army was bitterly defeated, suffering 339 casualties to the Confederates' 12. On July 18, the Union again attacked Wagner, led by the 54th Massachusetts Volunteer Infantry, the African American regiment that changed perceptions about the gallantry and capabilities of black soldiers. After two months under assault, the Confederates finally abandoned Fort Wagner on September 7. (Courtesy of Kurz & Allison-Art Publishers and the Library of Congress.)

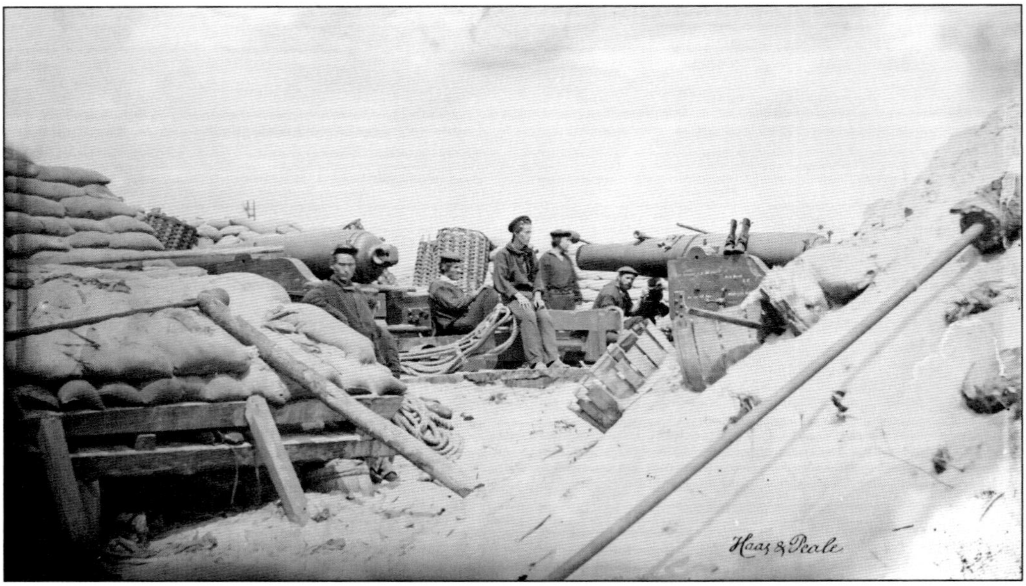

The two months it took the Union to take Fort Wagner was a disheartening campaign. During their approach, the Yankees dug a zigzag pattern across the beach, constantly working around the shallow graves of fellow soldiers who had perished in previous assaults. At times, bodies were used to fortify the walls of the trenches. After taking Morris Island, Union troops strengthened their batteries to begin an assault on Fort Sumter. Although they reduced Sumter to rubble, they were unable to force the surrender of Southern troops. (Courtesy of the Library of Congress.)

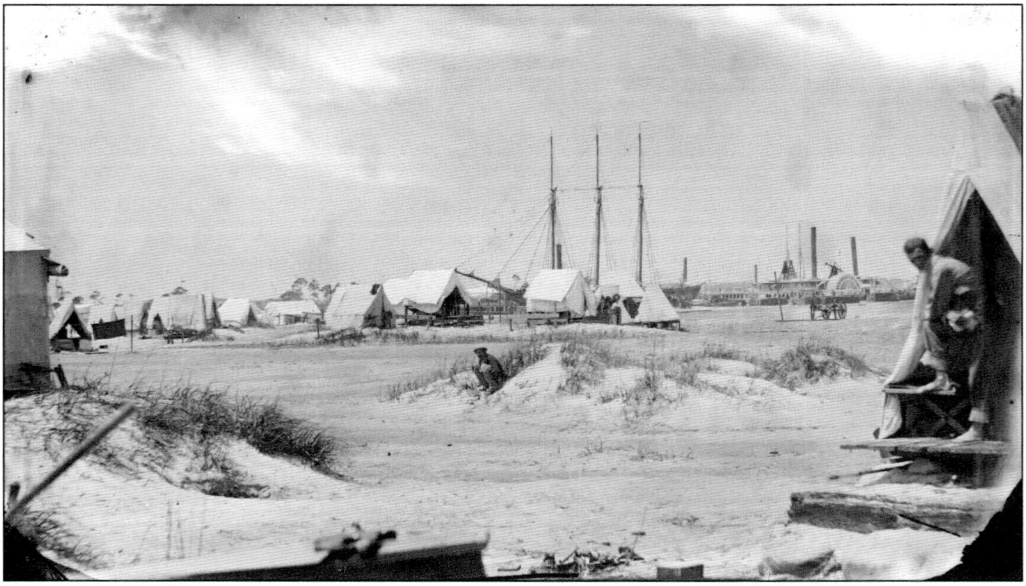

Life in the Union camps on Folly and Morris Islands was a constant struggle against fleas and rats. Garbage quickly piled up, worsening the infestations. Water quality was poor, and many of the soldiers subsisted on meager food rations and the occasional bottle of scotch smuggled into camp. In this photograph, Union soldiers camped on Morris Island in August 1863 make eyes at the camera. A schooner and ferryboat are behind the camp in Lighthouse Inlet. The trees in the back left are across the water on Folly Island. (Photograph by Haas & Peale, courtesy of the Library of Congress.)

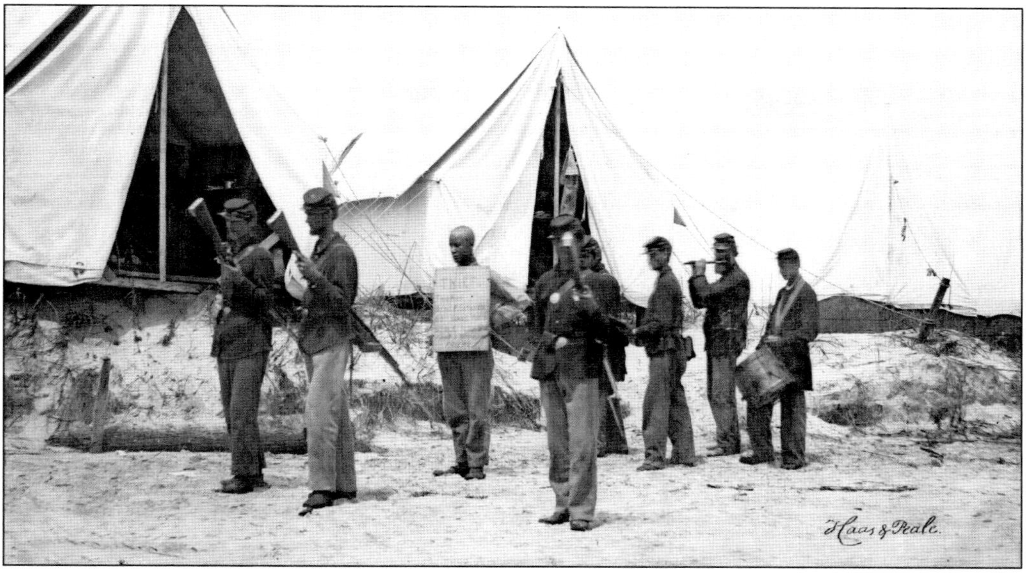

Poor conditions in the beach camps tempted many soldiers to act out. In addition, the Federal government was slow to pay the three black regiments stationed on Folly, who were often assigned the most laborious and dangerous jobs. After one black soldier in the 55th Massachusetts was accused of mutiny in June 1864, his fellow soldiers were ordered to execute him. In this photograph, another soldier accused of theft walks the "rogue's march" through camp. Note the accompanying musicians. (Photograph by Haas & Peale, courtesy of the Library of Congress.)

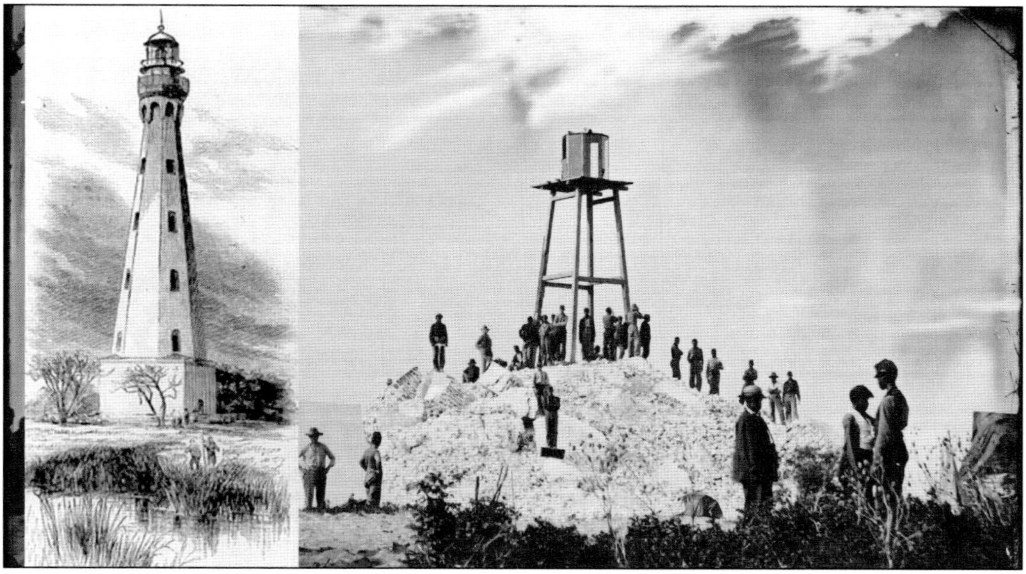

In January 1861, the Union took proactive steps to prevent the seizure of lighthouses along the Southern coast, destroying the lens and lantern of the Charleston light on Morris Island, along with 164 more between the Chesapeake Bay and the Rio Grande. The original 40-foot lighthouse, built in 1767, was replaced in 1838 by a 102-foot lighthouse (inset at left), which was torn down by the Confederates during the war to prevent the Yankees from using it as a watchtower. The pile of rubble remaining is from a smaller beacon light, seen here after the Union occupation of Morris Island. Bricks from the original lighthouse may have been used for shelters and dune huts across the island. (Courtesy of the US Coast Guard and the Library of Congress.)

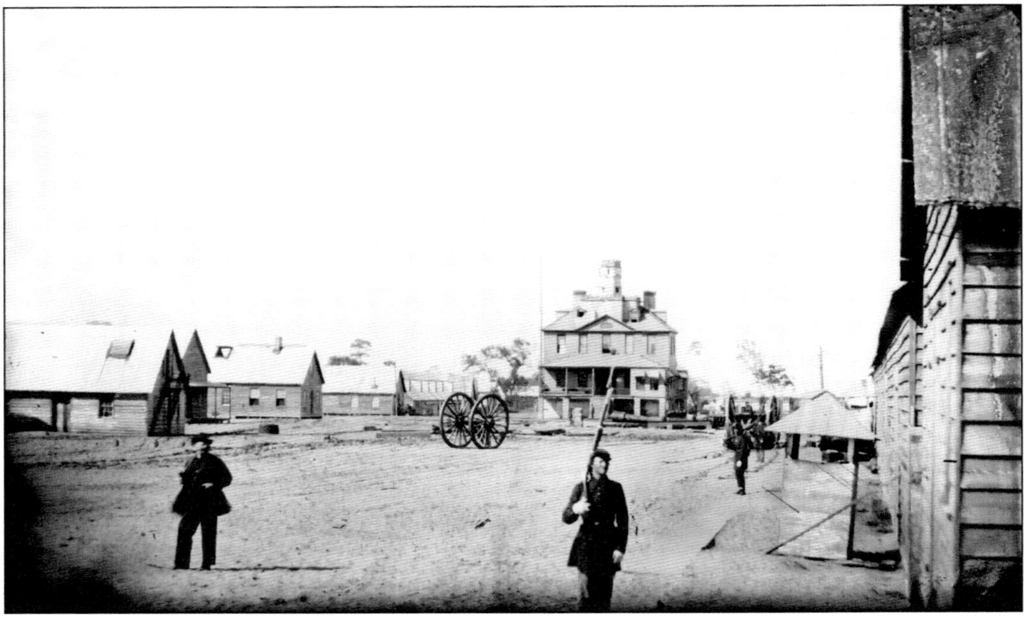

What appears to be before and after shots of the lighthouse keeper's Beacon House is most likely the other way around. Above, the buildings lining the thoroughfare leading to the house are new, built from wood gleaned from Folly and shaped into boards at sawmills the Union army built on Folly. After the Union's July 1863 attack on Morris Island, the Beacon House was reduced to a shell of itself (below). The Union quickly rebuilt the house (above) to serve as the headquarters of Gen. W.H. Davis of the 104th Pennsylvania and for use by Gen. Quincy A. Gillmore as a signal station. (Both, photographs by Haas & Peale, courtesy of the Library of Congress.)

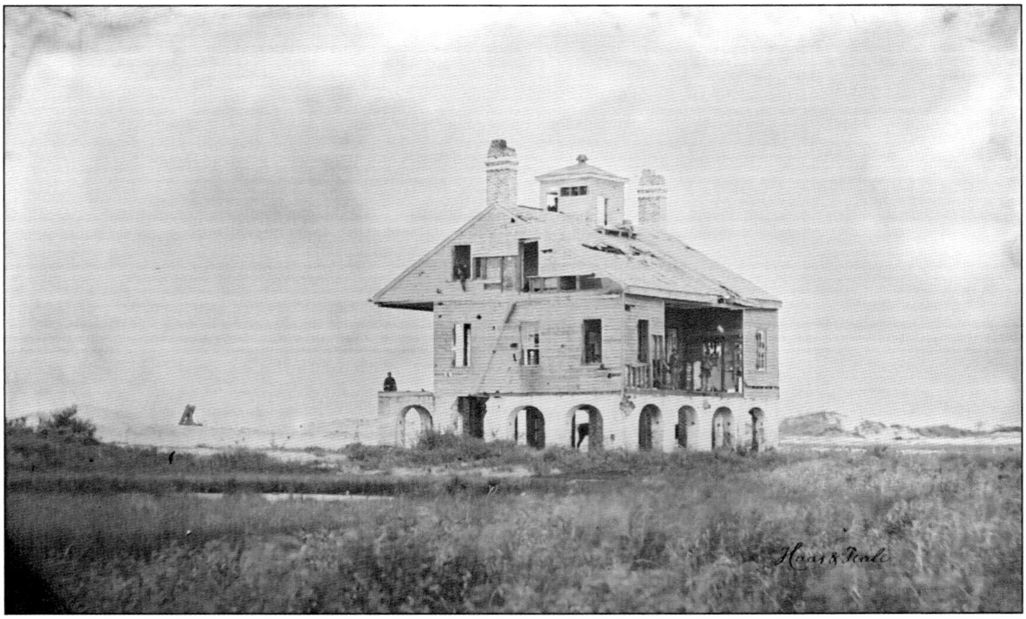

In June 1987, relic hunters Robert Bohrn and Eric Croen uncovered the find of a lifetime. Following the tracks of a bulldozer clearing the way for houses on present-day West Indian Avenue, their metal detectors alerted them to the presence of something below: the graves of 19 soldiers of the 55th Massachusetts Volunteer Infantry. Although early reports cited 14 bodies, later analysis revealed the bones of 19 individuals at the site. Arriving on Folly soon after the 54th Massachusetts that stormed Fort Wagner, the 55th remained on Folly long thereafter, clearing jungle, building fortifications, and hauling supplies. The only two fully intact skeletons were found in six-sided coffins, built from sawmills on Folly Island. (Courtesy of Robert Bohrn.)

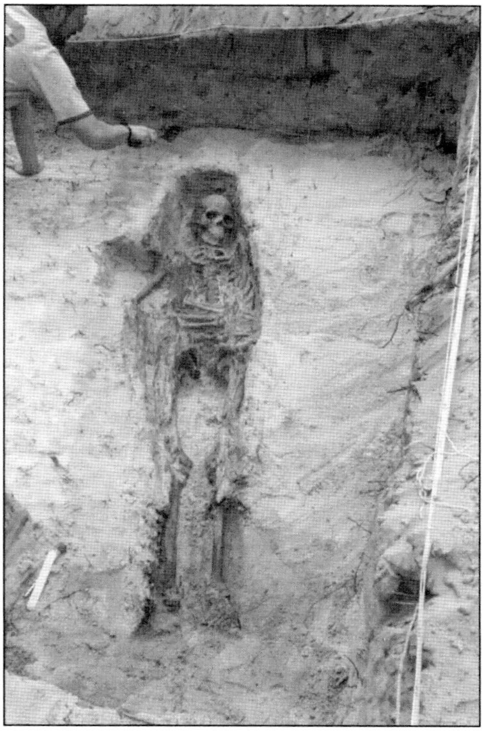

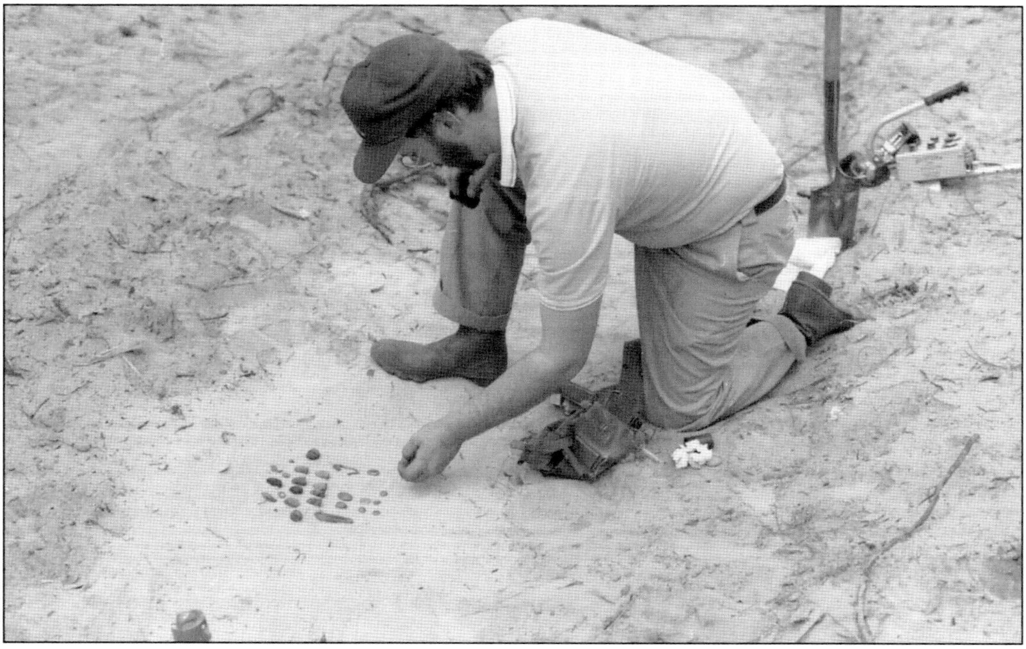

Bohrn grew up on James Island, and his passion for metal detecting stemmed from a deep fascination with the history of James Island and Folly Beach's role in the Civil War. In this photograph, taken on the day he discovered the bodies of the fallen soldiers, Bohrn looks over uniform buttons, bullets, and mini-balls that he collected at the site. Bohrn participated in the archaeological dig, eventually mounting a two-decade campaign to bring a national historical marker for the 55th Massachusetts to Folly Beach. (Courtesy of Robert Bohrn.)

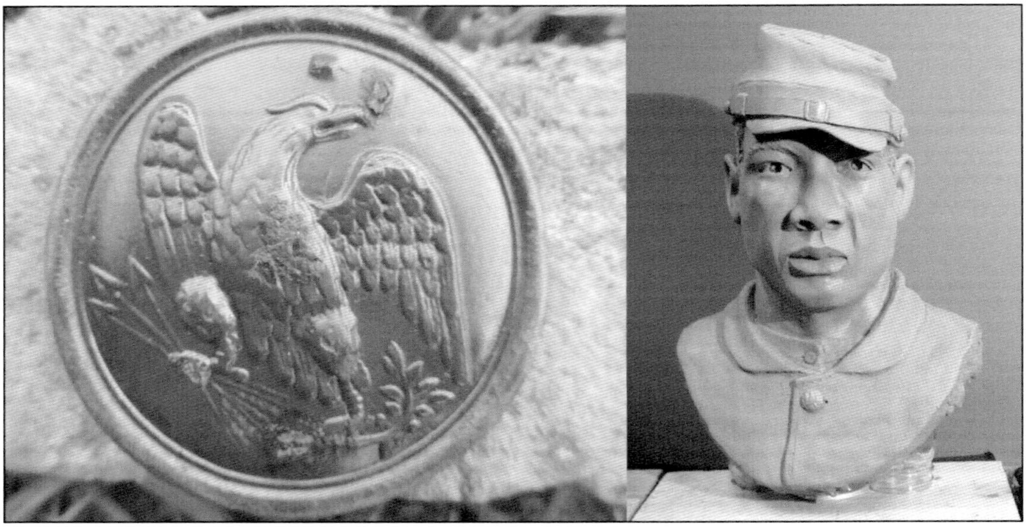

Union soldiers would have worn this eagle breastplate (left) over their heart, affixed to a leather strap that held their ammunition cartridge box. In theory, the emblem served to block a bullet from entering the body, but the requirement to keep the brass shined made them equally attractive to Confederate sharpshooters as targets. The bust on the right, created by forensic expert and sculptor Roy Paschal, is an approximation derived from one of two complete skulls recovered at the 55th Massachusetts Regiment's burial site. Although early analysis hypothesized that damage to the skull's teeth was caused by pulling ammunition from its cartridge, the marks were later attributed to smoking a pipe. Most likely, the soldiers found buried on Folly Beach died of dysentery, typhoid, and exhaustion, worsened by dehydration. (Courtesy of Robert Bohrn.)

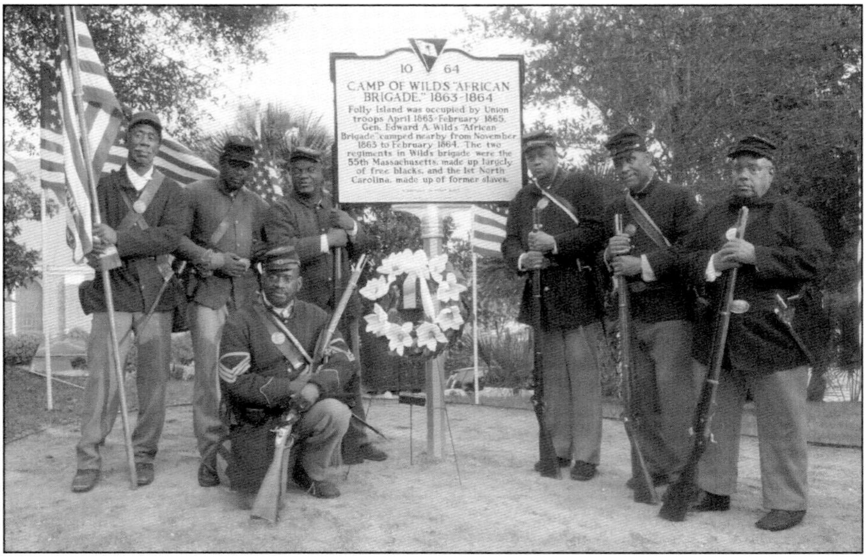

The recovered remains of the 55th Massachusetts soldiers were reburied with military honors at the Beaufort National Cemetery in May 1989. Thanks in part to the national attention the Folly Beach find received, Tri-Star Pictures made the Academy Award–winning film *Glory* based on the gallantry of the 54th Massachusetts Regiment's battles on James and Morris Islands. Many of the film's cast and crew, including Morgan Freeman, attended the burial ceremony. The soldiers were again remembered in July 2011 when Folly Beach's only national historical marker was dedicated to the regiments at Folly River Park. (Photograph by the author.)

Three

LAID BACK AND LOW KEY

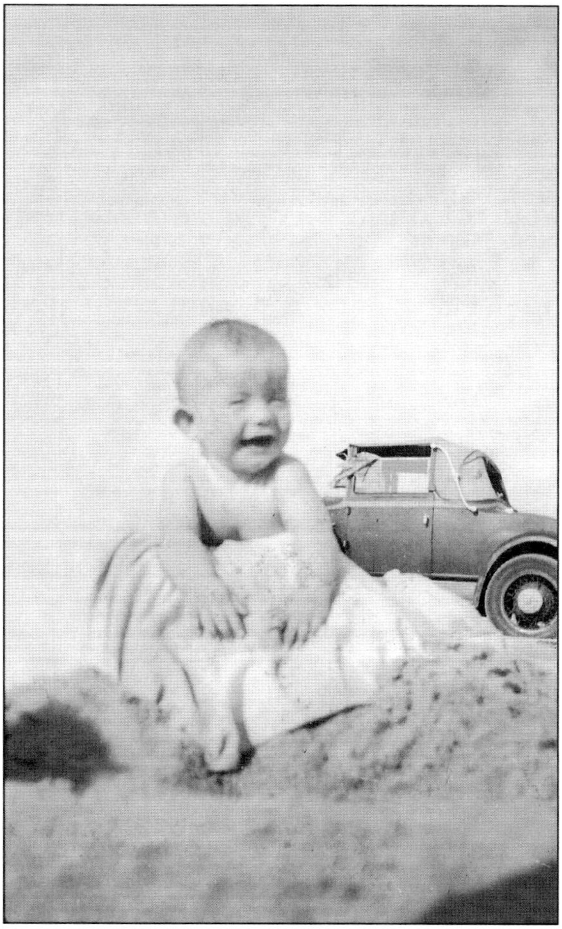

"Sunbathing should start early!" reads the caption on this photograph of five-month-old Betty Southworth (Schultz) in 1935. She remembers the family car in the background fondly for its rumble seat. After 50 years without much change, when the only route to Folly Beach was by boat, the island began to grow and attract visitors soon after World War I. (Courtesy of Betty Schultz.)

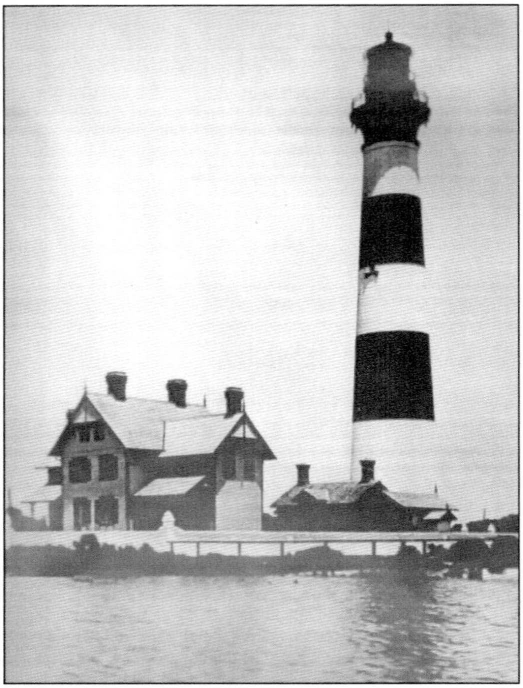

After the Civil War, Folly Island returned to obscurity for half a century. The Morris Island Lighthouse that still stands today, seen here around 1900, was constructed between 1872 and 1876, reaching 158 feet tall, but the decision to construct a new entrance into Charleston Harbor sealed the fate of the land surrounding it. The Army Corps of Engineers opted to replace the existing natural channel into Charleston Harbor with a manmade channel created by massive jetties, an obstruction of water and sand flow that afflicts Folly with erosion problems to this day. (Courtesy of Wallace Benson.)

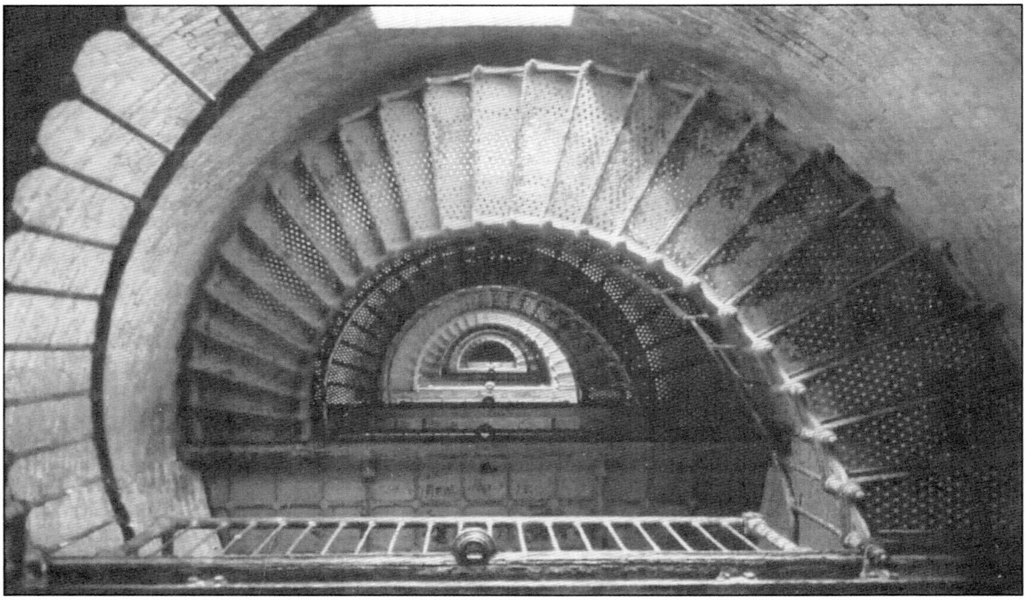

Returning to the South after his role commanding the Union troops on Folly, Gen. Quincy Gillmore spent much of the remainder of the century leading the construction of the jetties into Charleston Harbor. Cutting directly atop the sandbar that once ran from Sullivan's Island to Lighthouse Inlet, the rock obstructions claimed as much as 500 feet of shoreline from Morris Island each year. When the present lighthouse was built in the 1870s, it stood almost half a mile from the shoreline. Today, it is nearly 2,000 feet offshore at high tide. The interior of the light, seen here, remains much as it did at its creation, although volunteers from the Save the Light nonprofit organization must occasionally fill holes and clear out the debris and waste left behind by nesting birds. (Photograph courtesy of Save the Light and the Folly Beach Civic Club.)

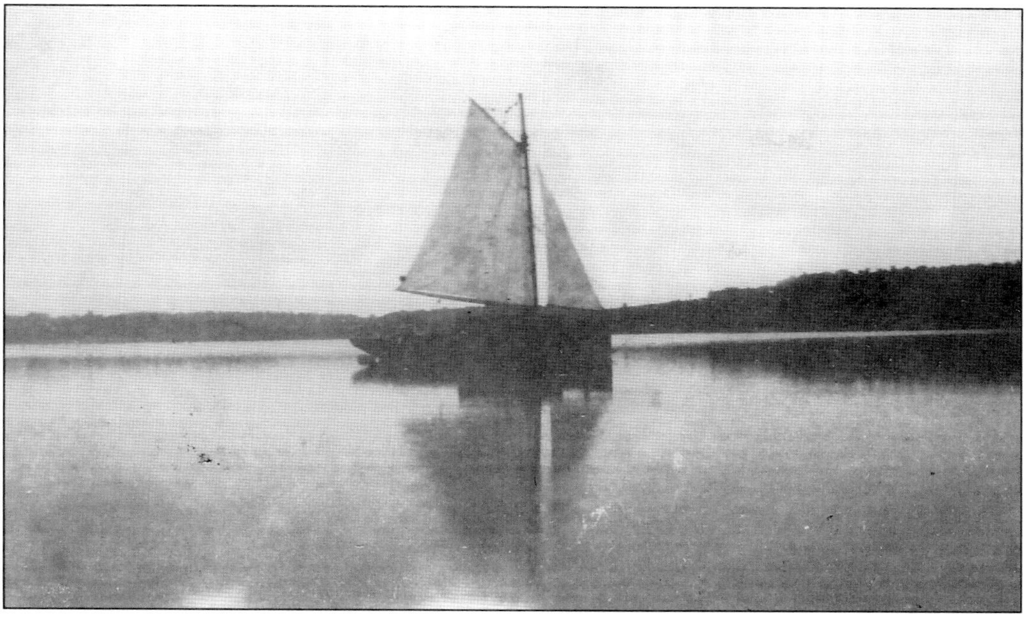

Prior to 1918, visitors to Folly Beach were more likely to stay in tents than in cottages. When World War I ended, the island was purchased by the Folly Island Company, which began to market Folly as a vacation destination. A road was built to the east of the current Folly Road, crossing Long Island and Little Oak Island on its way to the beach. The trip from Charleston took upwards of two hours by car or bus, and many still arrived by steamer and sailboat. This 1937 photograph shows *The Echo*, a sailboat built by Jack Southworth that was later used by the Coast Guard to patrol for German submarines off Folly Beach during World War II. (Courtesy of Betty Schultz.)

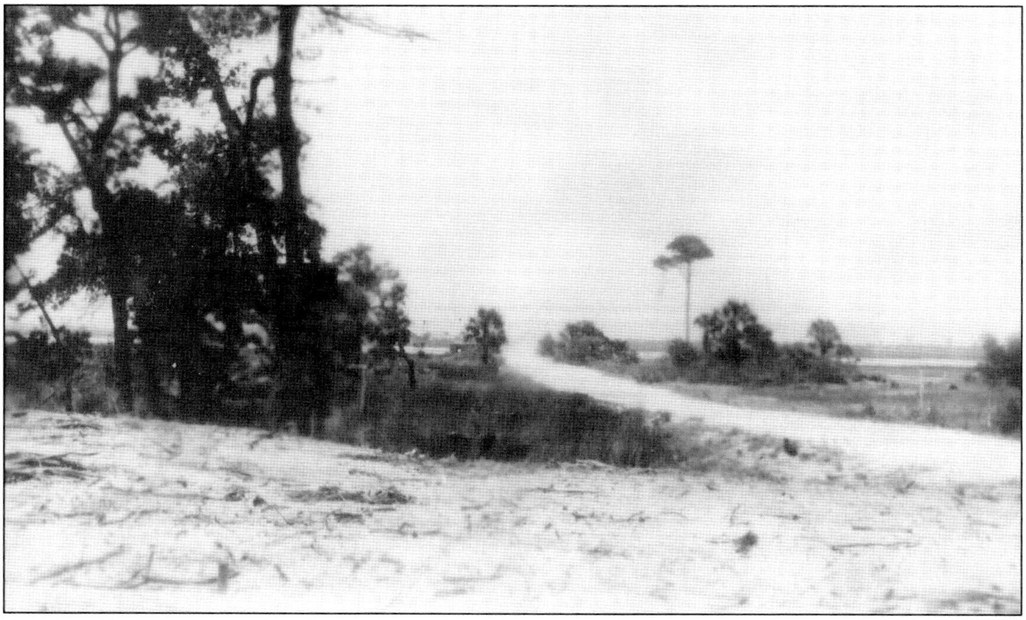

Until its boom in the 1920s, Folly was a quiet, isolated place. The first wave of tourists, in 1921, the year this photograph was taken, had only sandy thoroughfares to navigate across the island. (Courtesy of Patricia Jamison Wilbanks Bragg.)

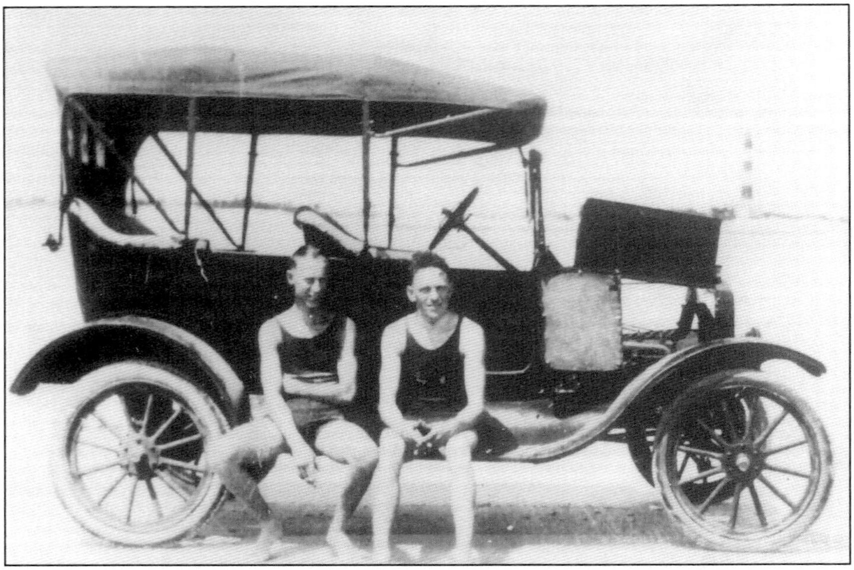

Two early tourists on Folly Beach, identified only as Glover and Judson, enjoy a drive on the east end of the beach. The Roaring Twenties were good to Folly, with the pavilion opening in 1921. Investors promoted and grew the island into a popular destination for day-trippers from Charleston. Round-trip fare on the steamer *Attaquin* or via bus cost $1, with full-day itineraries planned that included boat racing in the Folly River, surf fishing, and music in the evening on the pier. (Courtesy of Patricia Jamison Wilbanks Bragg and the Folly Beach Civic Club.)

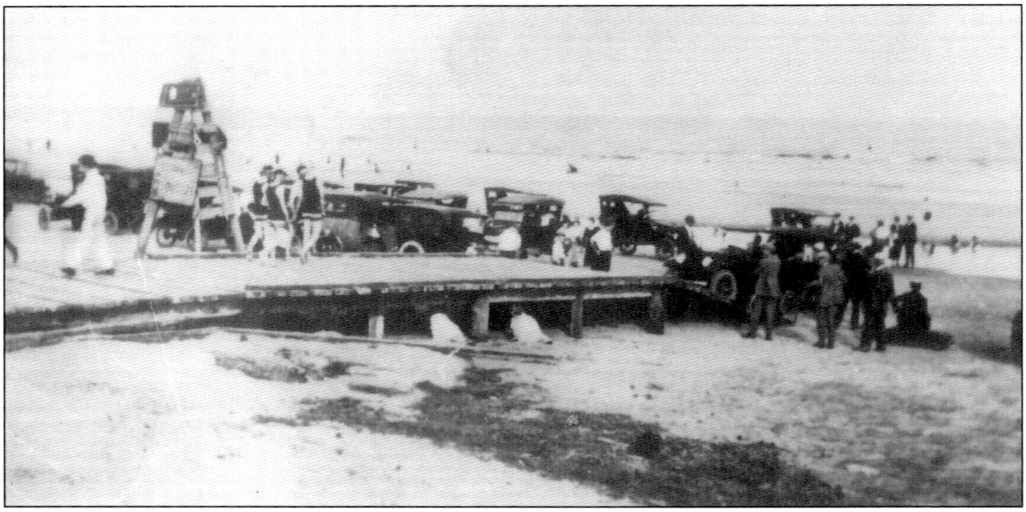

Many current Folly residents recall learning to drive on the beach. Until the 1960s, "if you could reach the gas pedal, you drove," recalls Patricia "Cookie" Bragg. "Nobody checked whether or not you had a license." Marlene Estridge, Folly's city clerk, remembers stripping the chrome off of her mother-in-law's 1949 Plymouth when she tried to drive it between the pilings of a house that had washed away. Estridge's father, Willis Browning, ran Doc's Service Station, at the current site of the Folly Beach Crab Shack. "Every day he'd pull cars out of the ocean," recalls Estridge. "The tide would come in and the people would be way down the beach somewhere. Half the people didn't have money, so he'd come home with watches and rings as payment." This 1920s photograph shows the wooden ramps that were used to drive through the soft sand of the dunes onto the harder beach. (Courtesy of Patricia Jamison Wilbanks Bragg.)

Before opening the first causeway road to the beach in 1921, developers sold lots on the island for as low as $1,000, with beachfront lots reaching $2,000. In the years that followed, the company began to partition off lots farther back from the ocean, selling 70-foot-by-150-foot parcels for as little as $550. "These lots are placed within the reach of every salaried man and woman in Charleston," claimed this advertisement for "Charleston's Most Accessible Beach." (Courtesy of Maebelle Barnett Bazzel.)

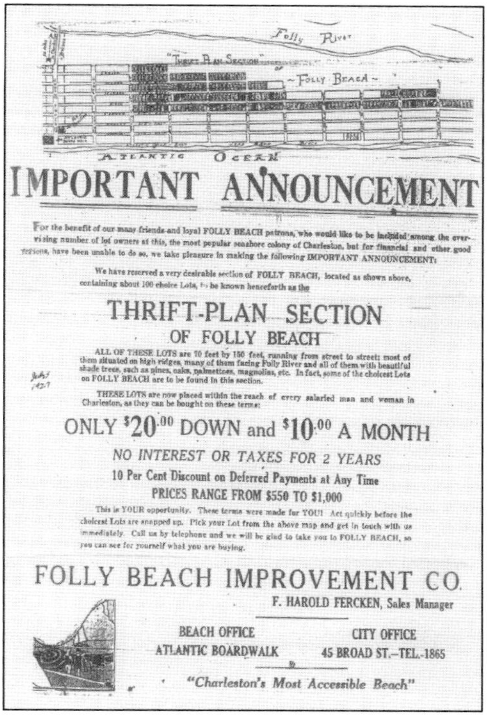

IMPORTANT ANNOUNCEMENT

For the benefit of our many friends and loyal FOLLY BEACH patrons, who would like to be included among the ever-rising number of lot owners at this, the most popular seashore colony of Charleston, but for financial and other good reasons, have been unable to do so, we take pleasure in making the following IMPORTANT ANNOUNCEMENT:

We have reserved a very desirable section of FOLLY BEACH, located as shown above, containing about 100 choice Lots, to be known henceforth as the

THRIFT-PLAN SECTION
OF FOLLY BEACH

ALL OF THESE LOTS are 70 feet by 150 feet, running from street to street; most of them situated on high ridges, many of them facing Folly River and all of them with beautiful shade trees, such as pines, oaks, palmettoes, magnolias, etc. In fact, some of the choicest Lots on FOLLY BEACH are to be found in this section.

THESE LOTS are now placed within the reach of every salaried man and woman in Charleston, as they can be bought on these terms:

ONLY $20.00 DOWN and $10.00 A MONTH

NO INTEREST OR TAXES FOR 2 YEARS

10 Per Cent Discount on Deferred Payments at Any Time

PRICES RANGE FROM $550 TO $1,000

This is YOUR opportunity. These terms were made for YOU! Act quickly before the choicest Lots are snapped up. Pick your Lot from the above map and get in touch with us immediately. Call us by telephone and we will be glad to take you to FOLLY BEACH, so you can see for yourself what you are buying.

FOLLY BEACH IMPROVEMENT CO.

F. HAROLD FERCKEN, Sales Manager

BEACH OFFICE
ATLANTIC BOARDWALK

CITY OFFICE
45 BROAD ST.—TEL. 1865

"Charleston's Most Accessible Beach"

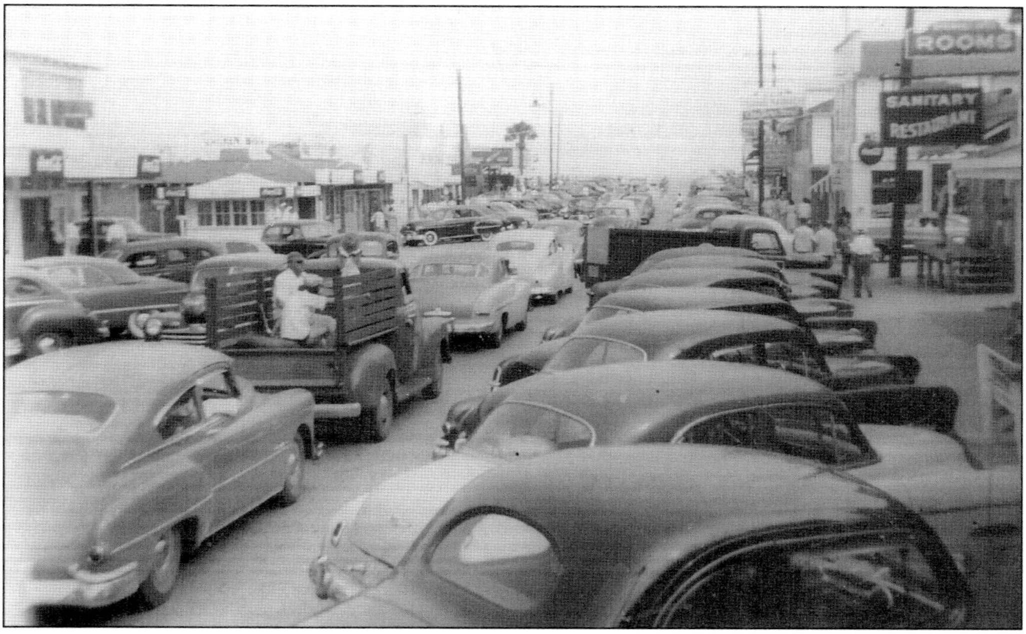

Traffic getting onto Folly Beach is nothing new. By the mid-1920s, Folly Beach was a busy scene on Sunday afternoons—as many as 200,000 people visited the beach in 1925 alone. Men wore wool shorts, while women often donned full-length dresses with stockings and head coverings. Swimming trunks were available for rent for those who did not own them or bring them to the beach. This 1940s shot shows the approach down Center Street toward the ocean, with the Sanitary Restaurant on the right. The island included hotels and plenty of cabins and guestrooms for rent within residents' homes. (Photograph by Boss Wilbanks, courtesy of Patricia Jamison Wilbanks Bragg.)

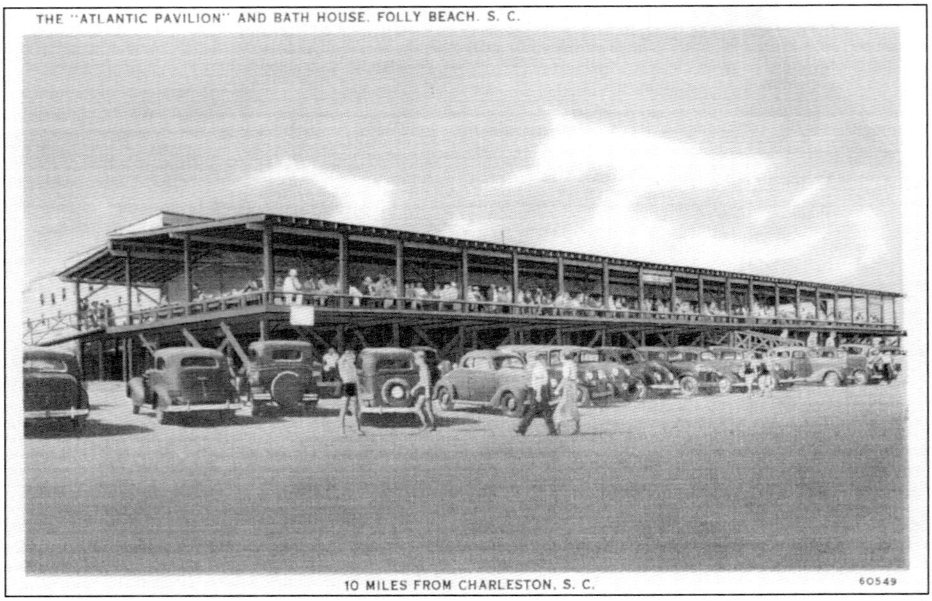

The Atlantic Pavilion opened in 1921, providing a central hub for beachfront activity. It suffered damage in the Hurricane of 1940. Carol McLendon Porter found this and several of the other Folly Beach postcards in this book at a flea market in northern Virginia. Her family often visited Folly in the 1950s, renting a cottage at Chastain's, on the front beach at 610 East Arctic Avenue. (Courtesy of Carol McLendon Porter.)

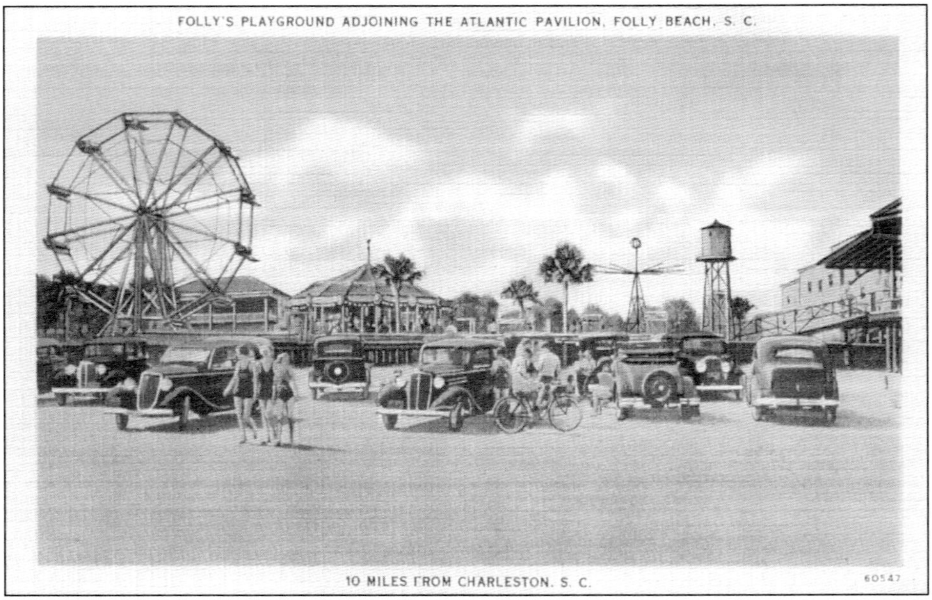

By 1937, more than 15,000 people celebrated the Fourth of July on the island. Folly's Playground amusement park was a primary draw for day-trippers to the island. Mary Barnett Herbert recalls the riotous atmosphere in local bars in the 1940s and 1950s, caused in part by sailors letting loose while on leave. "They had a small holding jail next to the bowling alley with bars for windows. I think that the heat and mosquitoes were probably the worst punishment that anyone had." (Courtesy of Carol McLendon Porter.)

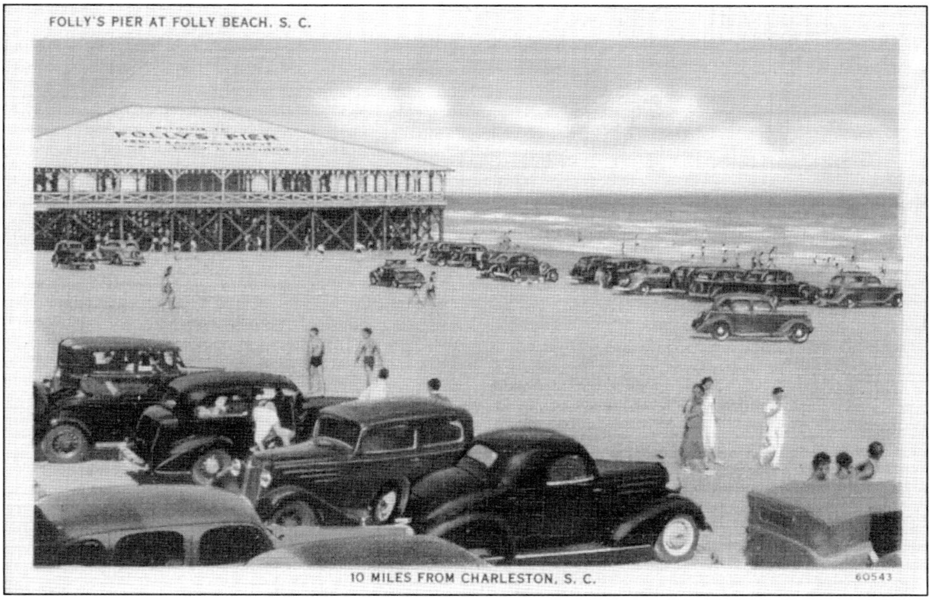

The back of this 1940 postcard reads, "Folly's Pier, where thousands enjoy dancing to the music of some of the finest orchestras in the country and located directly over the ocean." The Coca-Cola logo was painted atop the roof of the pier in the 1940s. The giant dance pier opened in 1931 and drew national musical acts, from Jerry Lee Lewis to Fats Domino to the Drifters. With air conditioning an expensive rarity on the island, residents grew accustomed to falling asleep with windows open and the sound of live music out over the ocean. (Courtesy of Carol McLendon Porter.)

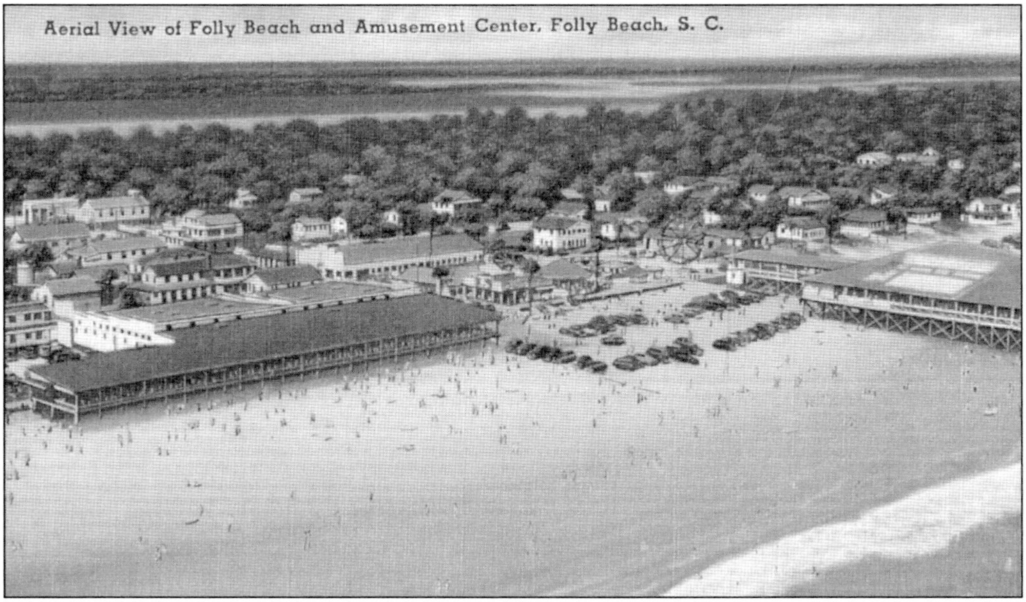

This aerial view of Folly Beach on a 1940 postcard shows the placement of the Atlantic Pavilion boardwalk, the pier, and Folly's Playground. Notice the amount of forest left throughout the center of the island. Many visitors in the postwar years came for the week, renting rooms at the pavilion's Oceanfront Hotel, the Wayne Hotel at 203 East Cooper Avenue, and Smoak's Hotel at 202 East Arctic Avenue, whose float stand employed many Folly Beach old-timers in their teenage years. (Courtesy of Carol McLendon Porter.)

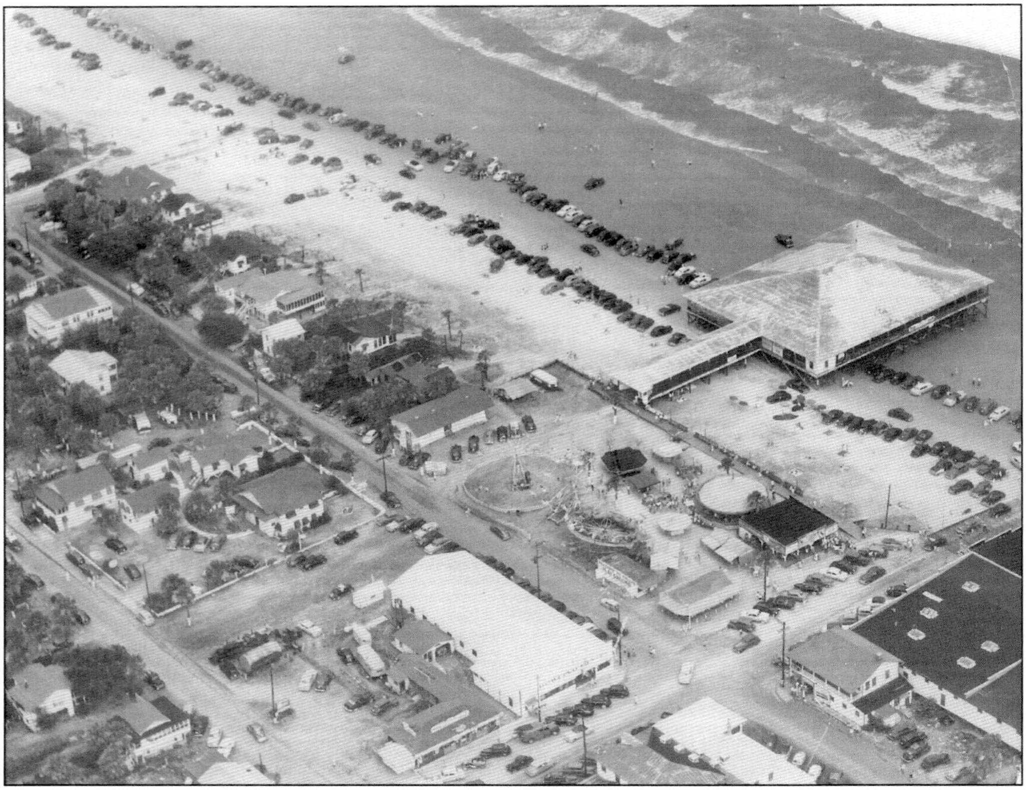

In the early 1940s, Folly's entertainment options included the pier, an amusement park, and a bowling alley. In this aerial shot by Robert E. Hubbard, notice the lines of cars along the beach. In the evenings, big bands performed on the pier, on a stage literally set atop the ocean. One of beach music's founders, Maurice Williams and the Zodiacs, returned to play the Follypalooza street festival in 2009. (Courtesy of Patricia Jamison Wilbanks Bragg.)

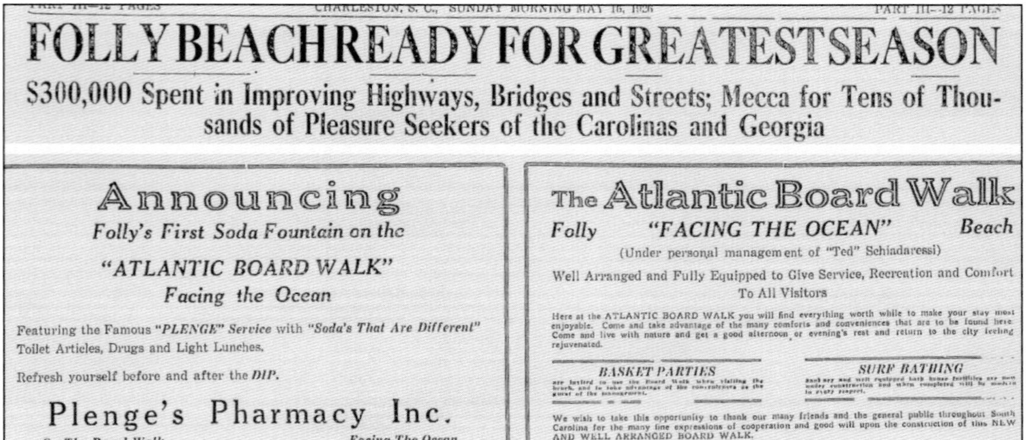

FOLLY BEACH READY FOR GREATEST SEASON

$300,000 Spent in Improving Highways, Bridges and Streets; Mecca for Tens of Thousands of Pleasure Seekers of the Carolinas and Georgia

Announcing

Folly's First Soda Fountain on the

"ATLANTIC BOARD WALK"

Facing the Ocean

Featuring the Famous "PLENGE" Service with "Soda's That Are Different"

Toilet Articles, Drugs and Light Lunches.

Refresh yourself before and after the DIP.

Plenge's Pharmacy Inc.

On The Board Walk — Facing The Ocean

The Atlantic Board Walk

Folly "FACING THE OCEAN" Beach

(Under personal management of "Ted" Schindaressi)

Well Arranged and Fully Equipped to Give Service, Recreation and Comfort To All Visitors

Here at the ATLANTIC BOARD WALK you will find everything worth while to make your stay most enjoyable. Come and take advantage of the many comforts and conveniences that are to be found here. Come and live with nature and get a good afternoon or evening's rest and return to the city feeling rejuvenated.

BASKET PARTIES

SURF BATHING

We wish to take this opportunity to thank our many friends and the general public throughout South Carolina for the many fine expressions of cooperation and good will upon the construction of this NEW AND WELL ARRANGED BOARD WALK.

Headlines and advertisements throughout the 1920s touted the progress made to open up Folly Beach to visitors. Operated by Ted Schiadaressi, the Atlantic Board Walk was the focal point of Folly on weekends and holidays in the 1920s and 1930s. Traveling exhibitions, including the Mabel Cody Flying Circus, also frequented the beachfront. (Courtesy of the *News and Courier*.)

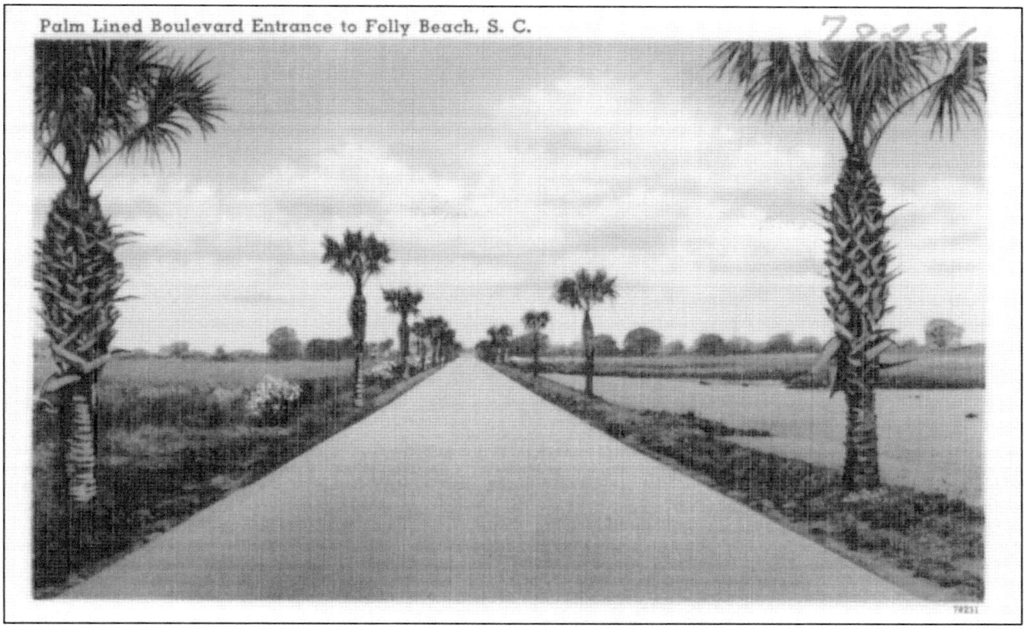

An improved causeway to Folly Beach opened in 1925, easing the journey from Charleston to the island by car. Books of 30 tickets for the tollbooth cost $5.25. This postcard shows the road to Folly Beach in the early 1940s. The elimination of the toll in 1943 was a cause for celebration. Businesses along Center Street welcomed the added tourists that free entry brought to the island. To mark the occasion, a motorcade including Sen. O.T. Wallace traveled from Marion Square in downtown Charleston to the beach. A French aerialist was hired to perform at the pier as part of the festivities. (Courtesy of the Boston Public Library.)

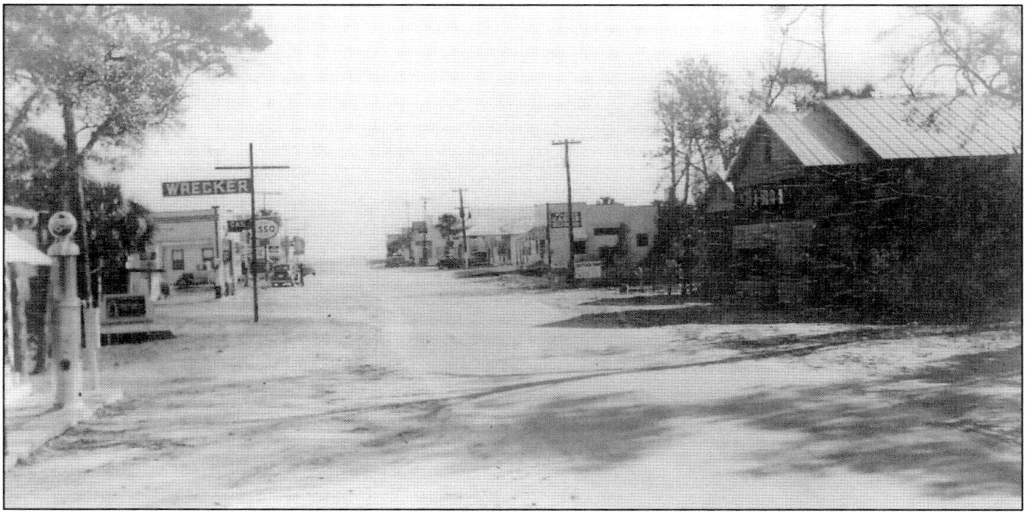

On weekdays in the 1940s—and still today, at least in the offseason—Center Street returns to a quiet, locals-only thoroughfare. After the Hurricane of 1940 washed away 50 beachfront houses, Folly Beach gradually rebuilt, even providing homes to as many as 1,000 workers at the Naval yard throughout World War II. During the war, however, there were fewer dances at the pier, and house windows were covered at night to prevent German submarines from spotting the lights. The Wrecker sign on the left was Doc's Service Station, where the Crab Shack now stands. (Photograph by Charlie Yarnell, courtesy of Maebelle Barnett Bazzel.)

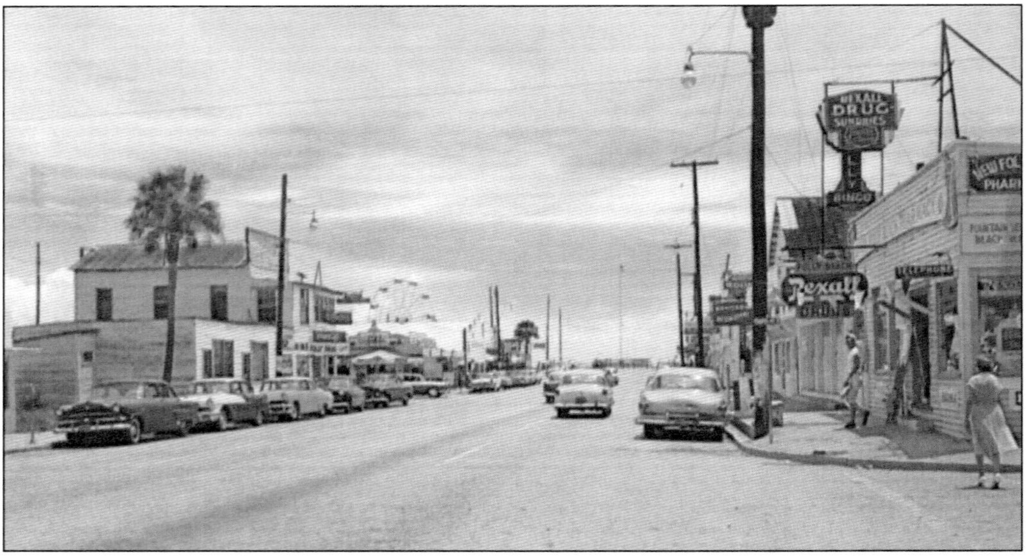

With the Ferris wheel poking up in the back left, Center Street was a welcoming place in the postwar years. The old dancing pier was situated in the same spot as today's fishing pier, with the boardwalk just to the west. A skating rink existed just behind the pavilion, and next to the amusement park was a bingo tent with gypsy fortunetellers. "The gypsies lived at what is now Mr. John's [beach store]," recalled Mary Barnett Herbert in a July 2011 article in *Island Life* magazine. "They were handsome people who called themselves Syrians. When a baby was born to one of the family members they had a feast and invited everyone. They cooked for days." In 1964, palm reading was banned on Folly Beach. (Courtesy of Maebelle Barnett Bazzel.)

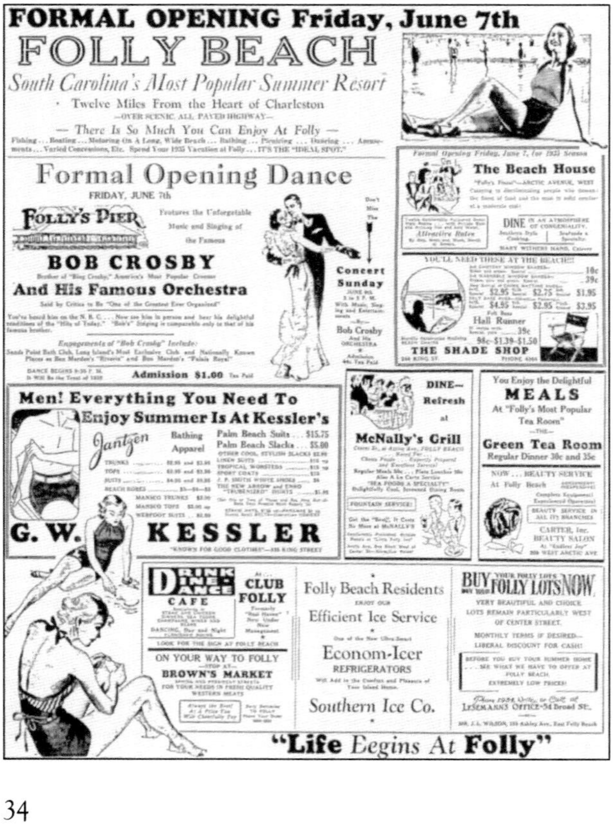

The Folly pier was built in 1931, leading to the opening of restaurants and stores that served the influx of seasonal visitors. Throughout the 1920s, Folly's investors and boosters worked to improve the road from Charleston and the thoroughfares on the island itself. In the mid-1920s, Atlantic, Arctic, Ashley, Erie, Cooper, Hudson, Huron, and Indian Avenues were cut and given their names. This June 6, 1935, advertisement from the *News and Courier* touts the opening of the pier for the summer, featuring a performance by Bing Crosby's brother Bob. (Courtesy of the *News and Courier*.)

In June 1934, composer George Gershwin visited Folly Beach to collaborate with DuBose Heyward on a musical adaptation of his novel *Porgy*. He remained for a month, likely honing the music for the iconic song "Summertime" from the resulting musical, *Porgy and Bess*, while on the island. Gershwin mingled with locals throughout his time on the island, even visiting African American churches on James Island to collect inspiration for the musical's score. (Courtesy of the Library of Congress.)

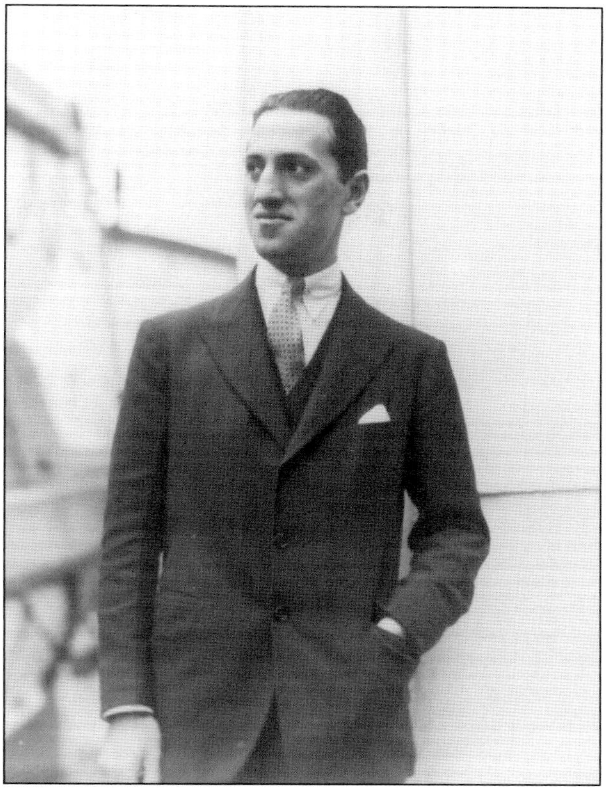

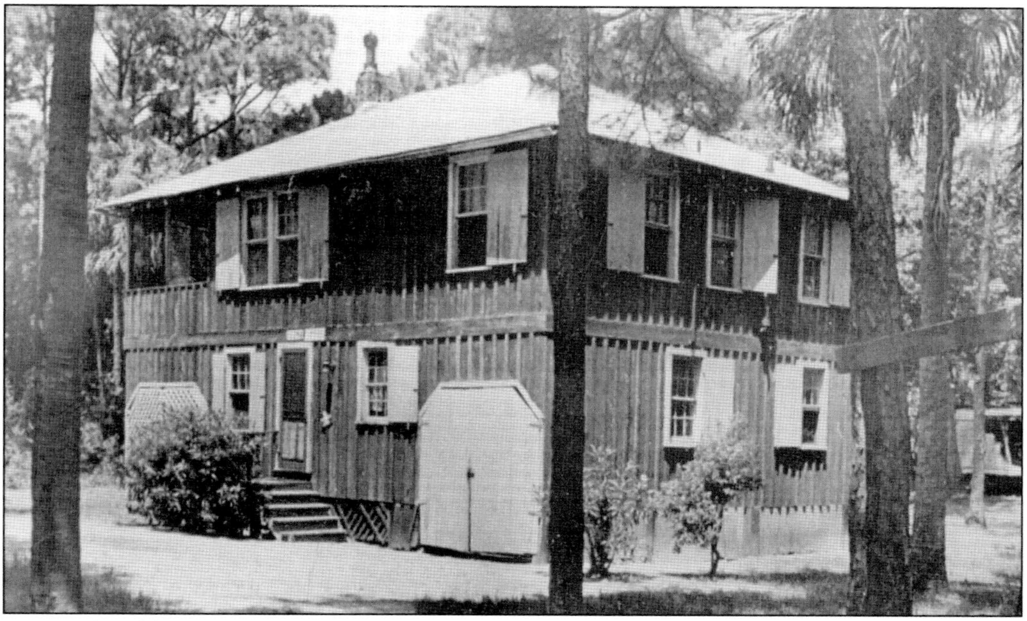

Heyward and his wife, Dorothy, lived in a home they called Follywood. When Gershwin visited in 1934, he stayed at a home across the street on the front beach. Although the term Follywood is still in use among local businesses today, a 1944 initiative promoted by Warner Brothers to rename Folly as Gershwin Isle fell flat in a town council vote. (Courtesy of Paul Chrysostom and the Folly Beach Civic Club.)

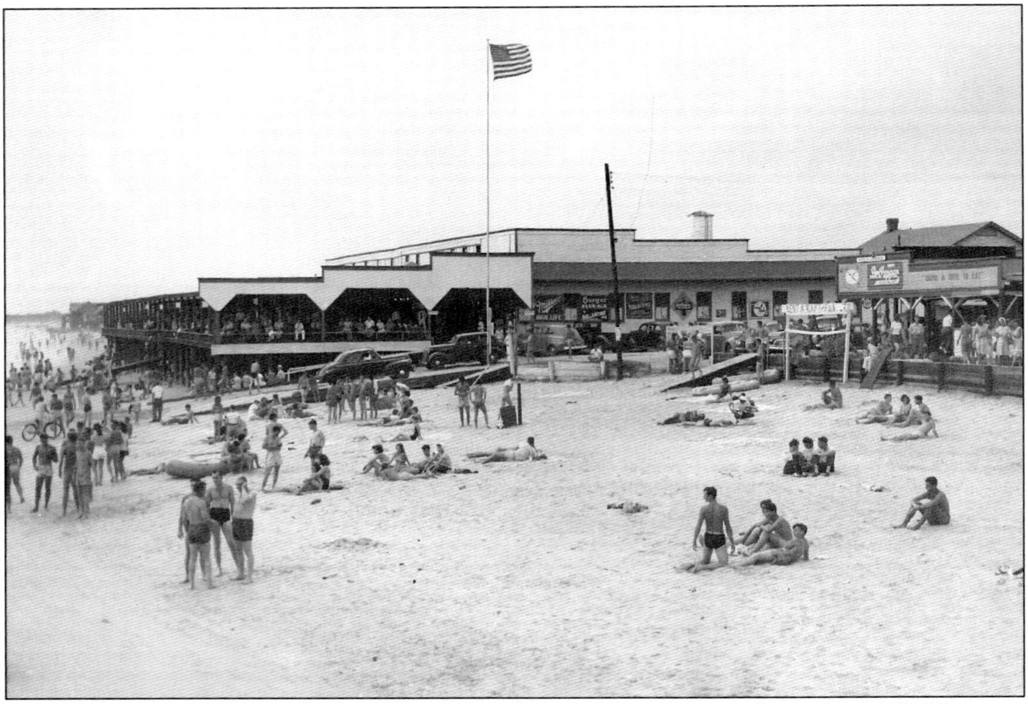
The original wooden boardwalk was the center of beachfront activity. It burned in 1957. (Courtesy of Patricia Jamison Wilbanks Bragg.)

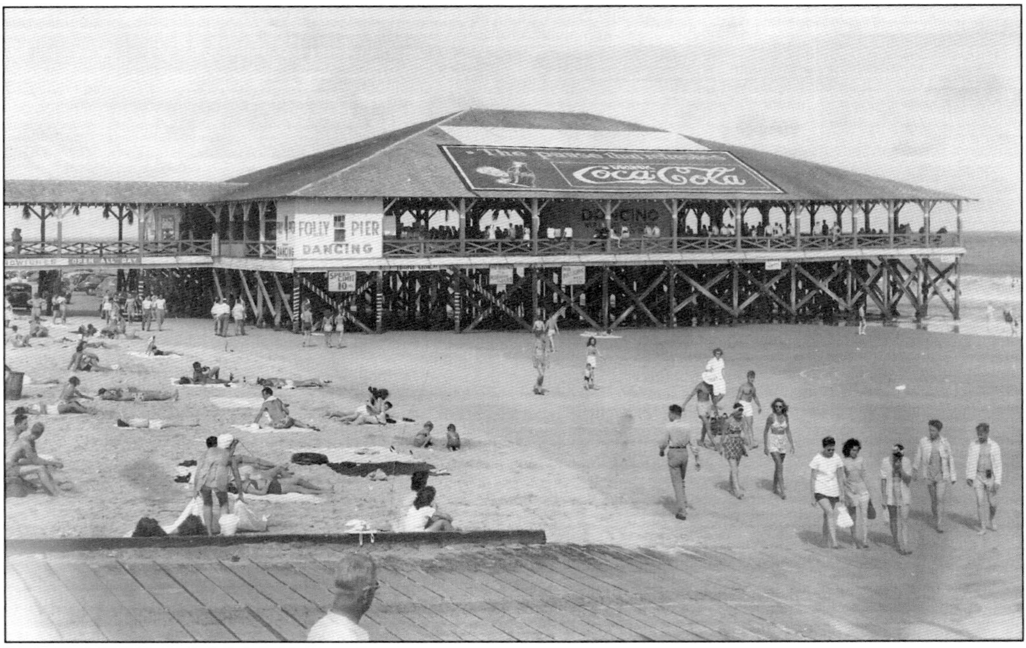

The pier was the hub of nightlife. In April 1965, Folly even experienced a small riot when Fats Domino failed to show up for a scheduled performance. Patricia "Cookie" Bragg grew up on the island, and recalls not being allowed to visit the pier or pavilion at night until she was married—she wed her sweetheart, Jack Wilbanks, at the age of 18. (Courtesy of Patricia Jamison Wilbanks Bragg.)

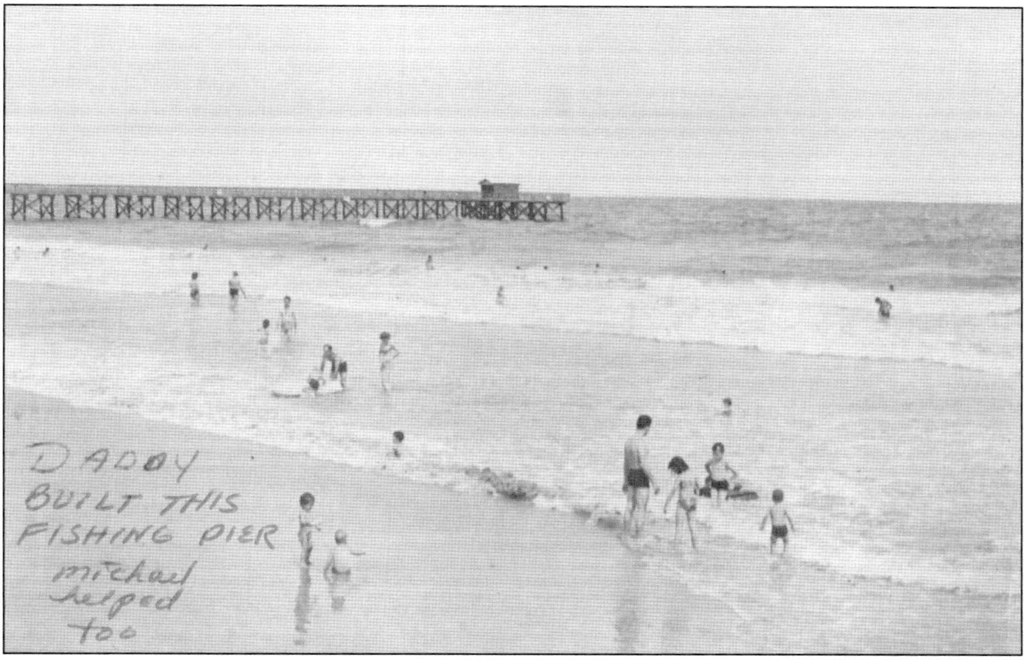

Jack Southworth built the Folly Beach fishing pier, adjacent to the dance pier, with his grandson Michael Schultz in the early 1960s. It was swept away by Hurricane Hugo in 1989 and replaced by the current Edwin S. Taylor Fishing Pier in 1995, named after the owner of the Atlantic House. (Courtesy of Betty Schultz.)

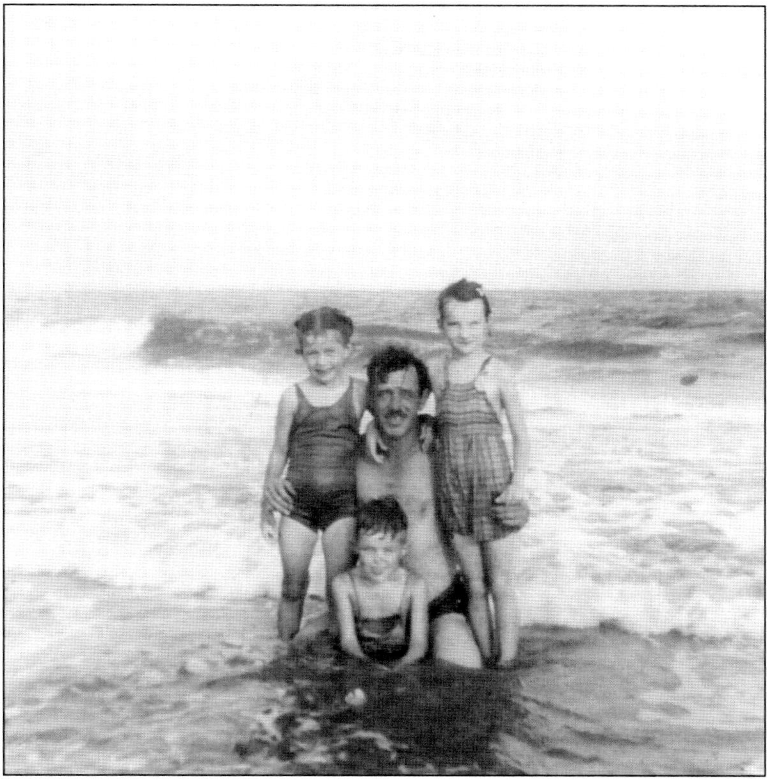

The Lowcountry has always been a magnet for people from the north. Betty Schultz's father, Austin "Jack" Southworth, was a jack-of-all-trades who made his living repairing the steeples of the churches in downtown Charleston. A proud father, he poses here with his children, Betty (left), John (center), and a friend in the waves at Folly Beach in 1941. (Courtesy of Betty Schultz.)

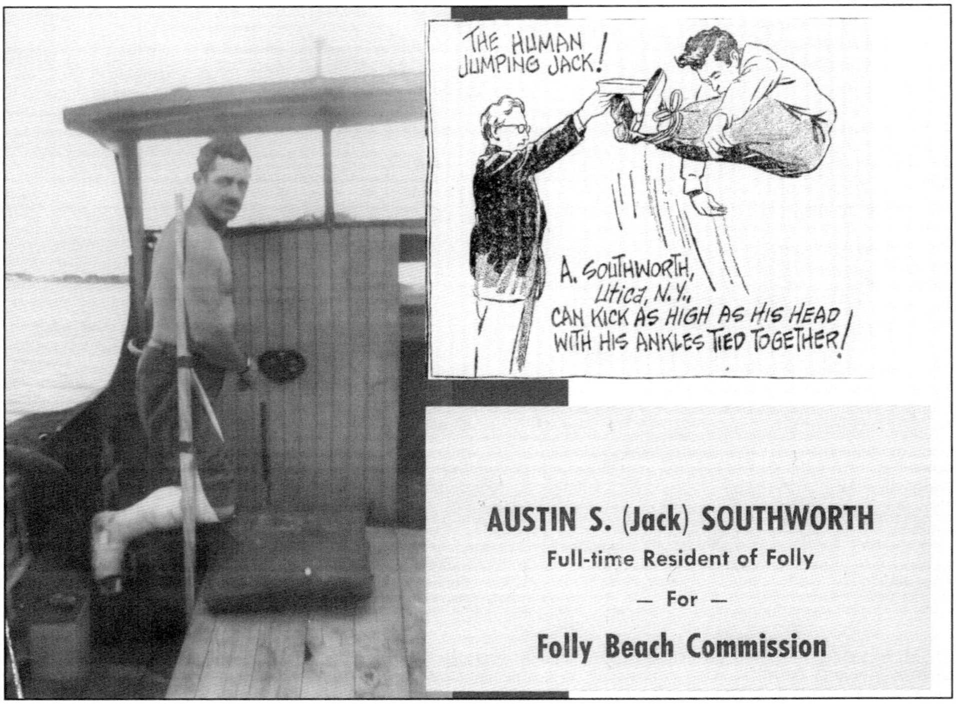

Earning the nickname Jack for his ability to do anything, including feats of human strength and dexterity, Jack Southworth and his wife, Jane, built a boat and sailed from New York to Charleston in 1935. Their daughter, Betty Schultz, of East Erie Avenue, was born en route, in Richmond, Virginia. In this photograph, determined to remain mobile, Jack wears a homemade crutch for a broken leg. Years later, he ran for Folly Beach Commission to represent the township formed to self-represent the island in 1936. (Courtesy of Betty Schultz.)

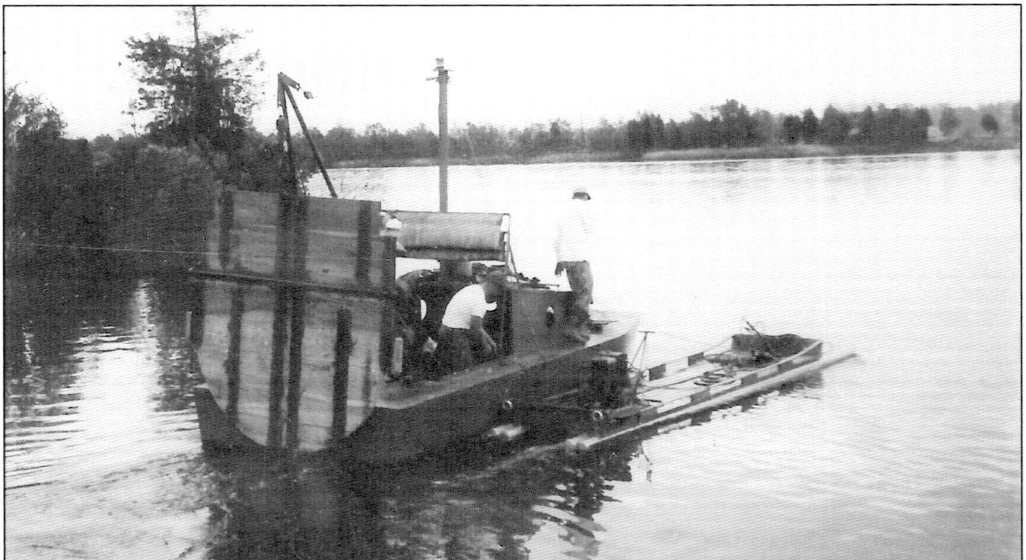

Southworth's boats were built for their purpose, from sailing the eastern seaboard to clearing out areas of the marsh. His unique boats had names to match, from *The Echo* to *Swamp Boogie*. (Courtesy of Betty Schultz.)

Regulations protecting the salt marsh were far more lenient—or nonexistent—in the 1940s than they are today. Cutting new channels and blasting out areas of the marsh with dynamite were common practice. (Courtesy of Betty Schultz.)

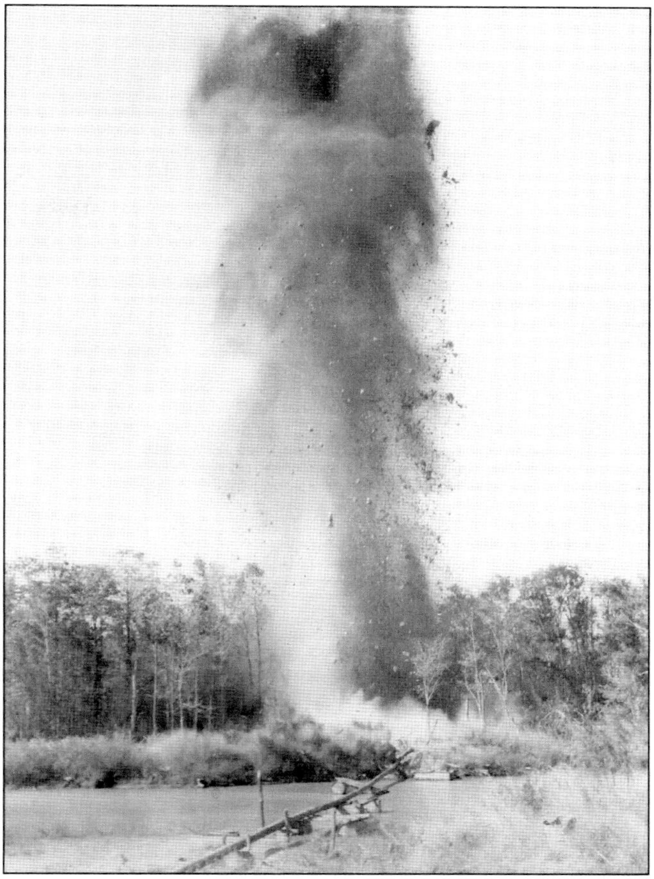

Heating oil had to be delivered well into the mid-1900s on Folly Beach. Boss Wilbanks owned Folly Fuel Supply, filling up his truck in Charleston and delivering to his neighbors on the beach. His son Jack is driving in the photograph below. (Courtesy of Patricia Jamison Wilbanks Bragg.)

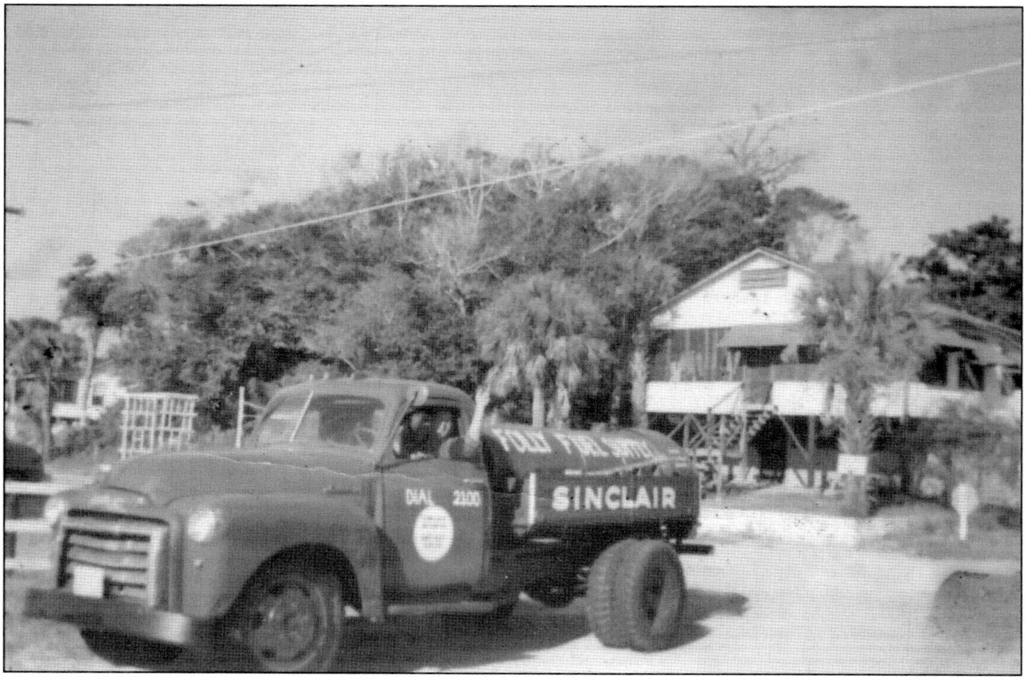

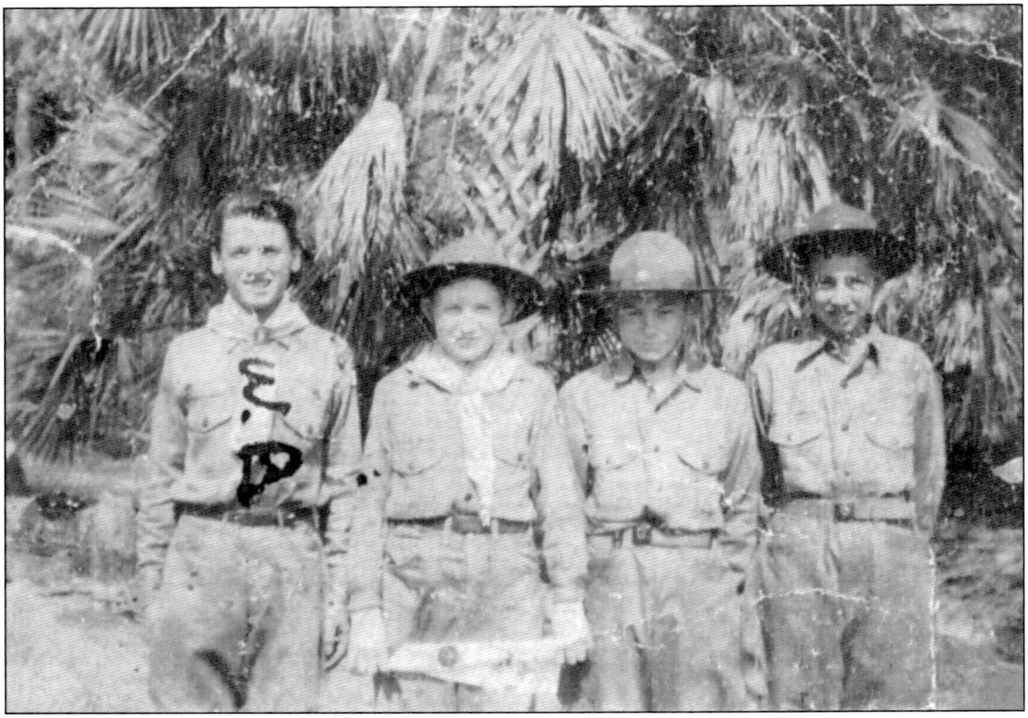

In 1942, the Boy Scouts of Folly Beach had plenty of open land and jungle-like forests to explore. William Barnett stands at attention on the left. (Courtesy of Maebelle Barnett Bazzel.)

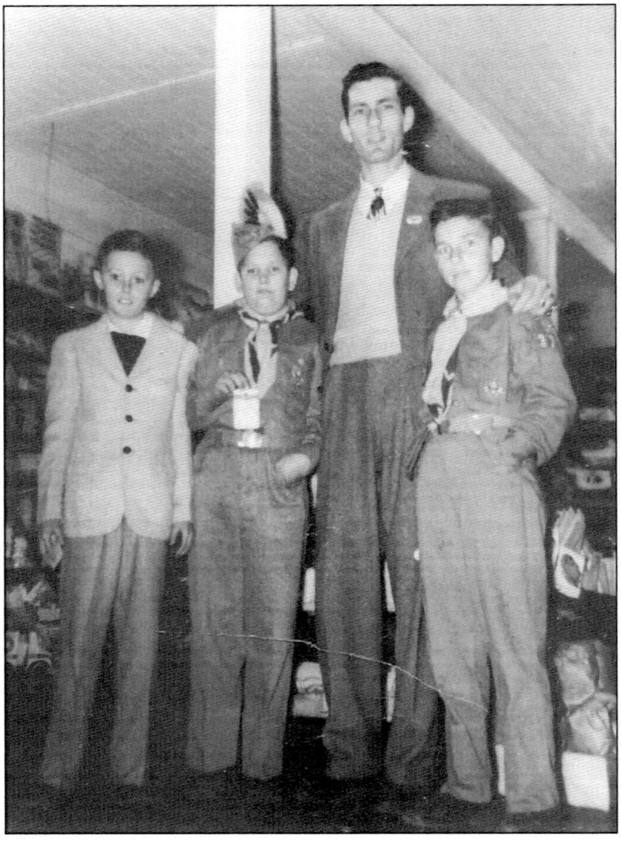

Boy Scout leader Bob Pratt stands with scouts (from left to right) Jimmy Owens, Jack Wilbanks, and Ralph Smith in the late 1940s. The Boy Scouts on Folly Beach were a relatively small troop compared to their counterparts in Charleston. (Courtesy of Patricia Jamison Wilbanks Bragg.)

In 1932, just nine families lived on Folly Beach, most of them originally from somewhere else. Walter and Cynthia Woods Barnett moved to Folly in 1941, relocating from Hell-for-Certain, Kentucky. The couple stayed in a small room on the pier and saved enough money for Cynthia to return home for their seven children. Their new house, at 702 ½ East Ashley Avenue, was a "world of wonders," with electric lights and a flush toilet. Walter served as a policeman and worked as a carpenter, constructing the old one-room city jail, the original civic center, and the skating rink that is now part of Folly Beach Baptist Church. (Courtesy of Maebelle Barnett Bazzel.)

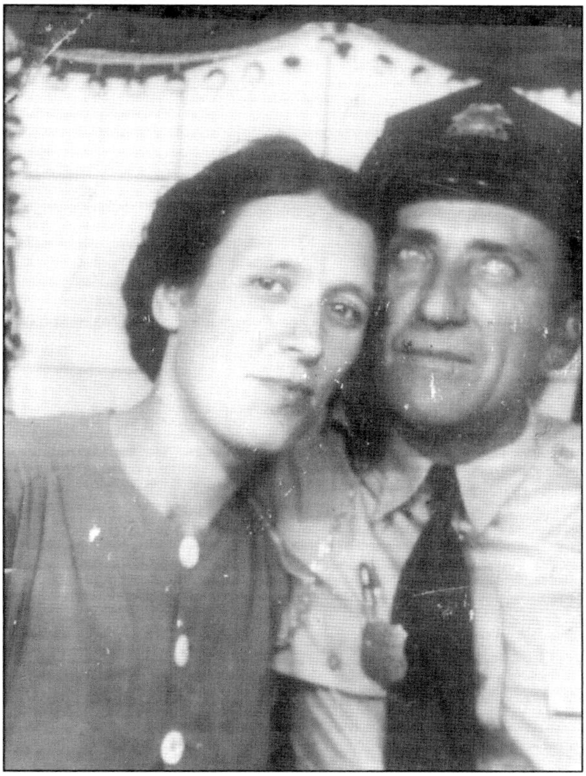

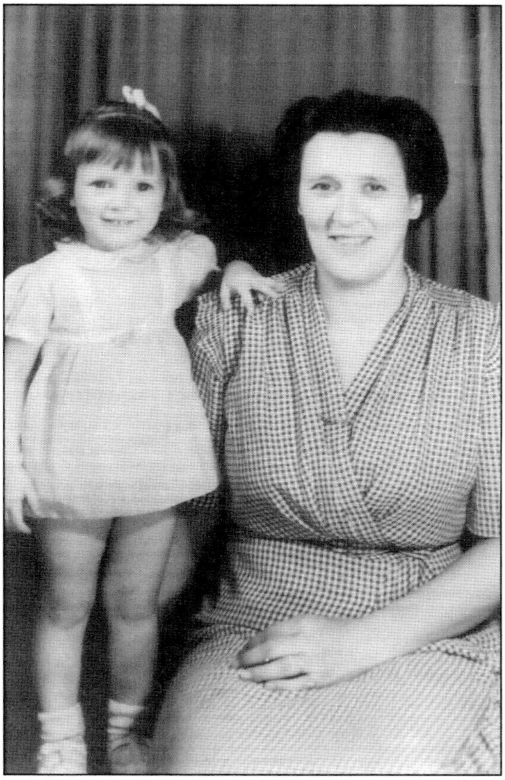

Cynthia Woods Barnett poses with her two-and-a-half-year-old daughter Maebelle in 1945, three years after moving to Folly Beach. Maebelle was born at The Sandpiper, a two-story house on West Ashley Avenue, behind the bus station on Arctic Avenue. Cynthia worked briefly at the Ocean Front Hotel, owned by Manning and Olive Bennett. Manning Bennett's sister, also named Maybelle, was married to Ted Schiadaressi, who built and operated the pavilion. Marshall Lee Hunt, a friend of Walter Barnett's and the island's police officer, was married to another woman named Maybell. Had she been a boy, the young Maebelle Barnett was to be named Teddy Lee after her father's friends. Her mother had planned to name a daughter Elizabeth Frances, but Walter signed the papers and wrote Maebelle, in honor of his friends' wives. Cynthia called her daughter Baby for most of the next year. (Courtesy of Maebelle Barnett Bazzel.)

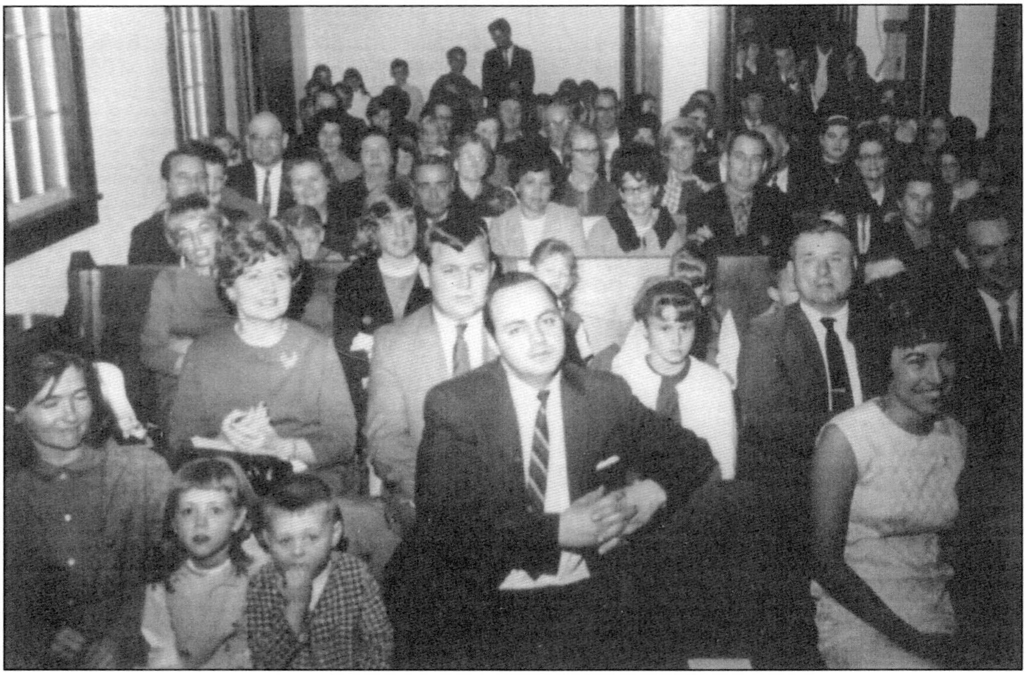

Sunday services were busy at Folly Beach Baptist Church in the mid-1960s. (Courtesy of Maebelle Barnett Bazzel.)

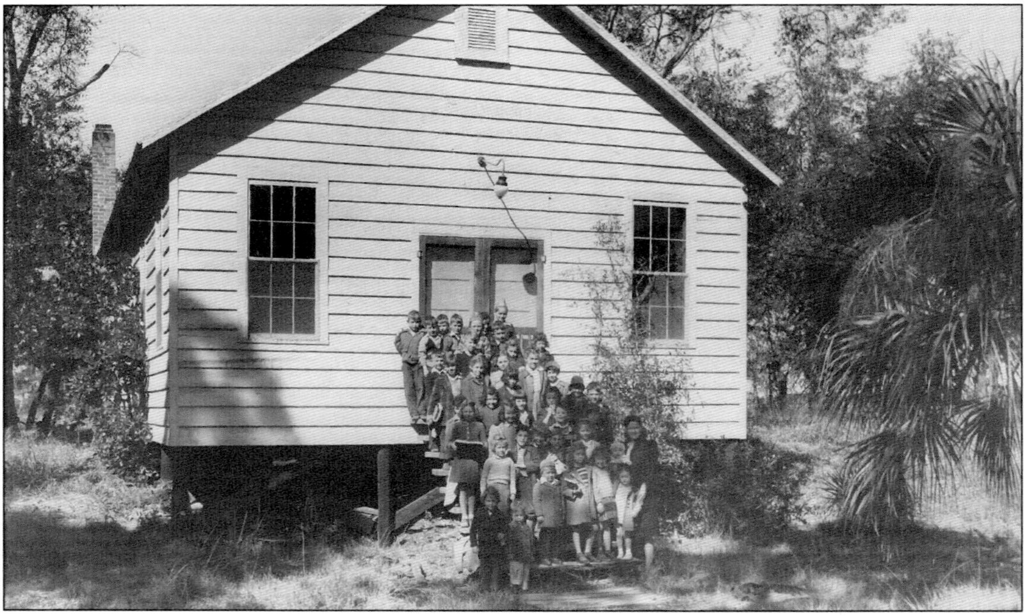

For many residents of Folly Beach today, Sunday church is still an opportunity to gather and share family news. This 1946 photograph of the Community Church shows Folly's children gathered on the stairs, including, in no particular order, Dorothy Turner, Bobee Browning, Bushy Peek, Helen Hubbard, Carolyn and Ben Nance, Eleanor Bentz, and Melton Demetre. This structure was built after the Faith Chapel burned. By 1947, the Folly Beach Baptist Church had been built, and this building became the Folly Beach United Methodist Church. (Courtesy of Patricia Jamison Wilbanks Bragg.)

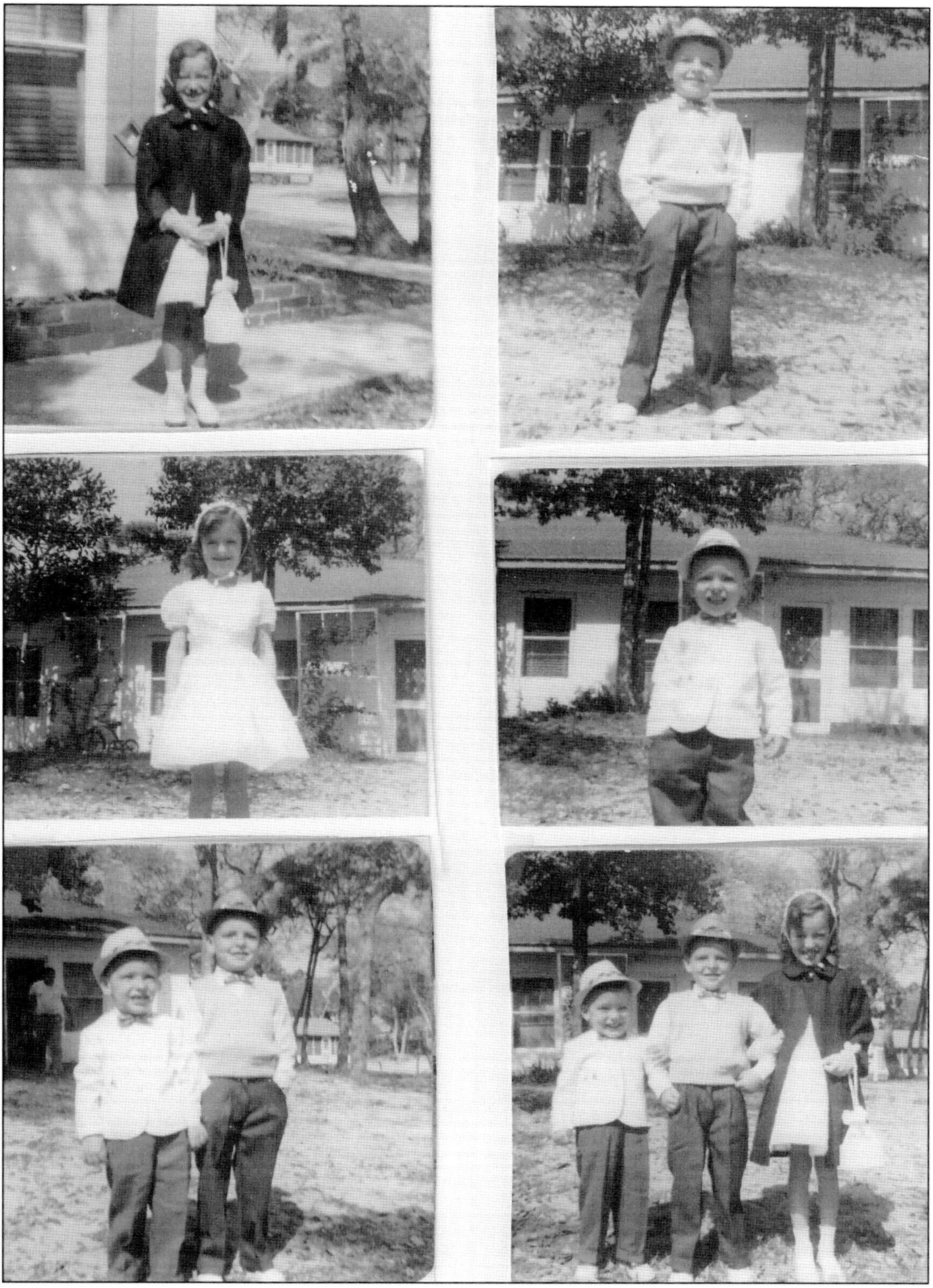

Easter Sunday remains a special time for family on Folly Beach. In this series of photographs from 1956, Cynthia Barnett (Norris) poses with her nephews Jimmy and Michael Blake. Cynthia's older sister, Stella, suffered from the disease Myasthenia Gravis and passed away in 1955. Stella's sons were raised with their young aunts as sisters on Folly Beach. (Courtesy of Maebelle Barnett Bazzel.)

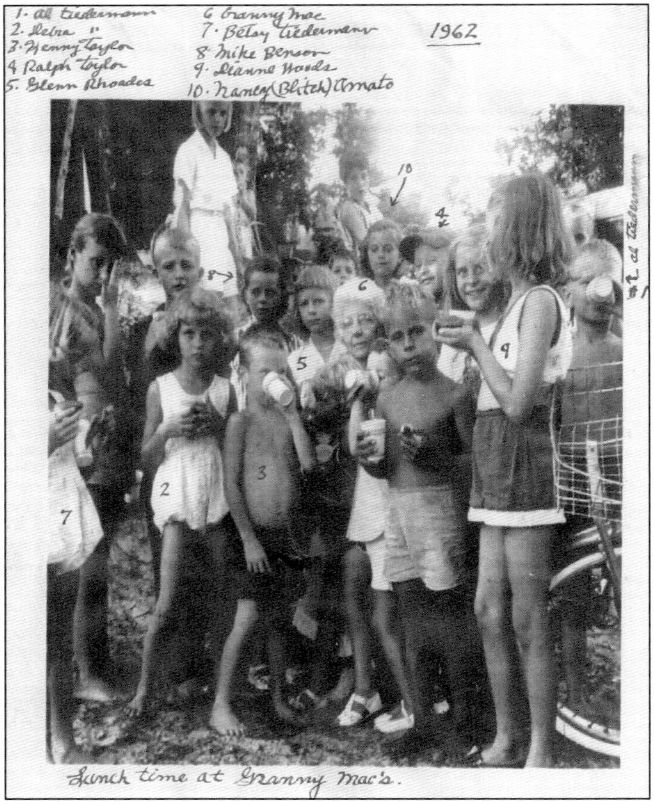

In the early 1960s, Maude C. McMillan (known to most as Granny Mac) was a neighborhood favorite of local children, teaching Bible school classes on Friday afternoons inside a bus parked on cinder blocks outside her home. If the children were attentive, Granny Mac rewarded them with cookies and Kool-Aid. (Courtesy of Wallace Benson.)

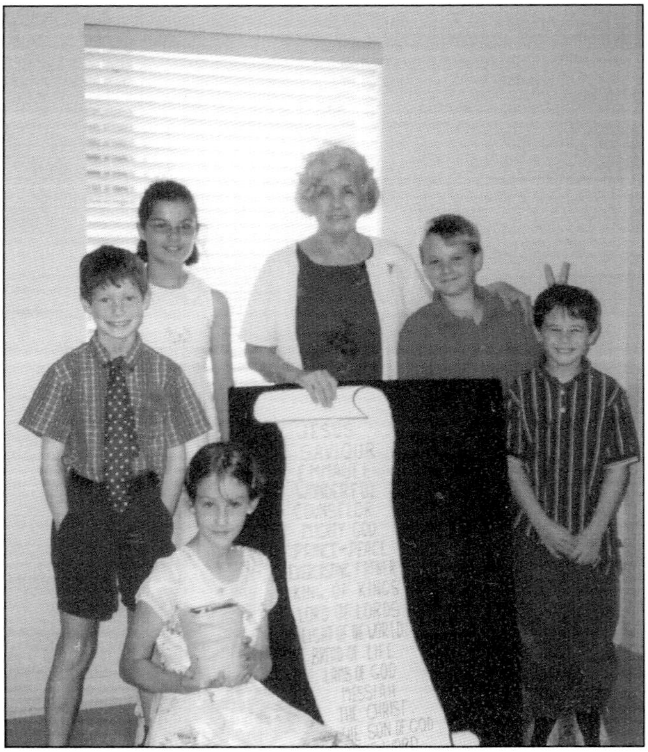

A devout Christian, Betty Schultz, seen here, taught Sunday school at the Folly Beach Baptist Church for more than 50 years. The church remains a focal point of the island community. (Courtesy of Betty Schultz.)

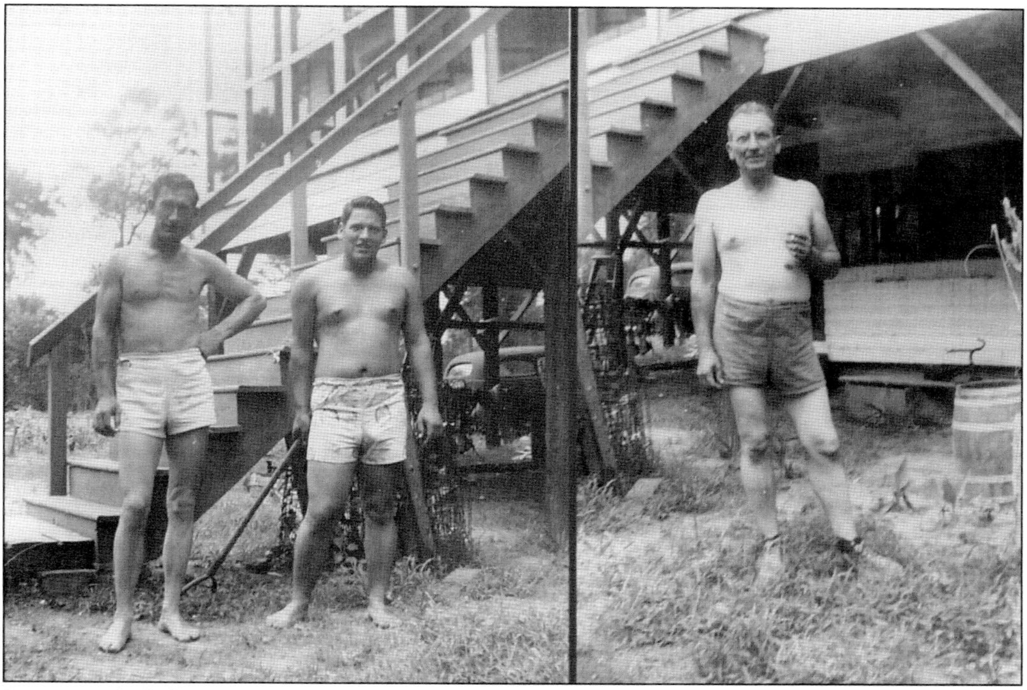

Dan Woods (left) poses with his nephew, Walter "Junior" Barnett, outside 1001 East Ashley Avenue after a day of fishing in 1949. Walter Barnett Sr. (right) joined them for the day on the water. (Courtesy of Maebelle Barnett Bazzel.)

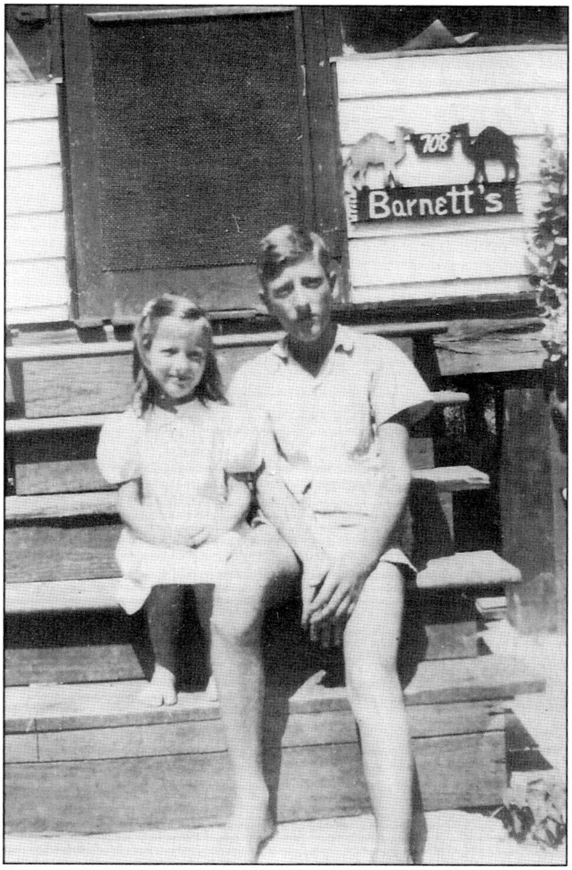

Siblings Maebelle and Breck Barnett sit on the steps of their home at 708 East Cooper Avenue. In this photograph, Breck was 13 and Maebelle was 5. "My brother was my hero," recalls Maebelle. When their father passed away, Breck was 16 and had four younger sisters. (Courtesy of Maebelle Barnett Bazzel.)

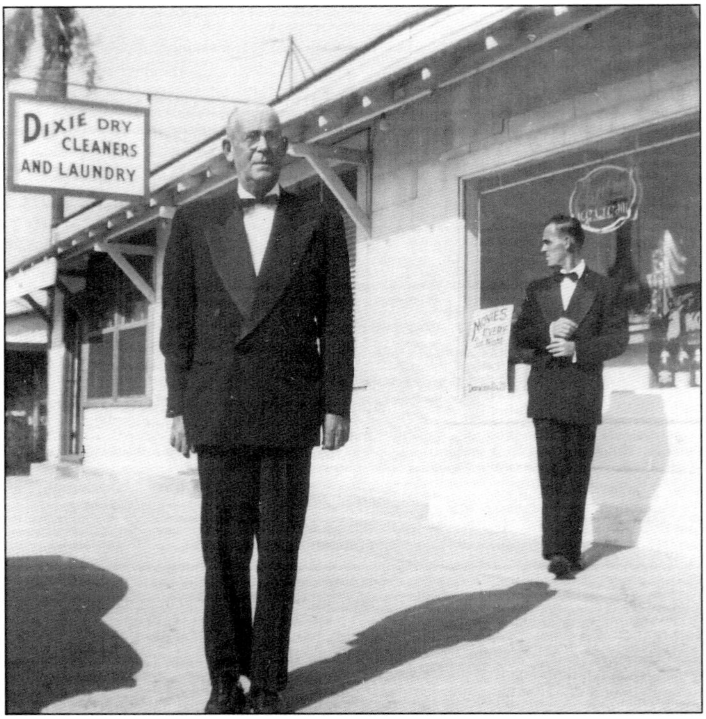

Billy Amos and his son Dick prepare to go to a wedding, posing for photographs outside Florence's Drug Store and Dixie Dry Cleaners, where Snapper Jack's is now located, at Center Street and East Ashley Avenue. (Courtesy of Patricia Jamison Wilbanks Bragg.)

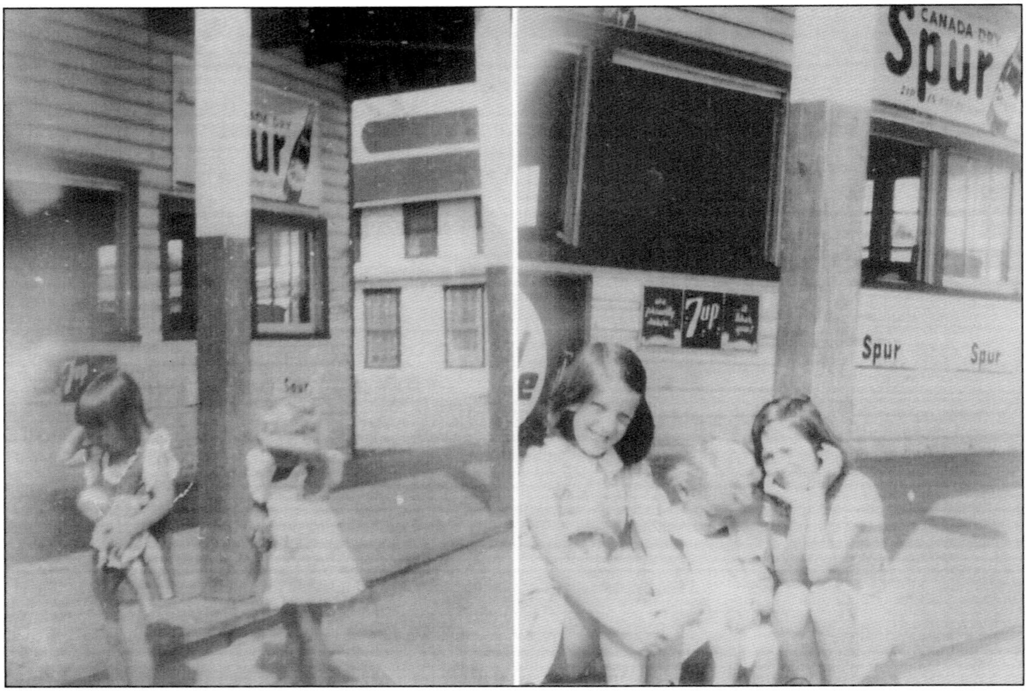

On the left, in front of the Little Atlantic in 1946, Maebelle Barnett and Paula Jean Baitinger cry over spilled ice cream. Immediately after, happy sisters Bonnie and Mike Barnett console Paula Jean (center). At the time, the Barnett family lived upstairs above the restaurant. The Little Atlantic later became Joe's Restaurant, and burned to the ground with the pavilion in 1957. (Courtesy of Maebelle Barnett Bazzel.)

In 1952, William "Bubbie" Barnett, a sharpshooter, returned home from duty with the Marines at Camp Pendleton in California after his father, Walter Barnett, passed away. (Courtesy of Maebelle Barnett Bazzel.)

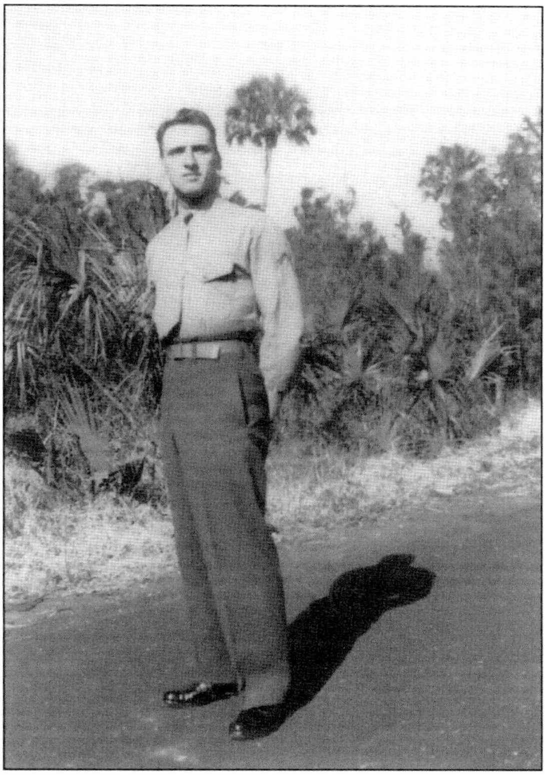

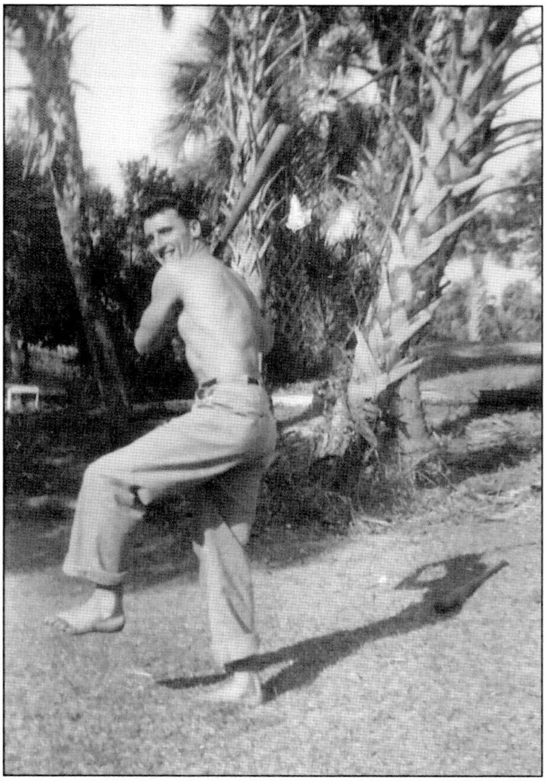

Bubbie Barnett returned to Folly with his young wife, Kathryn Bennett, for a happy trip in 1953. He is seen here playing ball in the yard. The game of half rubber developed around Charleston in the early 1900s, including on Folly Beach. Beachgoers still play the curious game, which utilizes half of a rubber ball, on Folly each summer. (Courtesy of Maebelle Barnett Bazzel.)

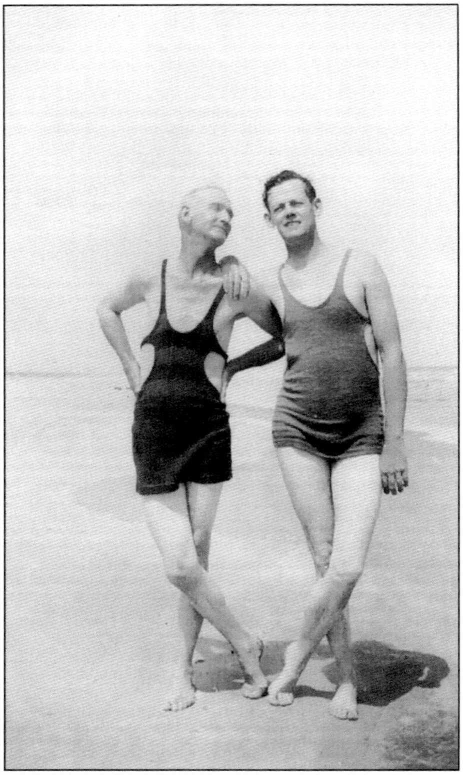

R.A. Adams poses with his friend Mr. Mann sometime before men's swimwear evolved into its current style. "My grandparents, Mr. and Mrs. R.A. Adams, lived to spend the day at Folly," says Cookie Bragg. "There were large family gatherings with several cars parked together and a 'tent' drawn across them for shade. The women were usually in dresses." (Courtesy of Patricia Jamison Wilbanks Bragg.)

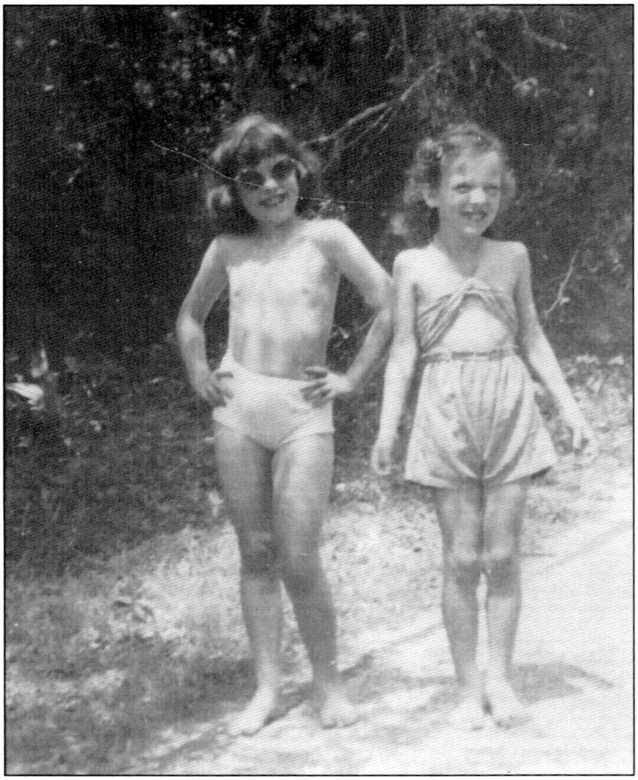

Barbara Hubbard (Johnson) (left) and Maebelle Barnett (Bazzel) smile for the camera around 1950. (Courtesy of Barbara Johnson.)

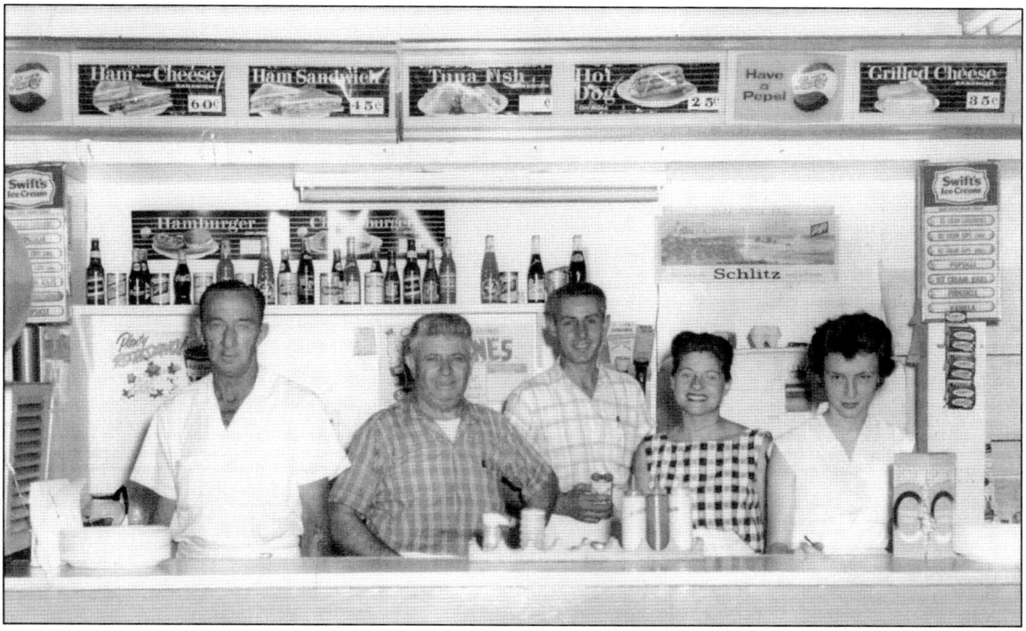

Paul Knight (left) stands behind the counter with Marie Smith (right) and three unidentified operators of the pavilion at the rebuilt Pavilion Bar on the boardwalk plaza in the early 1960s. (Courtesy of Maebelle Barnett Bazzel.)

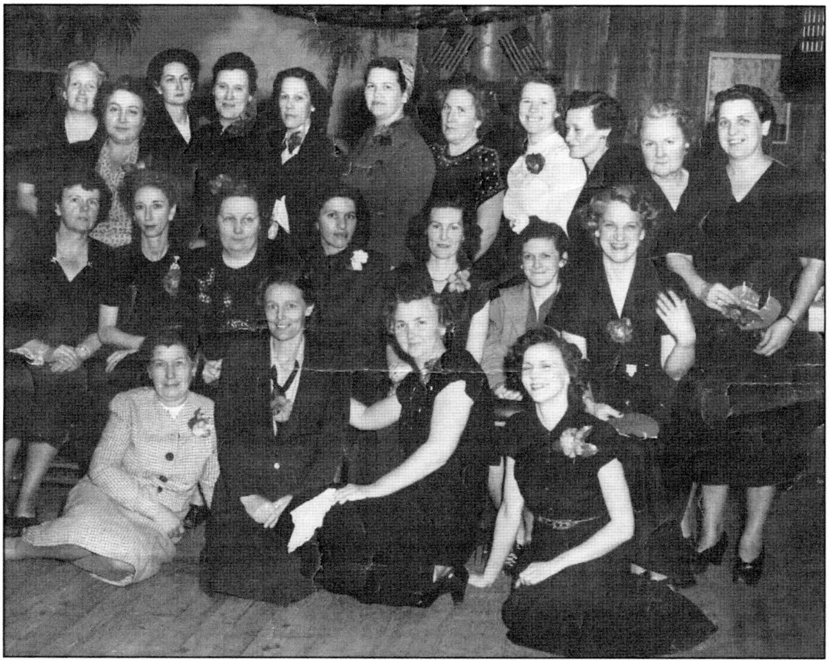

Folly Beach mothers pose at the Civic Club's 1948 Mother-Daughter Banquet. They are, from left to right, (first row) Stella Sharpe, Elizabeth Browning, Anne Donehue, and Mildred Howell; (second row) Eula Chastain, Emma Pauls, Eleanor Bentz, Clara Nelson, Mildred Goss, Evelyn Keith, and Mary Turner; (third row) Mary Smith, Ardelle Rivers, Miriam Murphy, Cynthia Barnett, Sue Danner, Dorothy Turner, Honey Hoppman, Cora Lee Nance, Margaret Owens, Hortense Fitzgerald, and Minnie Smith. (Courtesy of Maebelle Barnett Bazzel.)

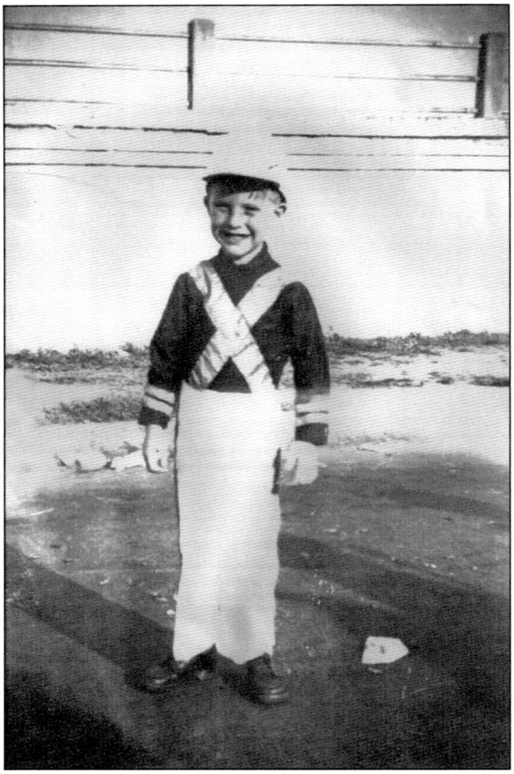

Five-year-old Wallace Benson jumped at the chance to head to downtown Charleston for parade day and "defend" Fort Sumter with his wooden gun. Benson's parents, Clifton and Thelma, met in Charleston when Clifton moved to town from Wilmington, North Carolina, to work at the shipyard. The pair soon moved to West Hudson Avenue on Folly because they loved the beach and because a quarter-acre lot was "real cheap." "We had a two bedroom house and four kids," recalls Benson. "Each kid had one drawer in the dresser and we had two bunk beds. Folly Beach was country back then, with goats roaming the island and chickens and horses all over the place. It was a simple life." (Courtesy of Wallace Benson.)

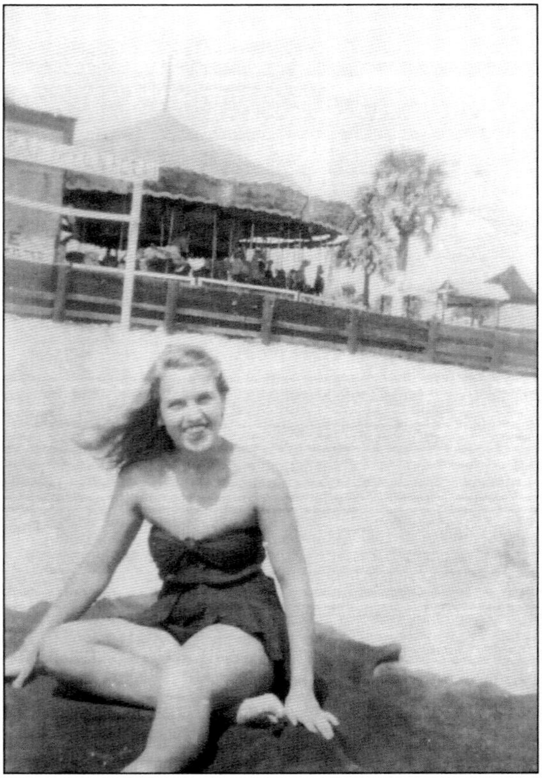

Lillian Owens, the daughter of Frank and Capitola Owens, sits on the beach in front of the merry-go-round on Folly in the 1940s. (Courtesy of Maebelle Barnett Bazzel.)

Bobbie Keller Weingarten enters the post office at 103 West Cooper Avenue with her son James (now Dr. James Weingarten) in 1953. The site of the old post office is now the Surf Bar. (Courtesy of Bobbie Keller Weingarten and the Folly Beach Civic Club.)

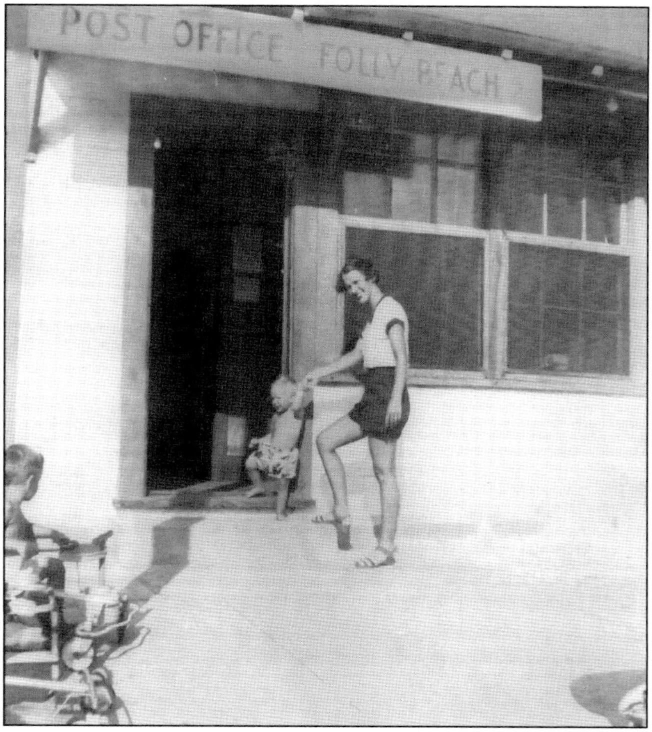

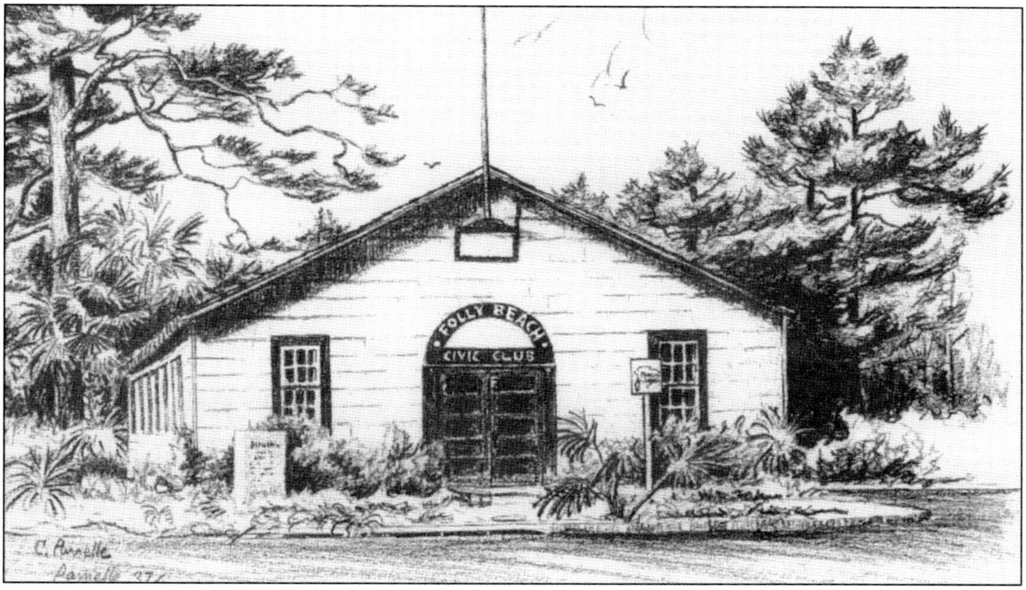

This drawing by Charles Parnell depicts the original Folly Beach Civic Club, built by Walter Barnett and his sons, Junior and William, using old boards salvaged from the construction of the dam on the Santee River that formed Lake Moultrie. Nails had to be removed from the warped boards, and the excess was used to help construct Folly's skating rink. The Civic Club is still integral to the community of Folly Beach, publishing a monthly newsletter, *The Sandspur*, which keeps citizens informed of the issues in city hall. The club also creates an annual calendar with photographs of the island over the course of its history, many of which appear in this book. (Courtesy of Maebelle Barnett Bazzel and the Folly Beach Civic Club.)

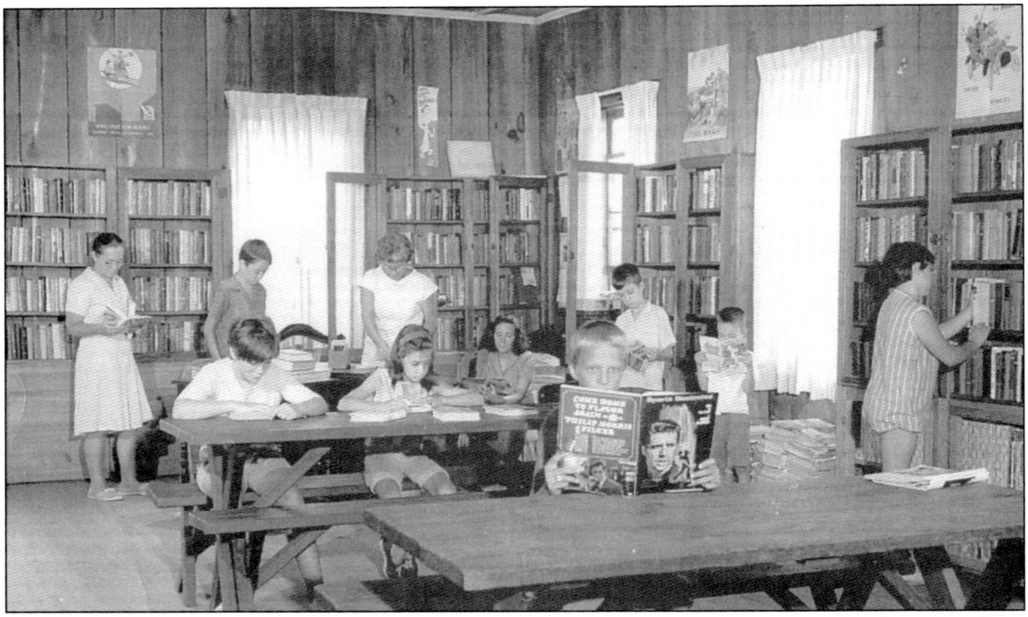

The island's original library was in the Civic Club until 1960. Dorothy Turner replaced Lottie Olney as the librarian, overseeing the many children who took advantage of books and a communal place to learn and read in the days before cable television. Olney, the original librarian for the Civic Club, was born on July 2, 1869, and passed away at age 86 in 1955 after a seven-year battle with breast cancer. Children and friends remember her as "the sweetest lady" on the island. (Courtesy of Kathy Nicklaus, Maebelle Barnett Bazzel, and the Folly Beach Civic Club.)

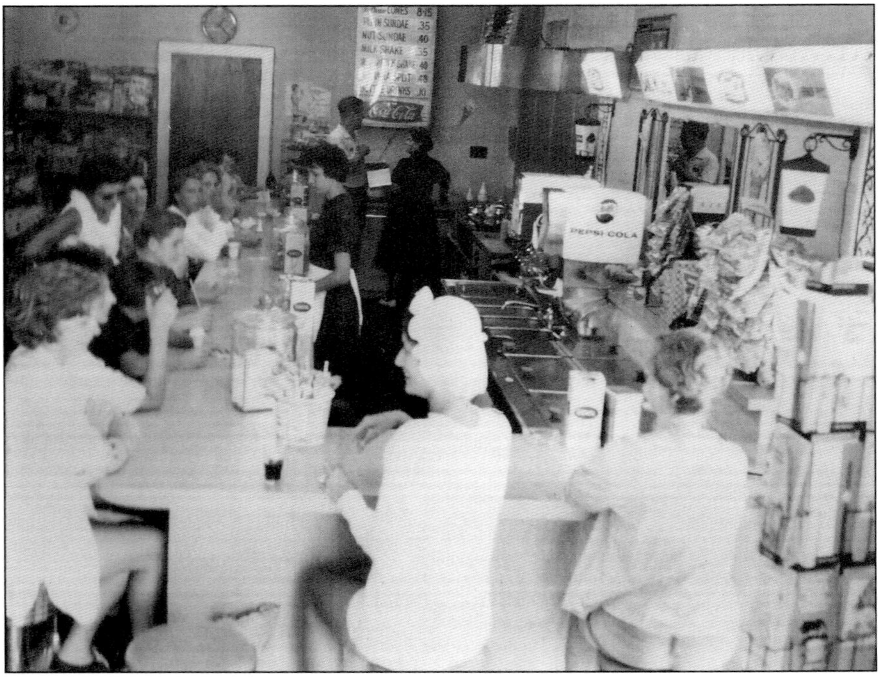

Center Street's drugstores were the hub of socializing and exchanging community news. This afternoon scene inside Folly Drug Sundries (Florence's) shows the lively scene around the counter. (Courtesy of Patricia Jamison Wilbanks Bragg.)

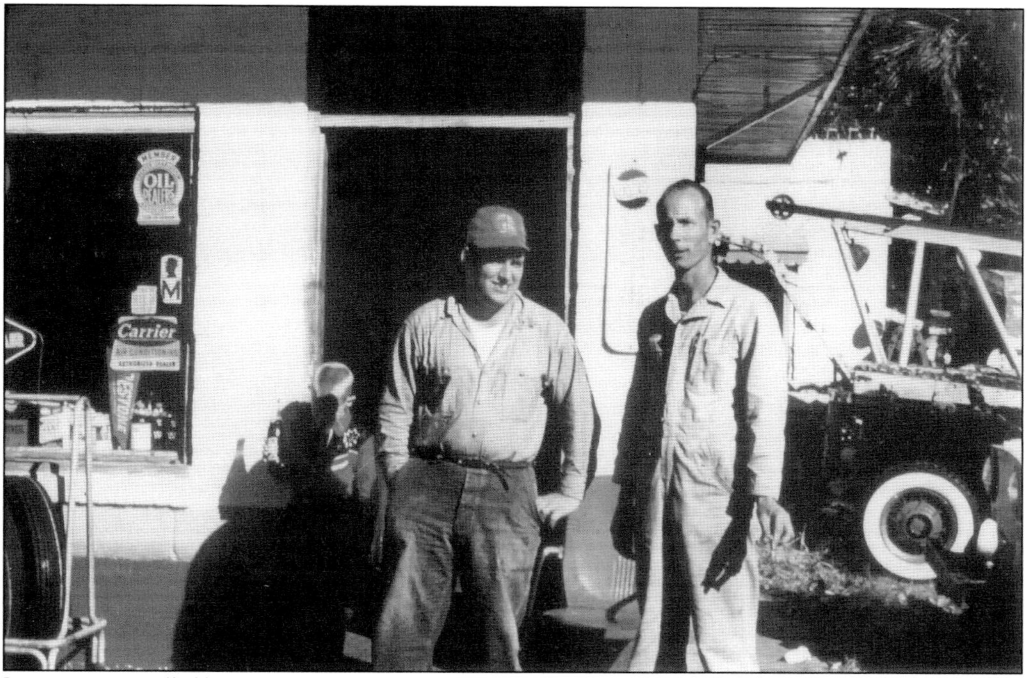

Junior Barnett (left) and Ernie Rhodes are seen here outside the Pure Oil station in the 1950s, the site of the current BP station on Center Street. Rhodes's brother Tom owned another station across the street, at the current site of the Grill on the Edge. (Courtesy of Maebelle Barnett Bazzel.)

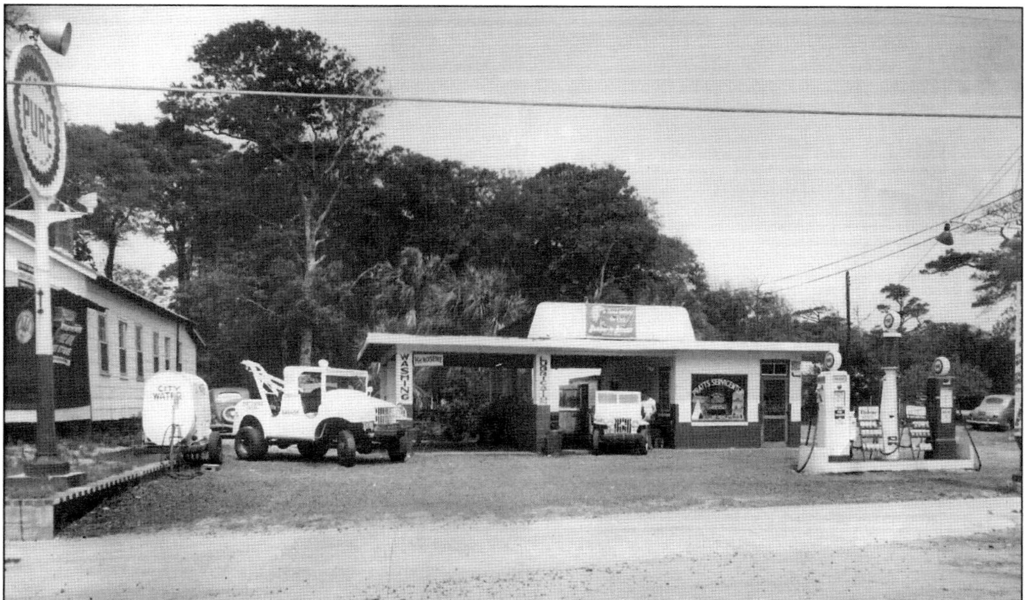

Folly once supported as many as three gas stations, but the cost of permits to keep underground tanks eventually led to just one surviving, the Pantry (now the BP/Kangaroo). In this photograph of Pratt's Pure Oil station, note the "City Water" tank to the left. Because well water on the island had a distinct mineral taste and smell, most visitors brought refillable jugs. A gallon at a city water tank cost 5¢ throughout most of the 1950s. (Courtesy of Wallace Benson.)

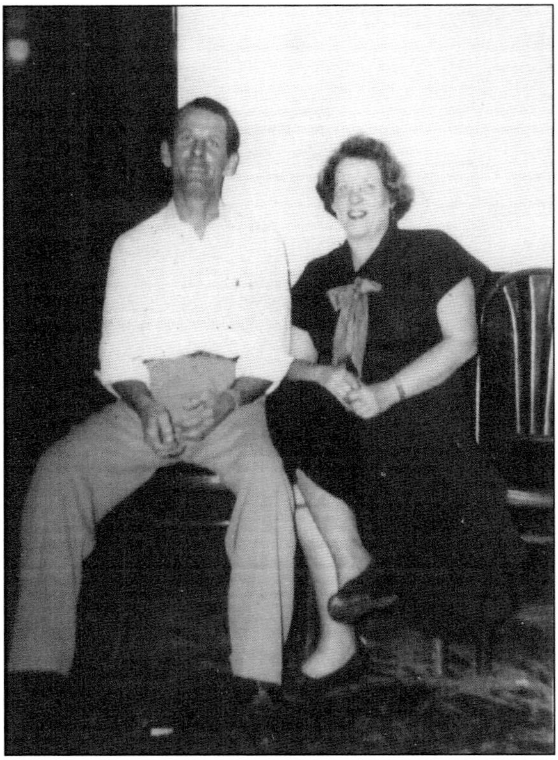

Boss and Florence Wilbanks owned Folly Drug Sundries, a fixture of Center Street throughout the 1950s. Maebelle Barnett recalls that Olive and Manning Bennett, who owned the Ocean Front Hotel, would give her and her siblings nickels, which they used to buy candy bars from the drugstore. (Photograph by Jack Wilbanks, courtesy of Maebelle Barnett Bazzel.)

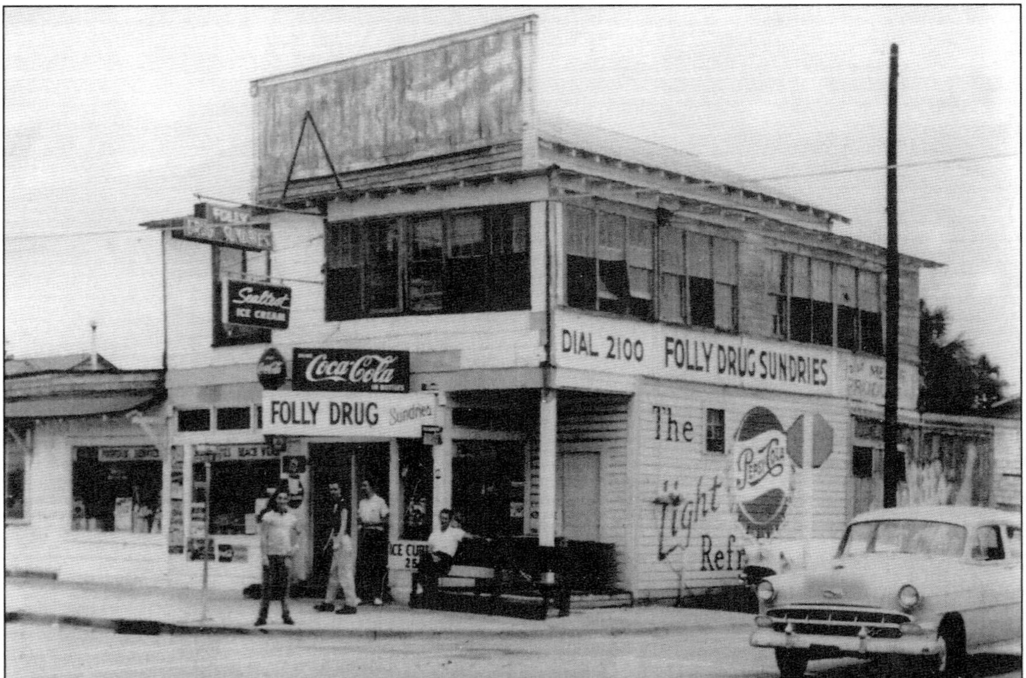

Known to locals as Florence's, Folly Drug Sundries seemed to employ every young person growing up on the beach at one time or another. Owner Boss Wilbanks kept a sign at the register that read, "I may not always be right, but I am always BOSS." (Courtesy of Maebelle Barnett Bazzel.)

A man hangs acrobatically on the Center Street sign. (Courtesy of Patricia Jamison Wilbanks Bragg.)

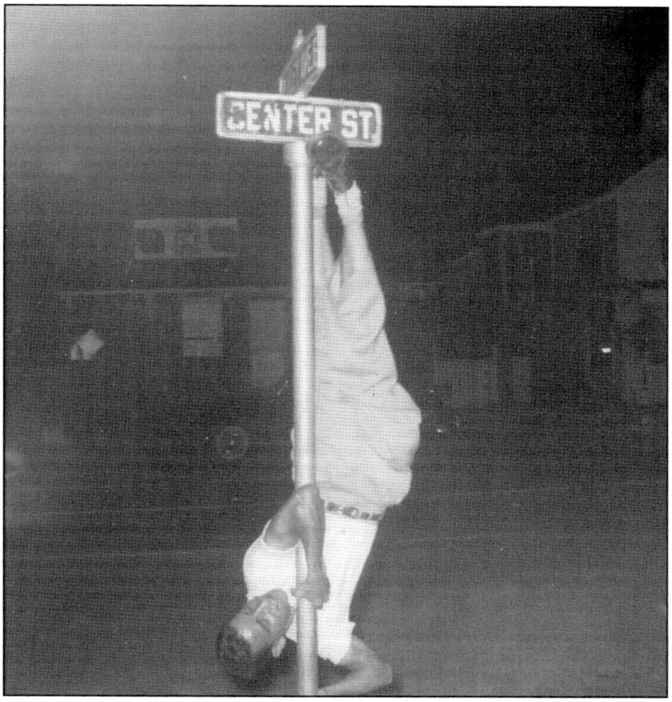

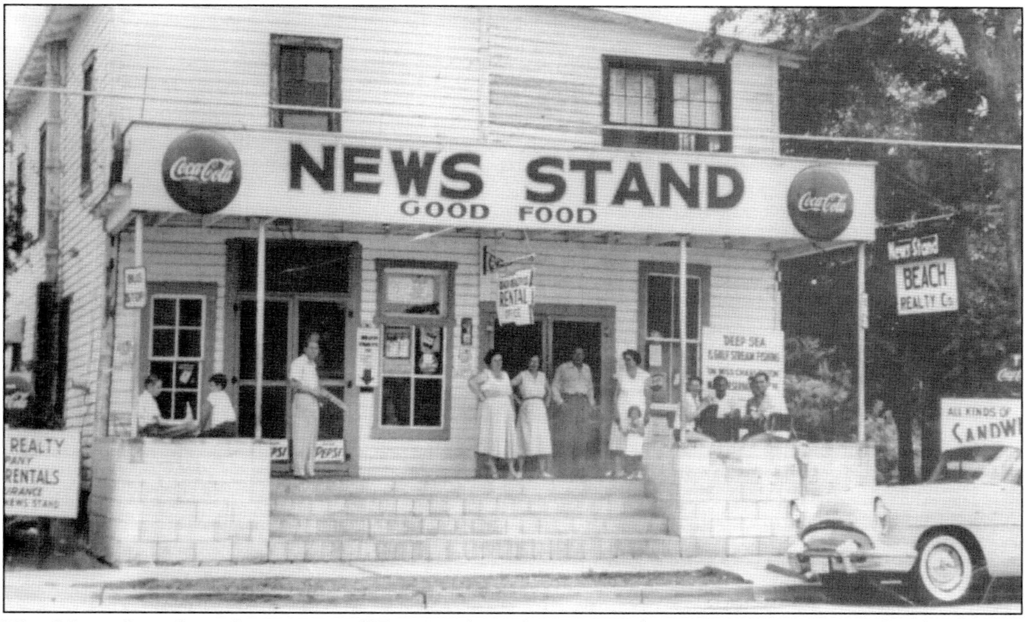

The News Stand, at the corner of East Hudson Avenue and Center Street, was a focal point of the community in 1957, popular for its fried chicken dinner and 15¢ hot dogs. Owner Tommy Weinges stands at the screen door, and his wife, Kitty, is the first woman on the right. Their daughter, Sallie, is the little girl standing at the front of the porch on the right. A magazine rack stood to the left when patrons entered the door. The porch also served as the bus stop for Folly Beach students riding to school in downtown Charleston. Marlene Estridge recalls that in the early 1950s, the bus only picked up about 10 students on James Island, most of which was still farmland. (Courtesy of Maebelle Barnett Bazzel.)

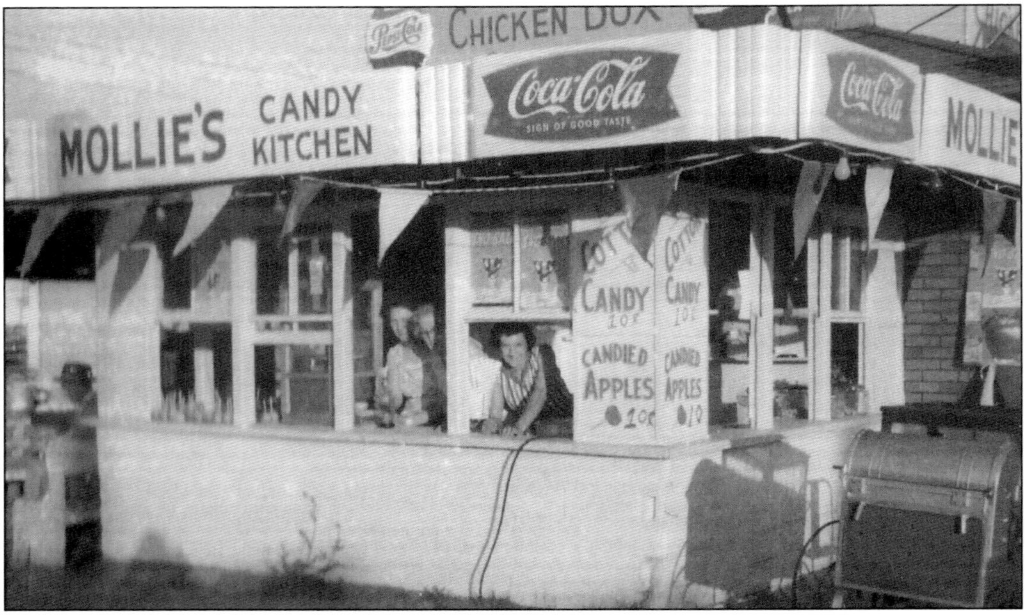

Restaurants come and go quickly along Center Street, often determined by which ones can weather the slow business during winter. The Chicken Box and Mollie's Candy Kitchen were popular food stands in the late 1940s. (Courtesy of Patricia Jamison Wilbanks Bragg.)

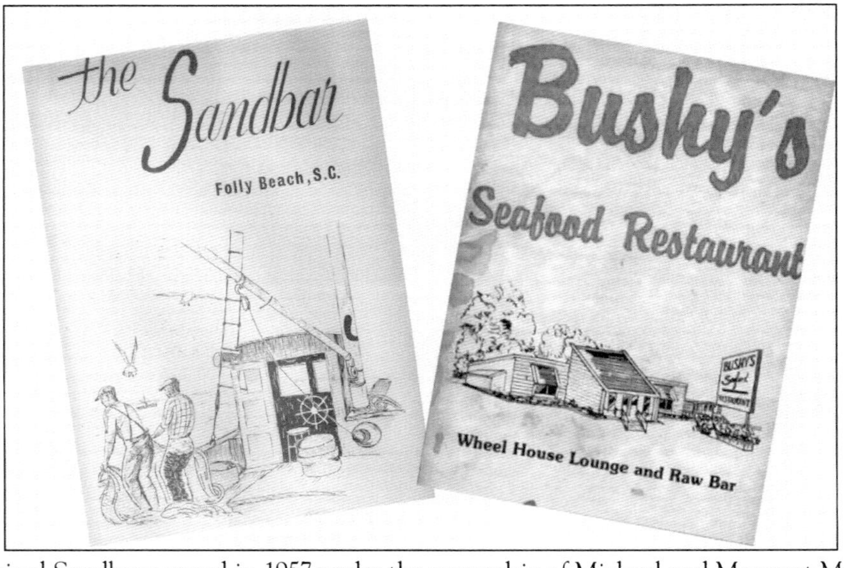

The original Sandbar opened in 1957 under the ownership of Michael and Margaret McCarthy and was purchased by Darus and Muriel Weathers in 1969. Mrs. McCarthy served her first plate of fried shrimp at the request of a hungry friend. Both a restaurant and a working seafood dock, there were typically several shrimp boats tied up there in the Folly River, until Hurricane Hugo took the dock in 1989. The Sandbar was a major employer on Folly Beach, accommodating as many as 600 guests at its peak as a two-story restaurant and banquet hall, used for birthdays, meetings, and weddings. In the mid-1970s, a combination seafood platter with shrimp, deviled crab, scallops, oysters, and fish cost $5.50. A pint of fish chowder was $1.50. Across the river, Bushy's occupied the spot now held by the Turn of the River condos. The Sandbar is still open. (Courtesy of Andie Weathers and Maebelle Barnett Bazzel.)

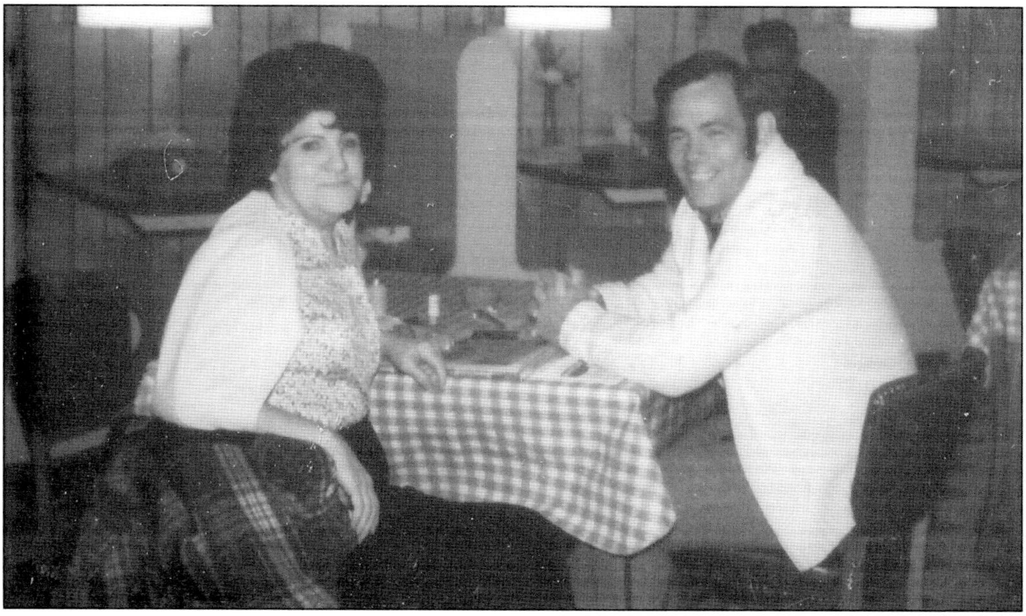

On Center Street, the Sanitary Restaurant was an institution for half a century. Founded by A.G. Kettas (Mr. Charlie to his customers) in the 1930s, the restaurant employed local youths like Cliff Harvey, who recalls Mr. Charlie hiding a nickel on tables for his wait staff when customers forgot to tip. "He was like a grandfather, and he didn't want us to get discouraged," says Harvey, who went on to become a Folly Beach police officer, rising to the rank of assistant chief. In 1964, Harvey's parents took over the Sanitary. In this photograph, Lotti Harvey sits with customer Harry Amtower, who tragically took his life with gasoline and fire at a Folly Road gas station. "He was always smiling," recalls Harvey. The Sanitary remained open until 1998, when the building became the original home of Lost Dog Café, adjacent to present-day Taco Boy. (Courtesy of Cliff and Martha Harvey.)

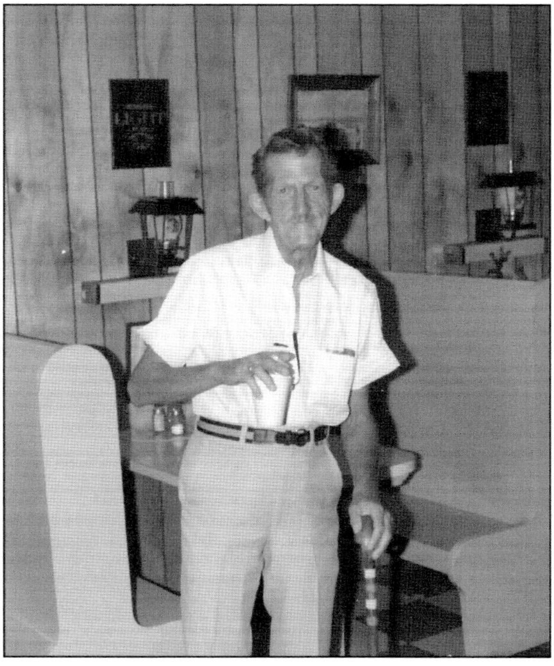

Seafood, steaks, and chops were the main attractions at the Sanitary Restaurant. Breakfast began at 6:00 a.m. with grits and coffee, with dinners available from 2:00 p.m. to 8:00 p.m. In the mid-1980s, a four-ounce rib eye sandwich and two slices of liver with onions were both $5 a plate. Paul Godfrey, seen here, a retiree from the Navy yard, was a daily customer until the day he decided he needed an adventure, buying a 1978 Oldsmobile convertible, a canoe and trailer, and camping gear, and setting out to rough it in the wilds. He soon returned. When Godfrey passed away, he was discovered in his home because his absence at the restaurant was noticed after two days. (Courtesy of Cliff and Martha Harvey.)

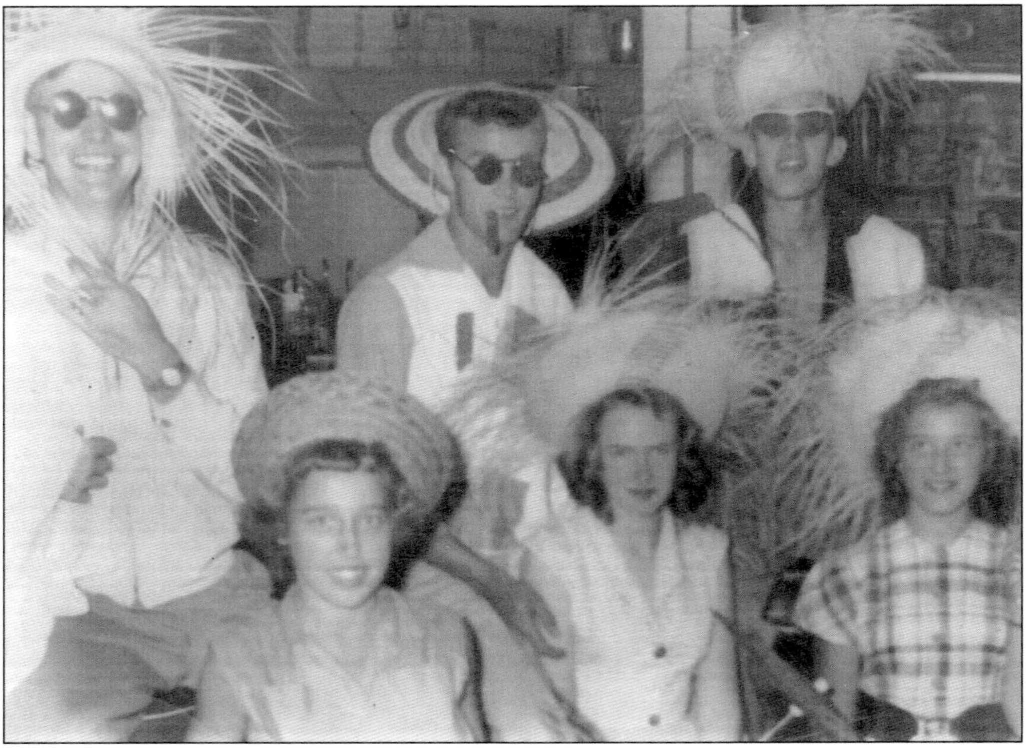

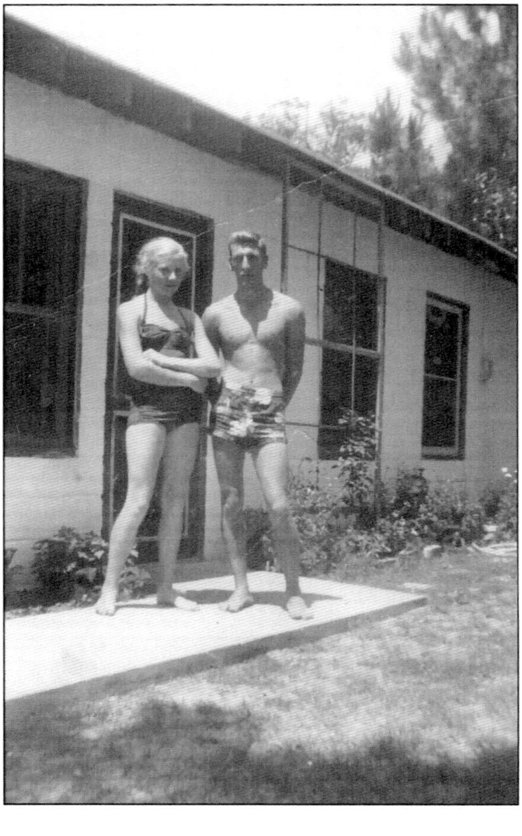

A senior in high school at the time, Marlene Estridge (front left) poses with her future husband, Marvin (back left), and her sister Betty (front right), who married and later divorced Jerry Donophan (back right). His brother, Raymond Donophan, is in the back center with his bride-to-be, Patsy (bottom center). The photograph was taken inside Folly Drug Sundries, and the cigars are fake. (Courtesy of Marlene Estridge.)

Nancy Leland and Breck Barnett met on Folly Beach and began courting when she was 13 and he was 18. They married when she turned 18 and went on to have eight children. (Courtesy of Maebelle Barnett Bazzel.)

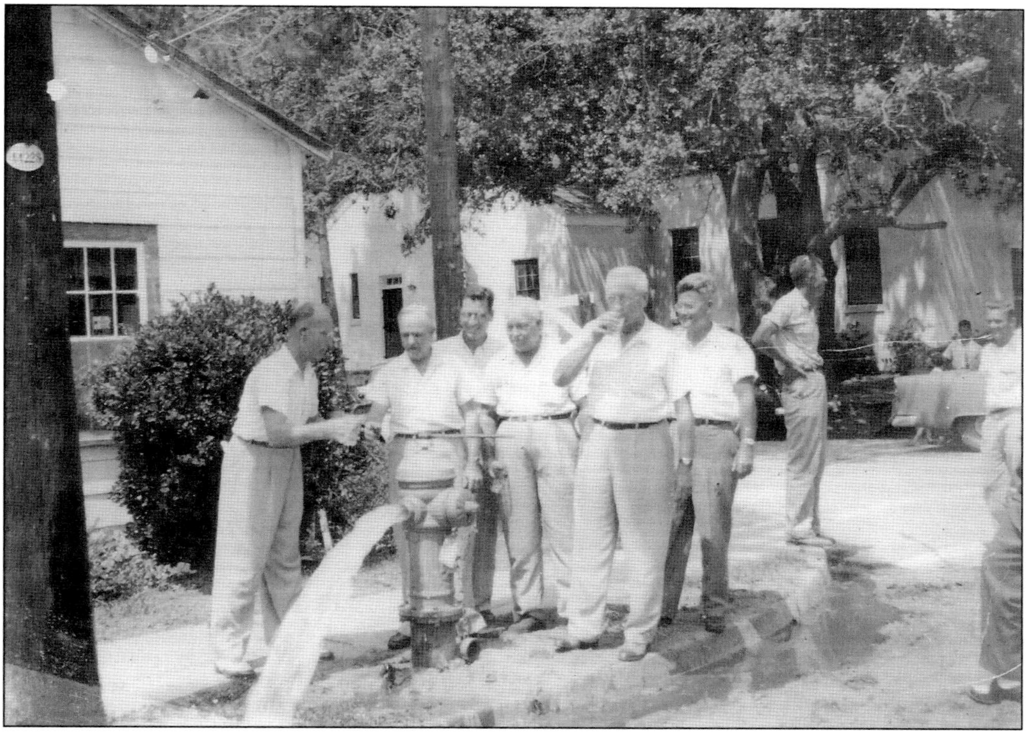

When city water came to Folly Beach in 1957, it was a cause for celebration. Here, Folly's leaders, from left to right, Fabian Smith, J.H. Thomson (of Charleston's waterworks), Ed Stringer, Jimmy Stuart, George Goehring, Curtis Winningham, and Tommy Wienges enjoy the first cup from the island's new hydrant. (Courtesy of Patricia Jamison Wilbanks Bragg.)

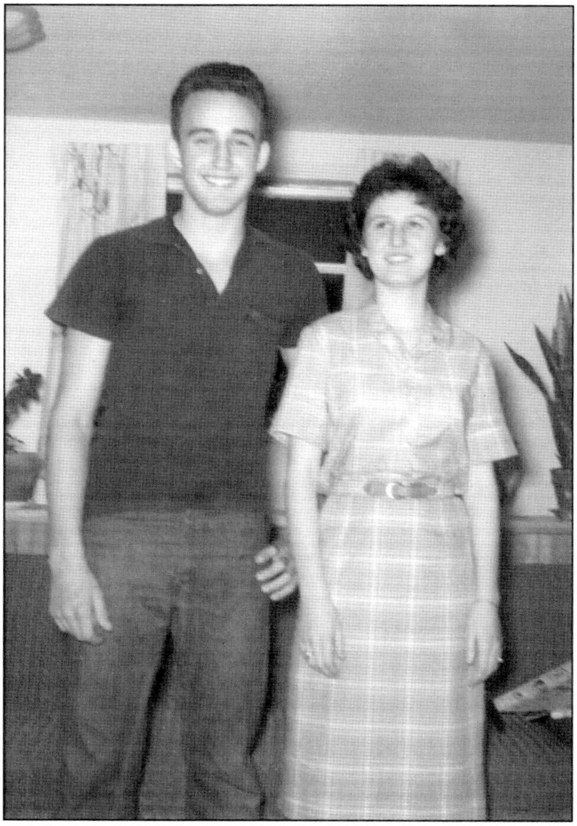

A 16-year-old LaJuan Leckie (Kennedy) poses with her brother Aven at 1110 East Cooper Avenue. LaJuan went on to own and operate Fred Holland Realty. Her husband, Regas Kennedy, was the mayor of Folly Beach from 1977 to 1980. (Courtesy of LaJuan Kennedy.)

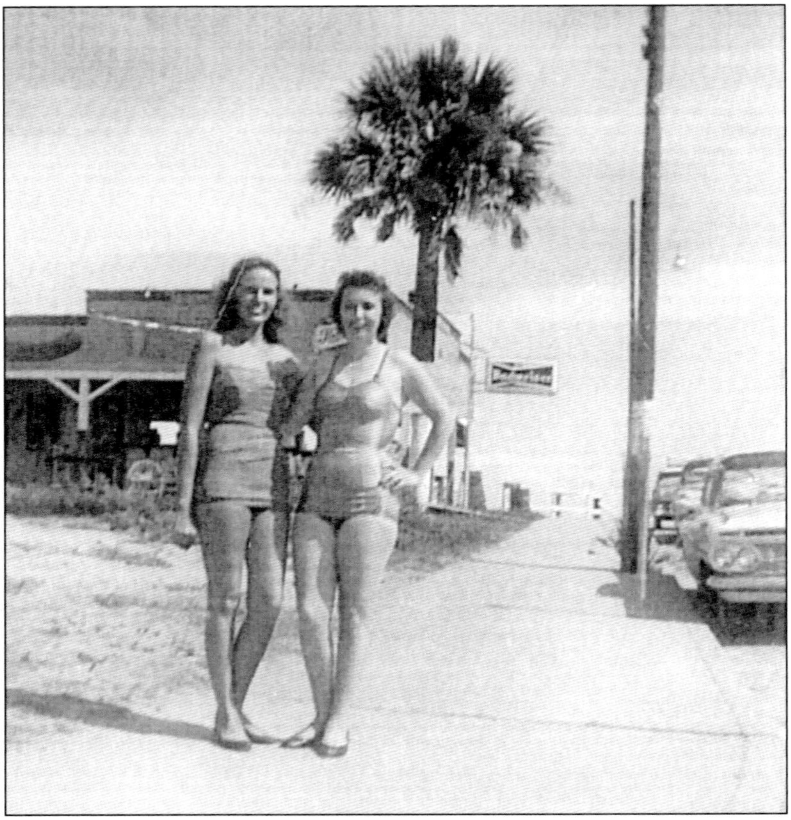

Vivian Blocker (Browning), at left, poses with her friend Edith Humphries on Center Street in the 1940s. Browning now serves the city as the assistant to city clerk Marlene Estridge. (Courtesy of Vivian Browning.)

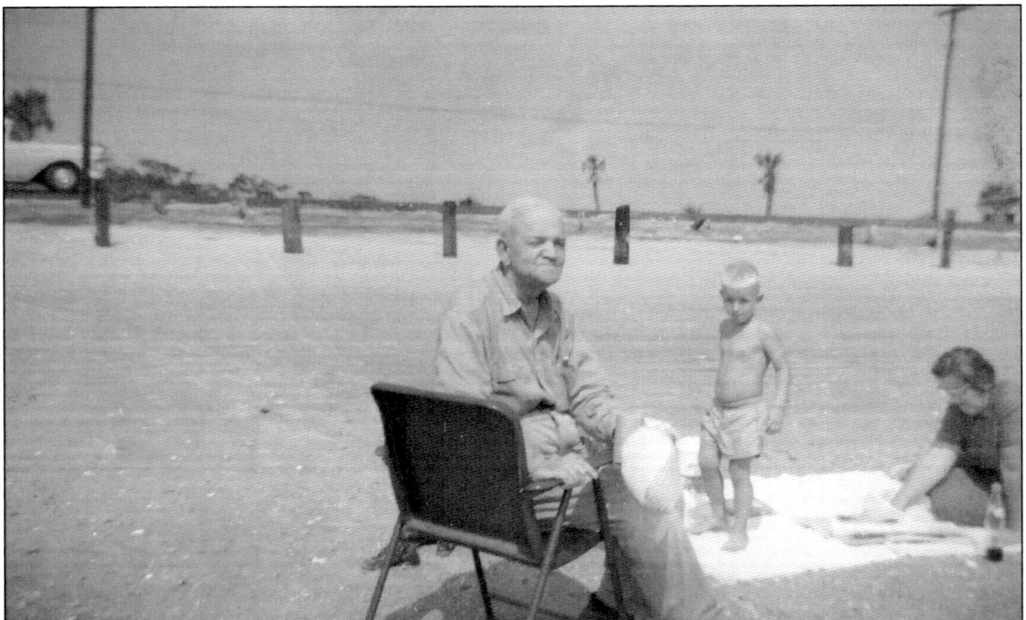

Four generations are evident in this 1961 photograph, taken at the Washout. Betty Schultz took the photograph of Mr. "Major" Smith, her husband Henry's grandfather. Her mother, Jane Southworth, sits on the right, while her son, Ivan Schultz, looks at the camera. (Courtesy of Betty Schultz.)

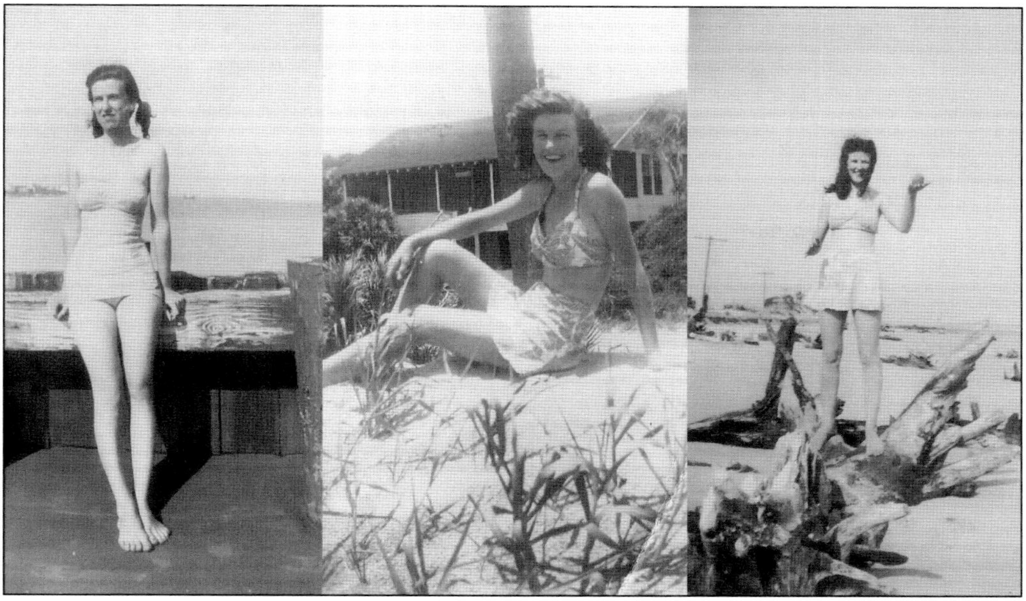

Wilma Brown (Maherg) grew up near the Navy base in North Charleston, but her summers and weekends were spent on Folly Beach. All three of these portraits were taken in 1946. (Courtesy of Greta Anderson.)

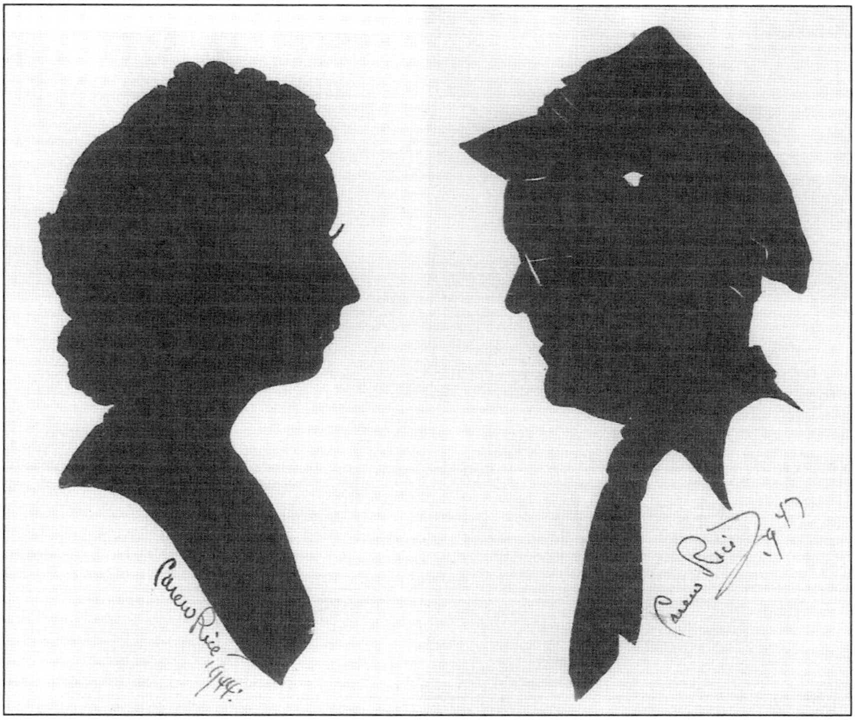

The late artist Carew Rice was nationally recognized for his silhouette portraits of Lowcountry scenes, and many Charleston residents have his silhouettes of family members on the walls. Rice regularly worked at the pavilion, cutting the pictures with tiny scissors. These silhouettes depict Robert "Bob" Hubbard, a deputy police officer, and his wife, Tilly. Carew's grandson, Clay Rice, carries on the tradition today. (Courtesy of Barbara Johnson and Marlene Estridge.)

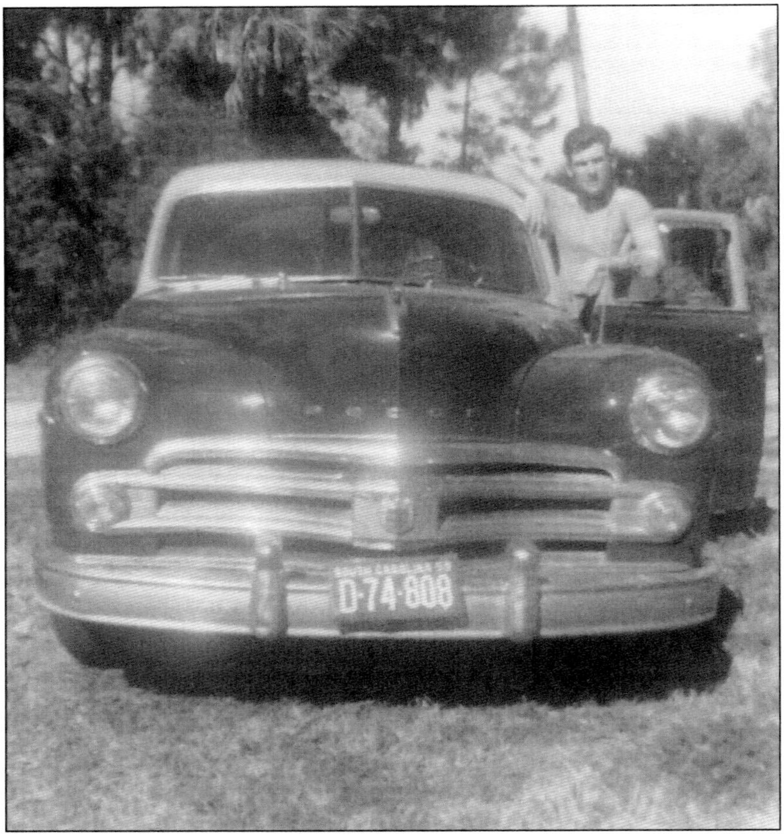

Harry Jacob Hinkel Jr. poses with his dark blue Dodge, which could not be parked on a hill. Hinkel married Bonnie Barnett, whose sister, Maebelle Barnett, borrowed the car and got it caught trying to turn around in the eroding dunes at the end of Center Street. "When I took my foot off the brake, it started rolling right back towards the drop off," recalls Maebelle. Eventually, two boys came to the rescue. (Courtesy of Maebelle Barnett Bazzel.)

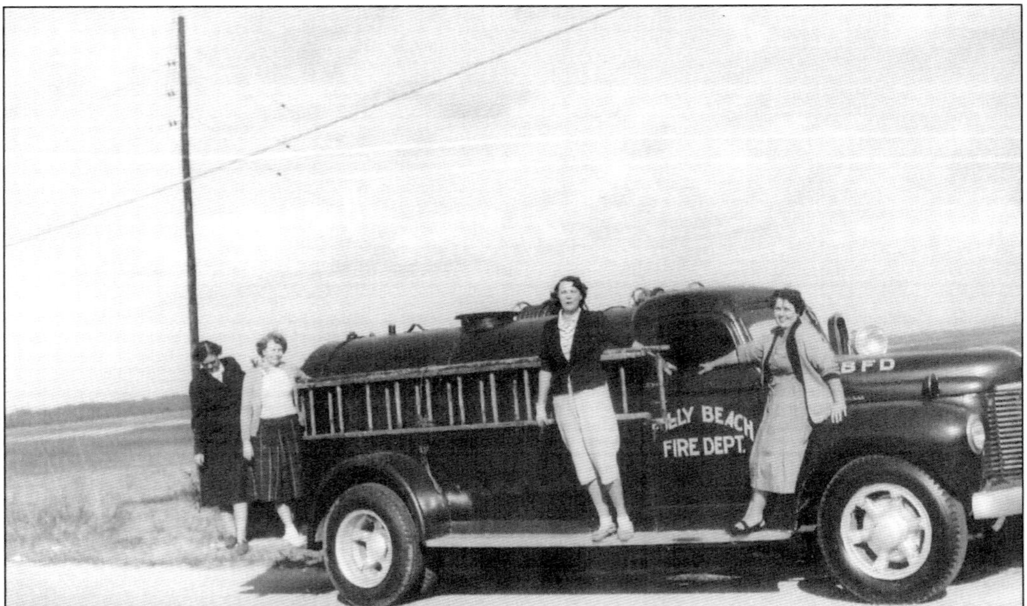

Folly Beach got its first fire truck, an International Harvester, in 1941. Here, local Folly women show off the new vehicle. They are, from left to right, unidentified, Marion Smith, Helen Barbery, and Maida Dudley. (Courtesy of John Jacobs and the Folly Beach Civic Club.)

On Kids Day in October 1974, local children got the chance to don fireman hats and cruise around Folly in the city's shiny 500-gallon-per-minute pumper truck. (Courtesy of Wallace Benson.)

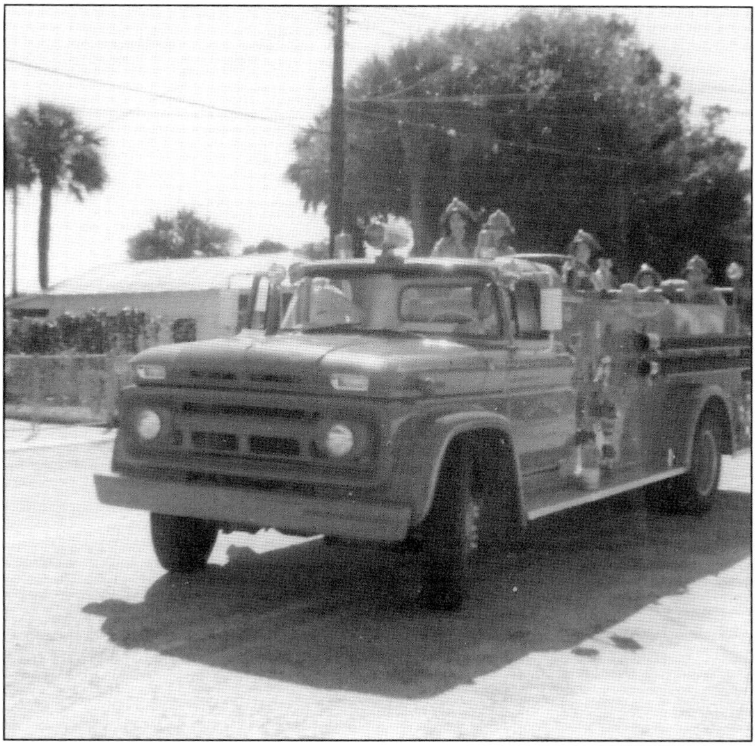

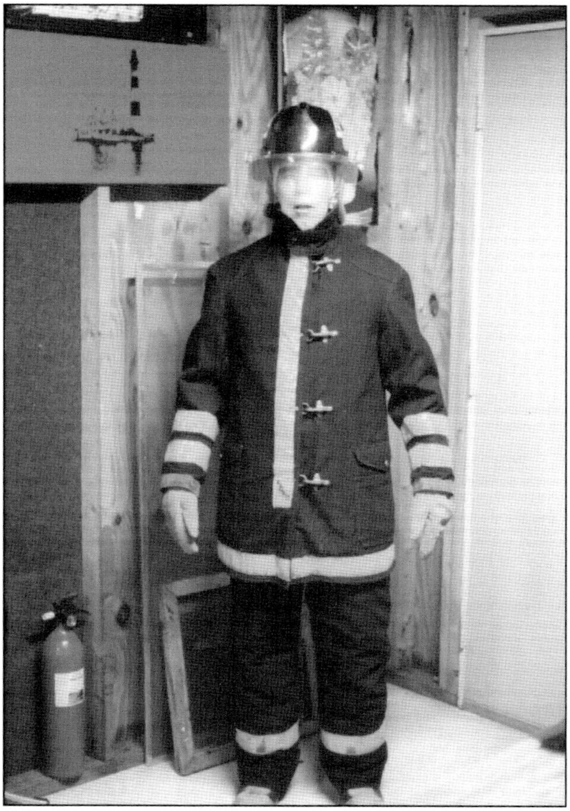

Until recent years, Folly Beach depended heavily on a volunteer fire department made up of community members. Here, volunteer fireman Bill Perry gets suited up in 1990. He fought fires on the beach as recently as 2012. (Courtesy of Bill Perry and Betty Sue Cowsert.)

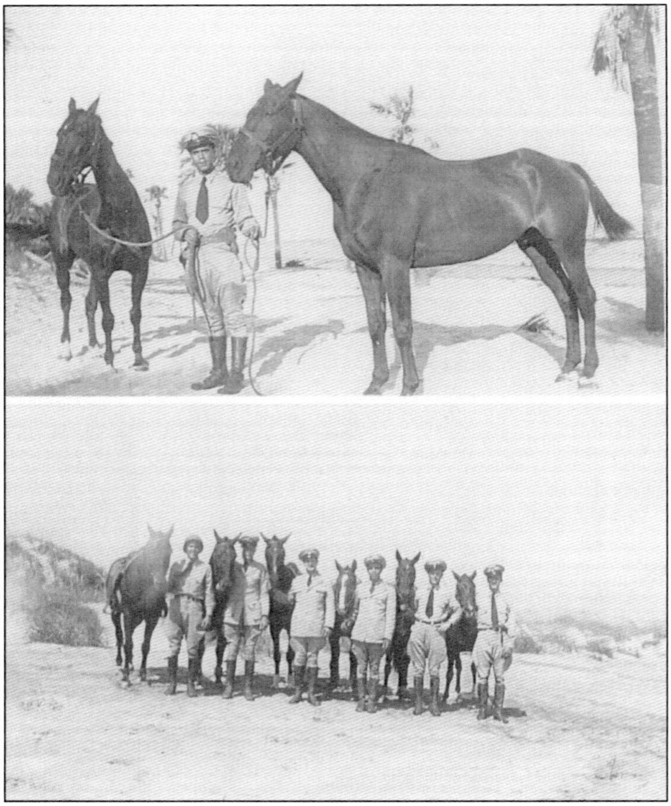

Throughout World War II, a 24-hour Coast Guard horse patrol rode up and down the beach looking out for German U-boats. Gasoline was rationed and in short supply, making horses a popular method of travel for residents as well. Floyd Harper, who commanded the horse patrol, often hitched a ride to Folly on the school bus to save gas. The man holding the two horses is identified only as Albert. The island's east end housed the Coast Guard's loran station from 1945 until its decommissioning in 1981, and it is now a popular, undeveloped park appreciated for its vistas of the Morris Island Lighthouse. Horseback riding was banned for the public on the island in 1967. (Courtesy of Vivian Browning.)

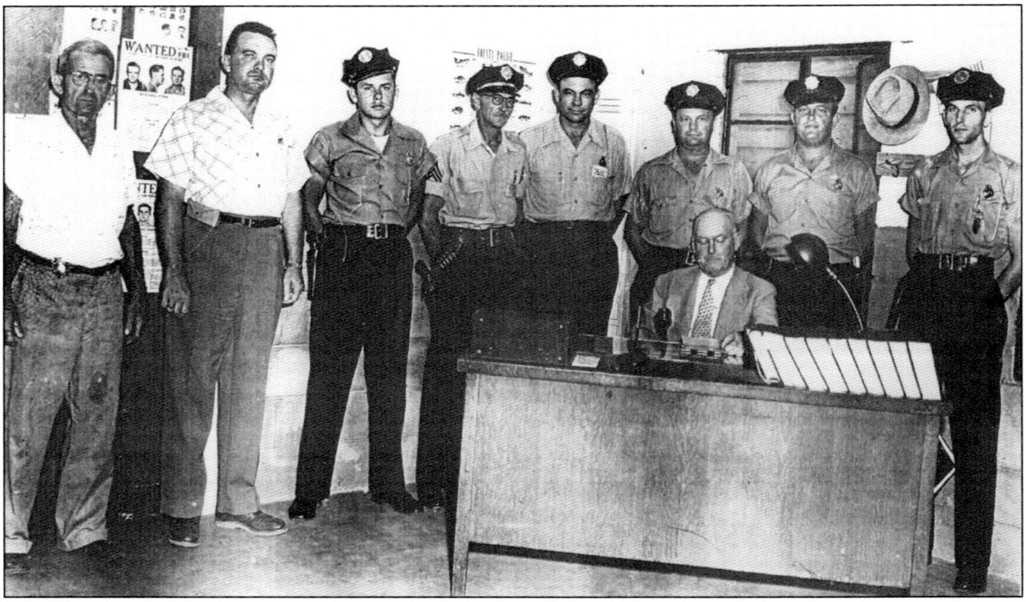

Folly's finest pose in the early 1950s. Commissioner G.B. Lynch is seated, and chief of police Dickie Bentz is at far left. John Harold Inabinett is fifth from the left and John Turner is sixth from the left. Commissioner Lynch's wife, Lura, was a third-grade teacher at James Island School and taught Bible verses to many of the island's youths. (Photograph by Jack Wilbanks, courtesy of Maebelle Barnett Bazzel.)

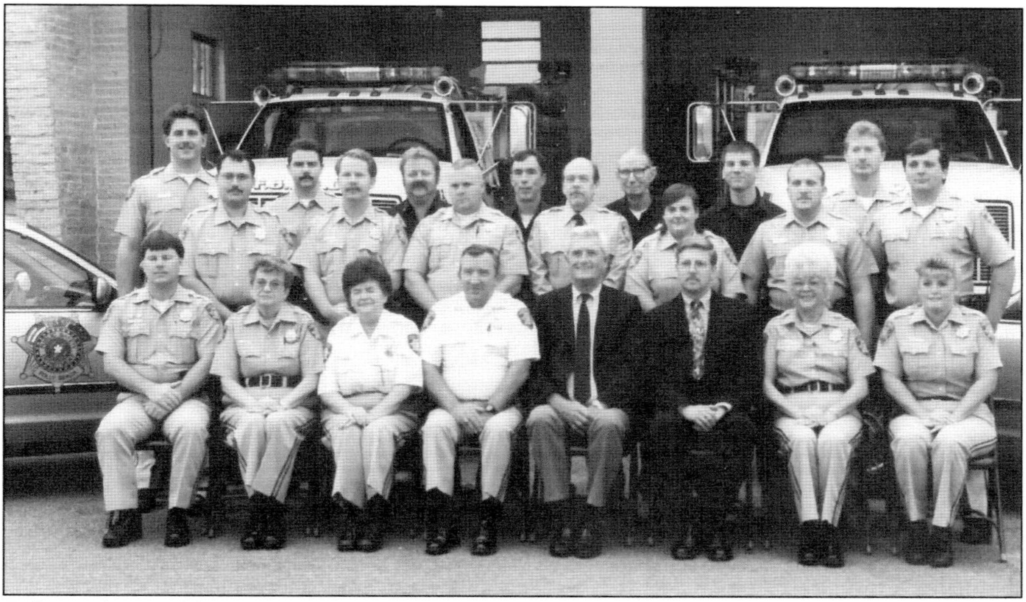

Folly's police and fire departments pose for a picture in the early 1990s, with Mayor Bob Linville seated in the middle with a dark tie, next to George Tittle, the chief of police. Cliff Harvey, an officer throughout much of the 1970s and 1980s, recalls that the Sanitary Restaurant served as an unofficial substation for the force. In those days, elderly residents did not hesitate to call the police for help changing a light bulb on their porch, and local police were typically first responders to fires and medical emergencies. Officers worked 12-hour shifts in the summer and 10-hour shifts in the fall, taking home around $125 per week after taxes. "We didn't do it for the money," says Harvey. "We did it because we enjoyed the people on Folly Beach." (Courtesy of Bill Perry and Betty Sue Cowsert.)

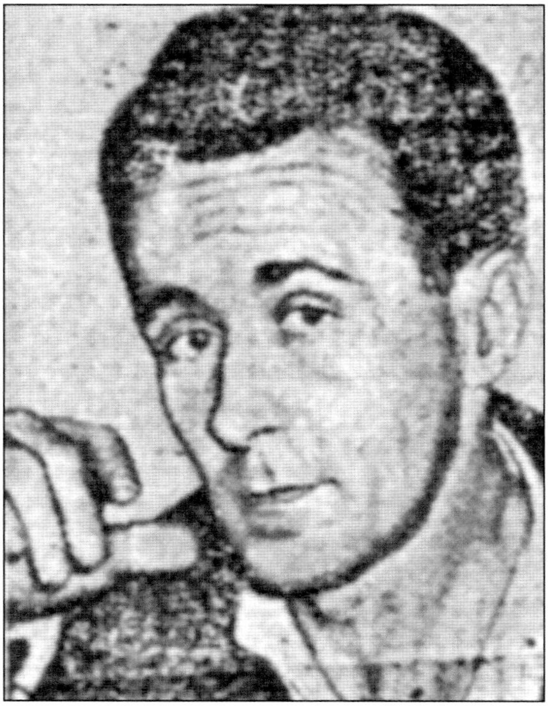

Folly made national news when Elmer "Trigger" Burke, a notorious 1940s hit man, was captured hiding out on the island in a rented bungalow. Burke participated in the Great Brink's Robbery, a famous holdup in Boston that netted nearly $3 million in 1950. After another attempted murder in 1954, he escaped from jail in Boston but was caught a year later on Folly Beach. In 1958, Burke was executed in the electric chair. "Sing Sing [Prison] also has iron windows—but no trees or breezes," wrote the *News and Courier* in its story about Burke's execution, along with a photograph of the iron-windowed house Burke had rented on Folly. (Courtesy of the *News and Courier*.)

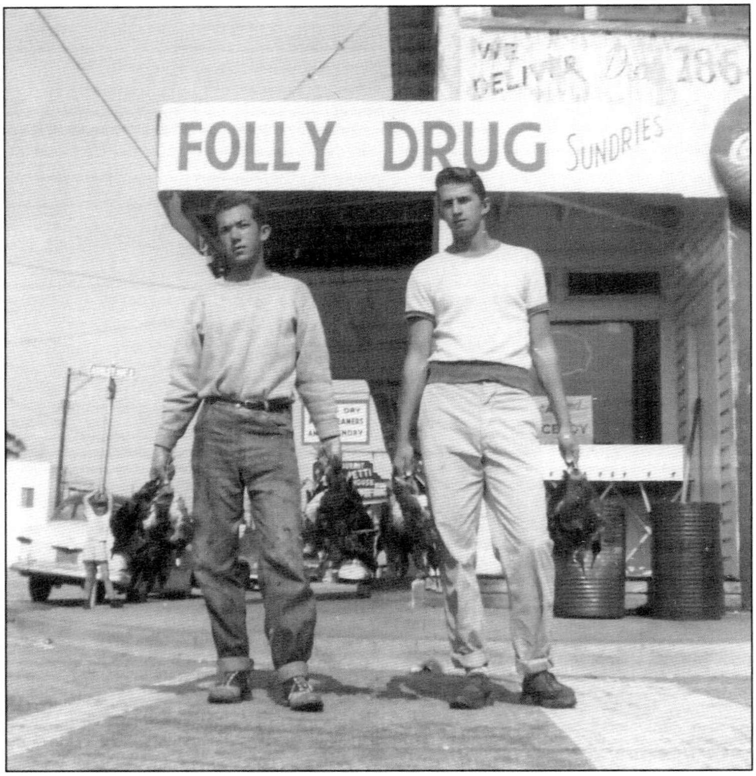

Arnold Droze and Michele Altine stand outside Folly Drug Sundries with an impressive harvest of birds. (Courtesy of Patricia Jamison Wilbanks Bragg.)

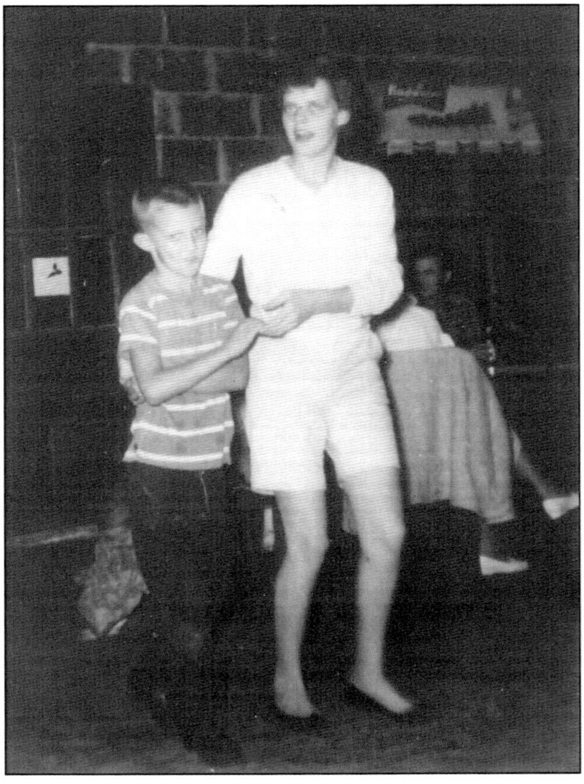

A young Robbie Barber, now the proprietor of Bowen's Island Restaurant and a former member of the South Carolina House of Representatives, dances with his aunt Patsy Kelly in the old dining room at Bowen's Island, before the walls were painted white. The room had a television and a jukebox and was a popular hangout throughout the 1950s and 1960s. Today, locals and visitors still congregate on the porch every evening to watch the sunset over the marsh. (Courtesy of Robert Barber.)

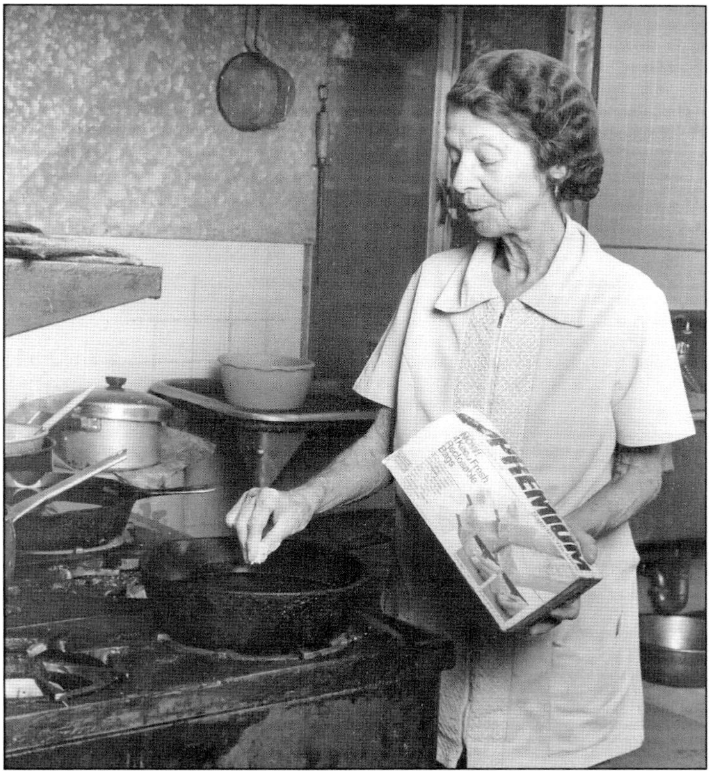

Jimmy and May Bowen opened Bowen's Island Restaurant in 1946, serving local seafood, including fried shrimp, oysters, and crab cakes. Their grandson, Robert Barber, took over the restaurant in 1989, and the menu remains relatively unchanged. In this 1979 photograph, May Bowen crushes saltines for her famous crab cakes. "It was light on the meat but had phenomenal flavor and a mustard base," recalls Barber. "They used to make them on Sunday morning when I'd be going to church, and unfortunately I never got that recipe." (Photograph by Bill Jordan of the *Post and Courier*, courtesy of Robert Barber.)

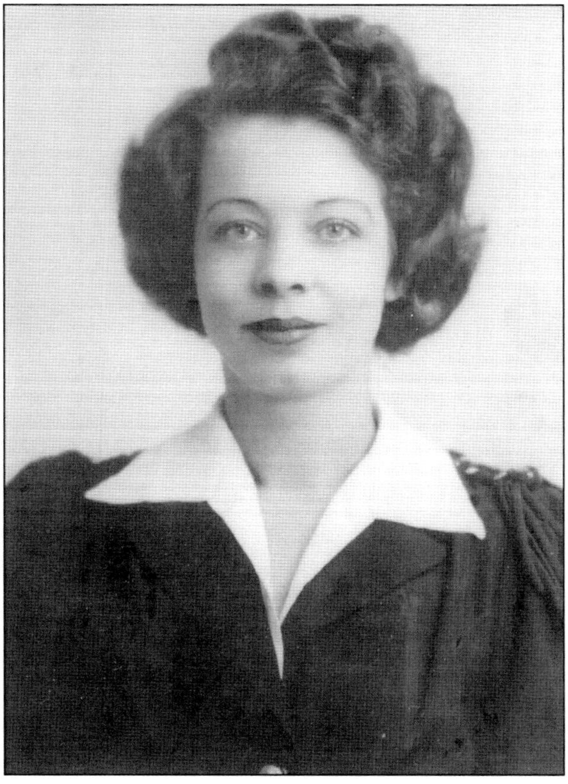

A young May Bowen, seen here in the early 1930s, was likely dressed up for a meeting of the Eastern Stars, the women's branch of the Masonic lodge. At Bowen's Island Restaurant, "May was the boss," recalls her grandson Robert Barber. (Courtesy of Robert Barber.)

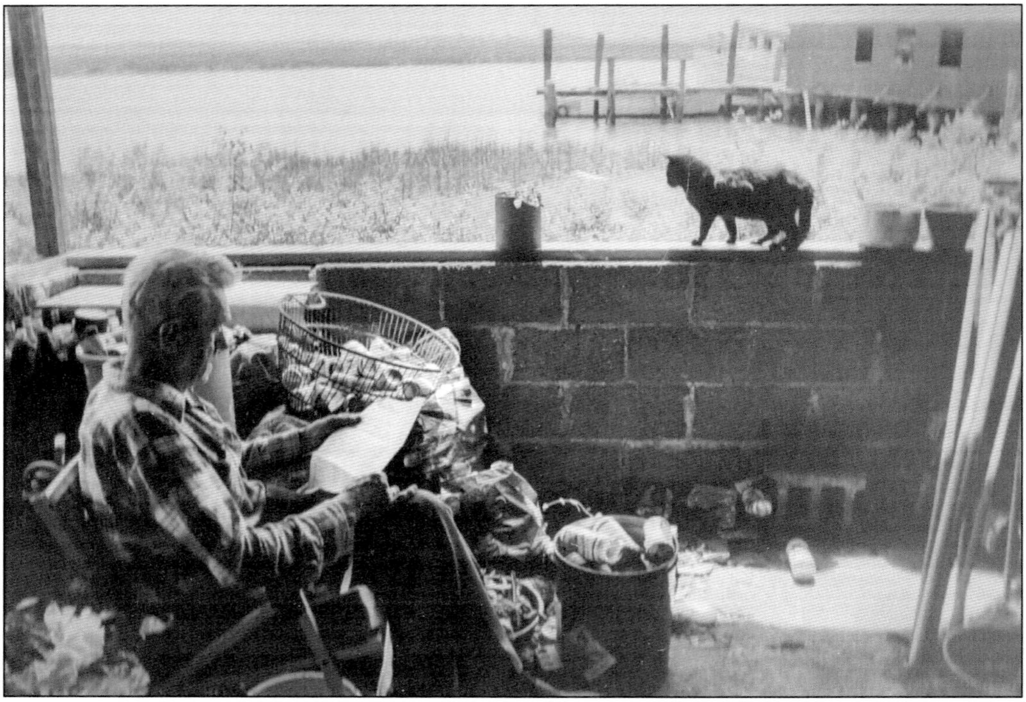

John Sanka served as manager and cook at Bowen's Island Restaurant from its opening in 1946 until 1985, living in a small one-room apartment behind the restaurant. Here, Sanka pauses for a moment to check paperwork amidst bags and buckets of empty Budweiser cans. The Bowen family bought their island at the end of World War II. Their building on Folly, Bob's Restaurant, became Mr. John's Sundries, operated by John and Rachel Chrysostom, whose son, Paul, still operates Mr. John's beach store at that location. (Courtesy of Cramer Gallimore Photography Studio.)

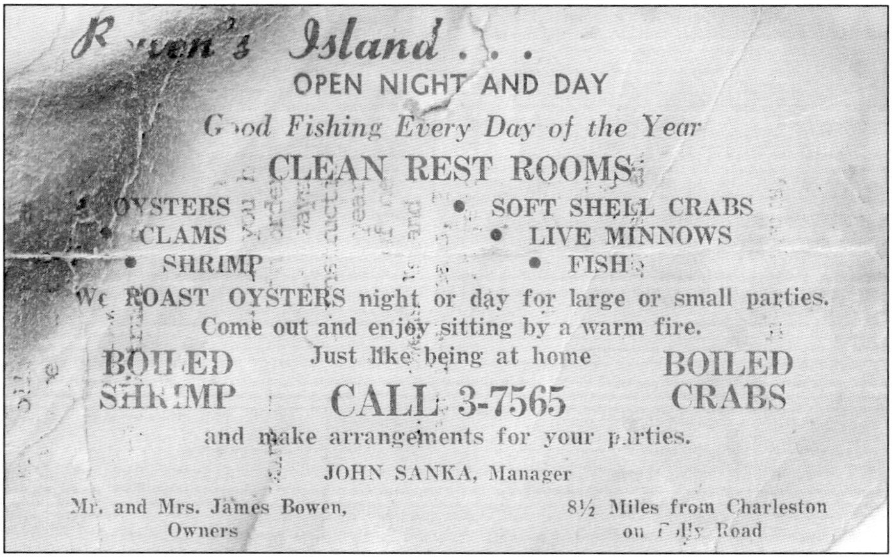

The Bowen family built a 250-yard causeway to their island in the late 1940s, opening a small fish camp that grew into Bowen's Island Restaurant. Most of the information on this advertisement from the early 1950s still applies six decades later, except for the shorter phone number. (Courtesy of Robert Barber.)

Manager John Sanka spent much of his life living and working at Bowen's Island Restaurant, which weathered fires in 2006 and 2012. After the 2006 fire took the dining room, owner Robert Barber rebuilt a wide deck and spacious bar, designed by Folly artist Carl Janes. The homey atmosphere and traditional seafood continue to attract national attention. (Courtesy of Robert Barber.)

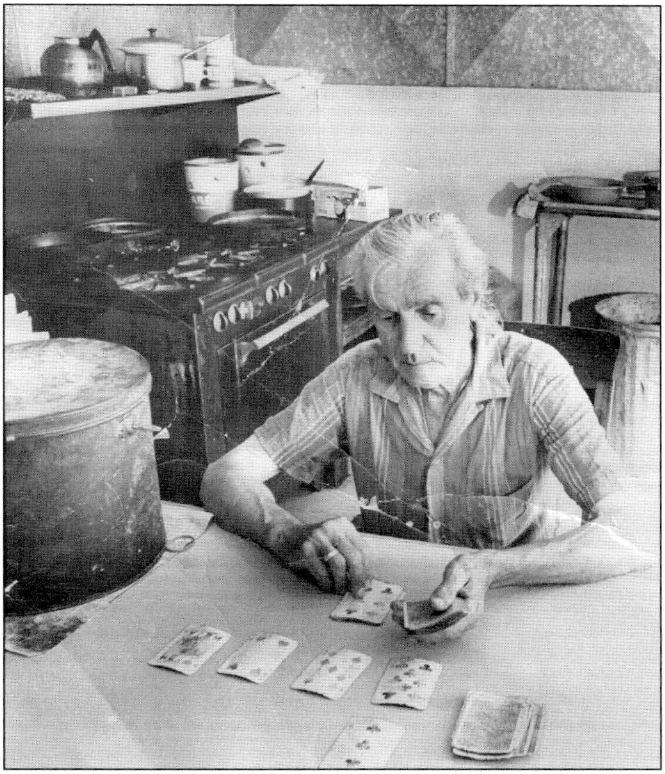

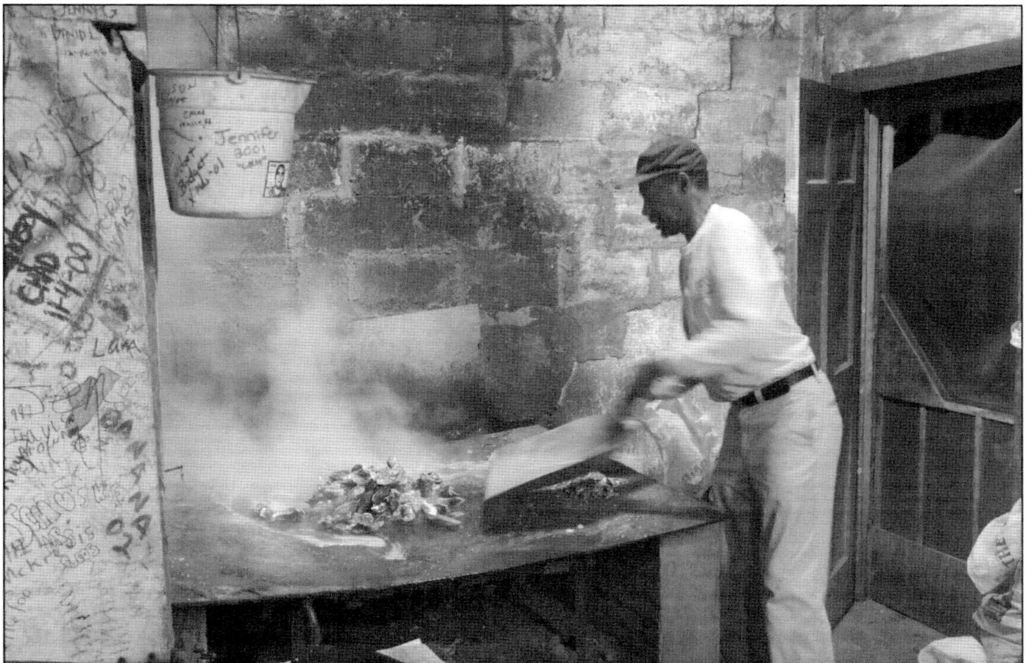

Oysters are still roasted in a traditional manner at Bowen's Island, on a hot slab of metal over an open fire. The piles of oyster shells surrounding the parking lot are evidence of the bounty of the surrounding waters. (Courtesy of Cramer Gallimore Photography Studio.)

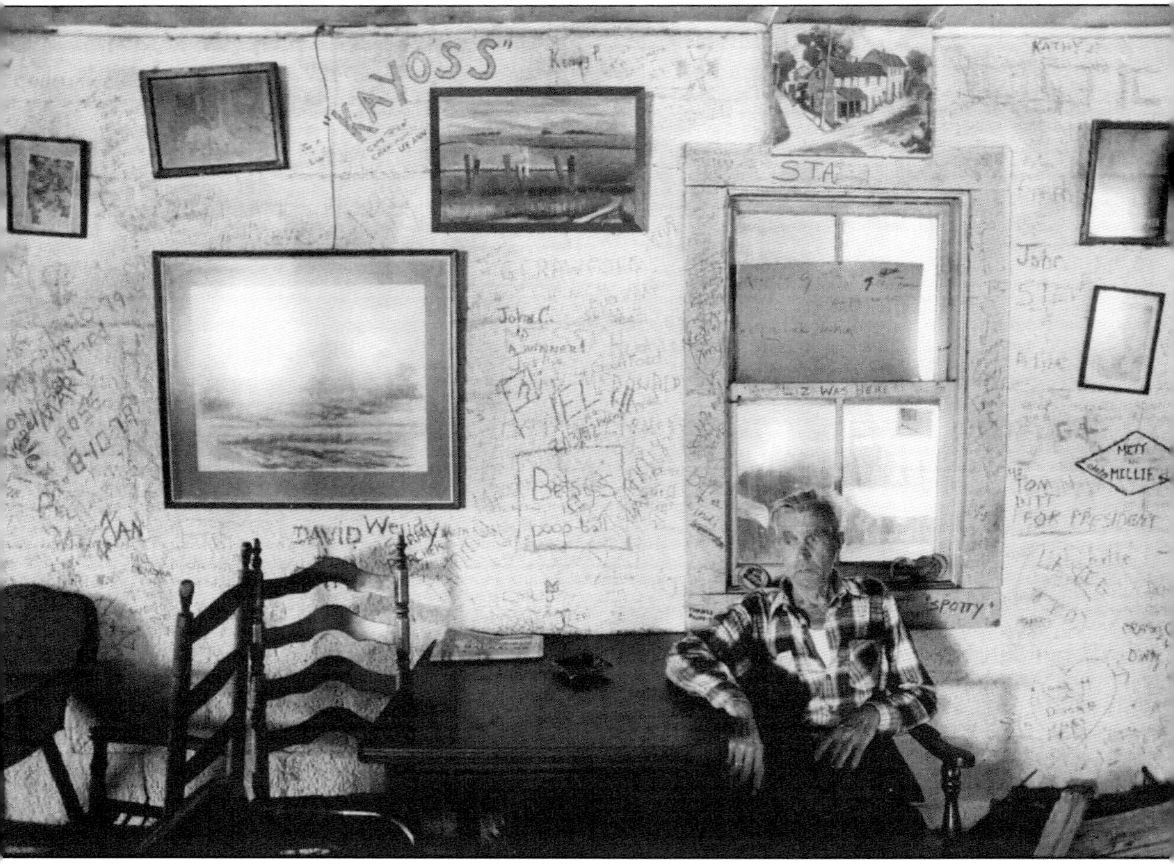

Before it burned in 2006, the walls of the old dining room at Bowen's Island contained the collective memories of generations of happy diners. (Courtesy of Cramer Gallimore Photography Studio.)

Bill Perry rows the *Sea Snark*, a styrofoam boat that he found on the side of the road and returned to seaworthiness. "It was broken in half, so we put plywood across it and used it to row out to our sailboat," Perry recalls. "It rode great and was self-bailing." This photograph was taken in 1978 in the river near ninth block on the west side. The cat rode out on the *Sea Snark* and jumped to the sailboat. (Courtesy of Bill Perry and Betty Sue Cowsert.)

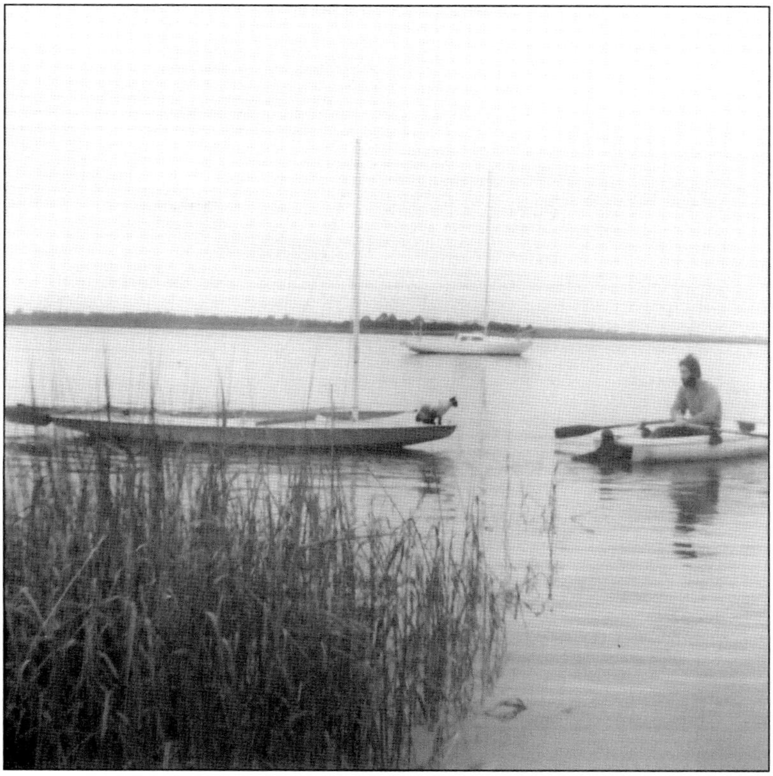

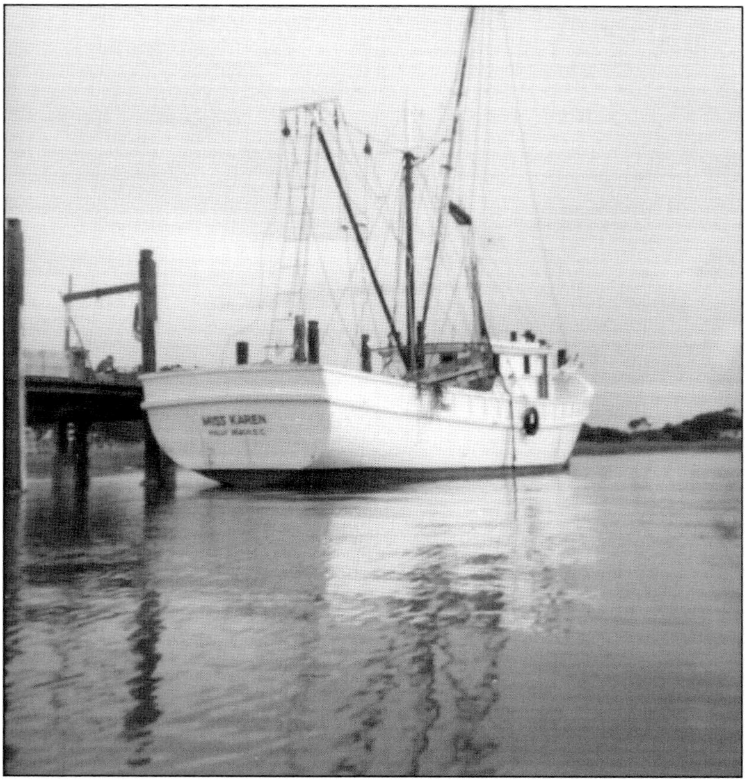

Shrimp boats were once kept at docks all around Folly Beach. This boat, the *Miss Karen*, was kept at Carl Ott's dock near ninth block on the west side. The docks often hosted fish fries, and this particular area became a popular gay bar and hangout in the 1980s. Some of the pilings from the dock are still visible in the marsh. (Courtesy of Bill Perry and Betty Sue Cowsert.)

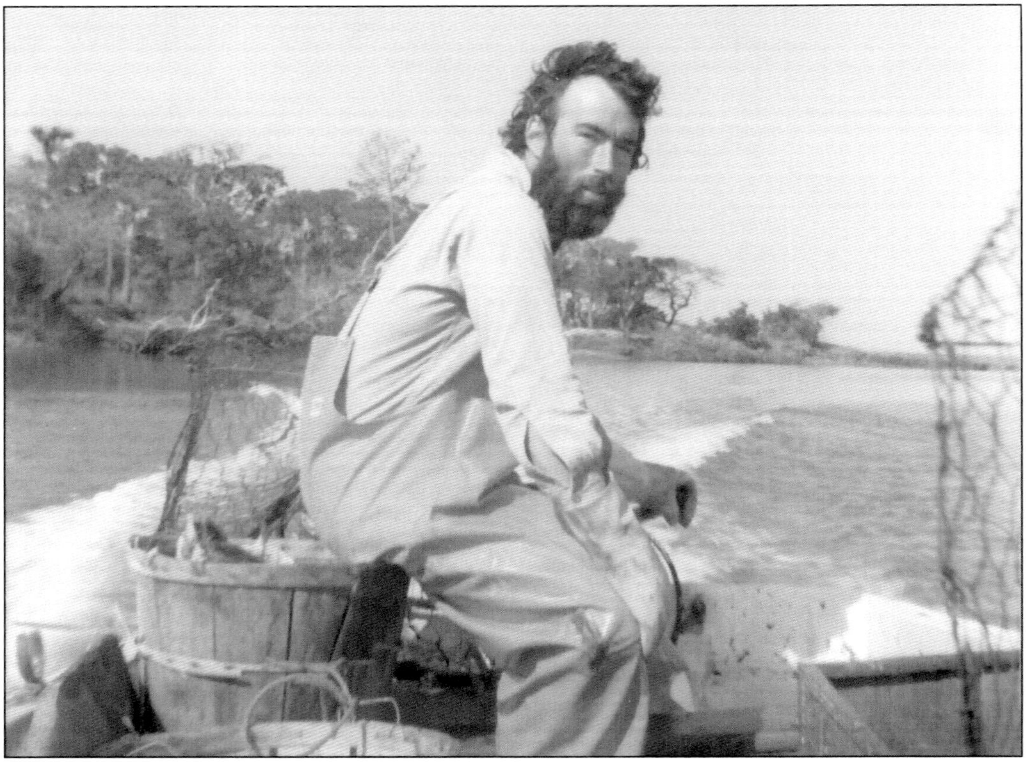

Shrimping and crabbing supported many Folly residents for decades. Before opening Oceansports Surf Shop, Bill Perry, seen here in September 1981, worked for years as a crabber. He and his wife, Betty Sue, checked their traps seven days a week. They unloaded their catch at Charlie Peyton's seafood dock, where Mariner's Cay condos and marina currently sits. In those days, drug smuggling on Folly Beach from the Caribbean was still fairly common. Perry recalls being offered $2,000 for a night's work by a couple of Cuban men who arrived at the dock one day. He politely declined. (Courtesy of Bill Perry and Betty Sue Cowsert.)

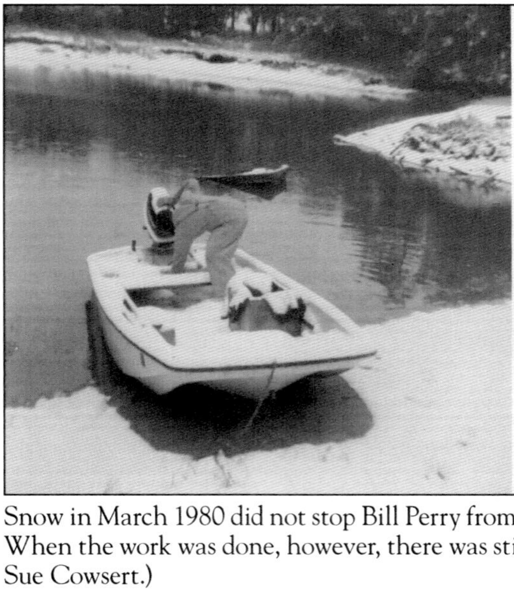

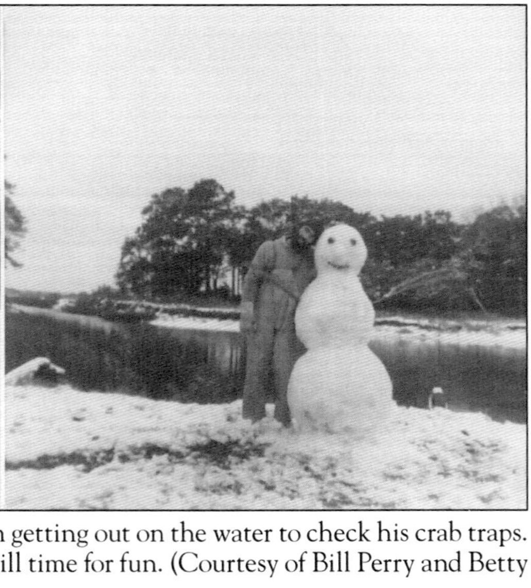

Snow in March 1980 did not stop Bill Perry from getting out on the water to check his crab traps. When the work was done, however, there was still time for fun. (Courtesy of Bill Perry and Betty Sue Cowsert.)

Folly's first commercial industry was likely Sea Island cotton in the 1700s. As recently as the 1970s, plots of undeveloped land could still be found to harvest homegrown produce. This garden, at Bill Lyle's house at ninth block on the west side, reverted to salt marsh after a dyke broke that had kept the property dry. "We drained it out and grew okra, corn, Jerusalem artichokes, asparagus, and corn in there," recalls Bill Perry, seen here on the "farm." (Courtesy of Bill Perry and Betty Sue Cowsert.)

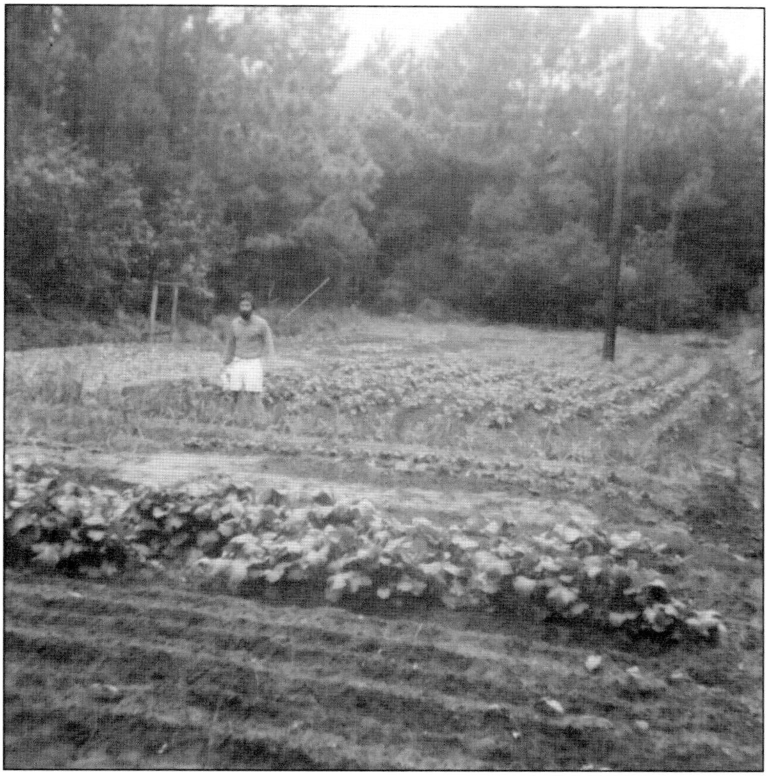

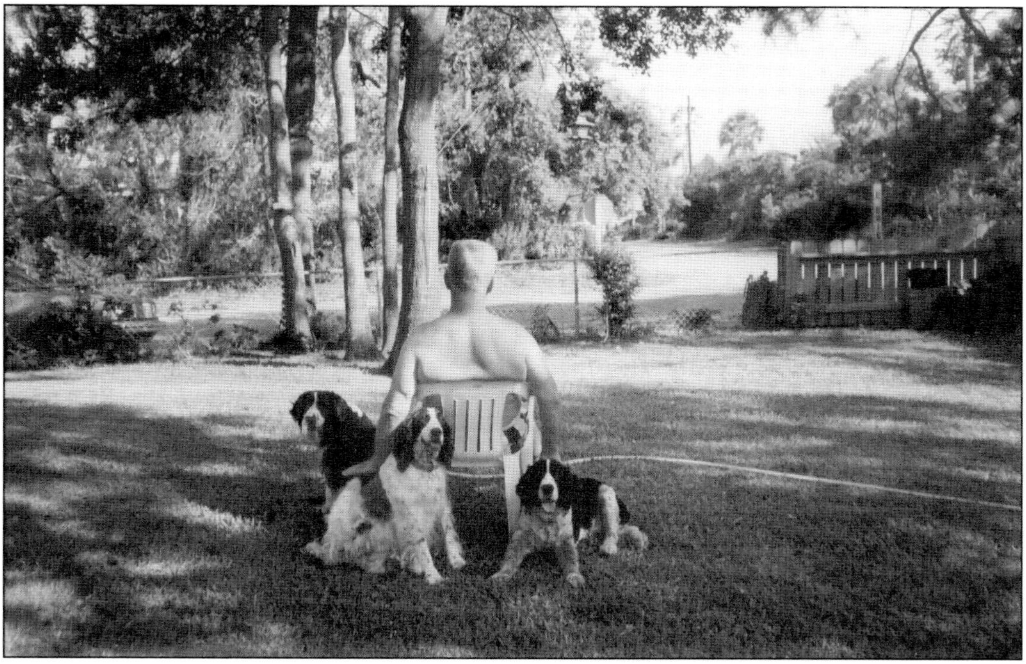

Henry and Betty Schultz love their springer spaniels. Here, Henry sits in the yard while Remington, Annie, and Patches pose for the camera. Annie, an escape artist who loved to explore, ran away one too many times from her previous home on Isle of Palms, requiring a lawyer and the Schultzs' open arms to secure her a new home on Folly Beach. (Courtesy of Betty Schultz.)

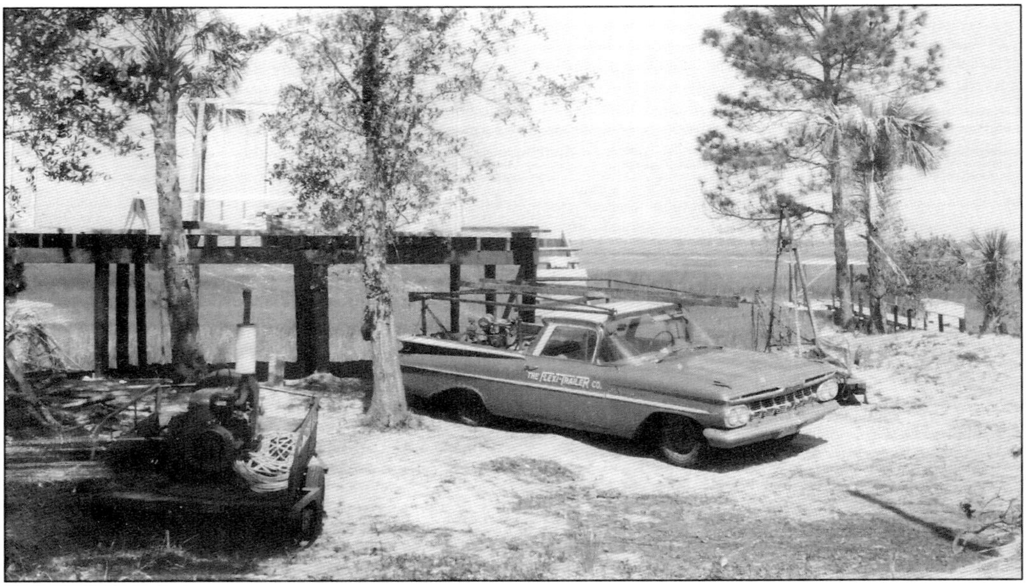

Henry and Betty Schultz moved to Folly Beach in 1966, building from scratch on two marsh-front lots that they bought for $650 each at what is now seventh block on East Erie Avenue, putting the title of the family car down for credit on that amount. There was no road, so building materials had to be driven through the woods to the site. Although city water came to Folly Beach in 1957, their isolated location meant they had no water or electricity in the early years. Fellow lifetime resident Andie Weathers recalls that when her father, Darus Weathers, was building their house in the mid-1950s, a concrete truck collapsed the wooden bridge to the island. From then on, he had to park his truck across the river, walk across what was left of the bridge, and carry his supplies and tools four blocks to the homesite. (Courtesy of Betty Schultz.)

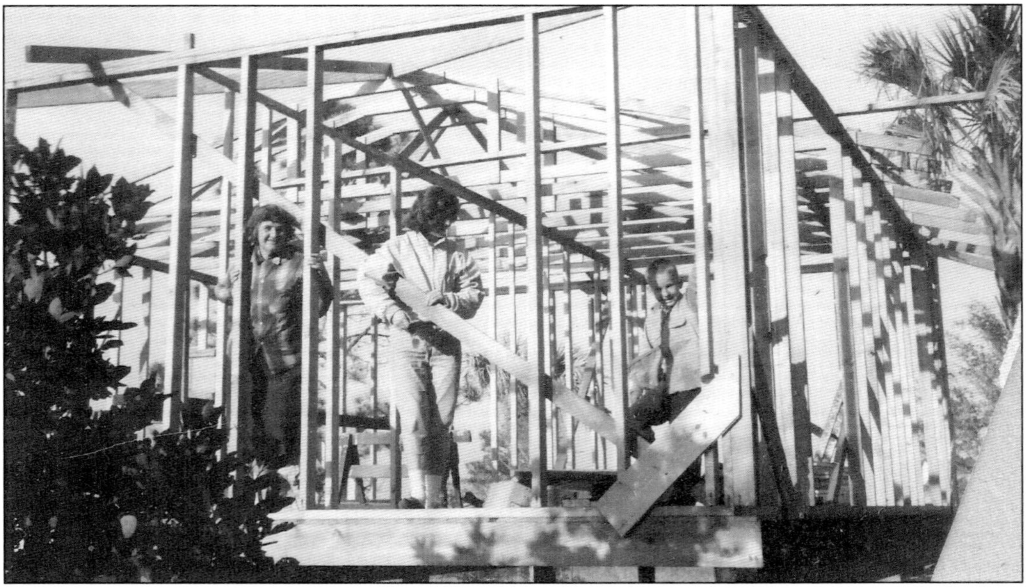

Building was a family effort, without the convenience of electric saws and axes. Three generations of Schultzs and Southworths lived at their homestead in its early years, enjoying biscuits in the morning, picnics in their outdoor dining area, and afternoons spent swimming and crabbing. (Courtesy of Betty Schultz.)

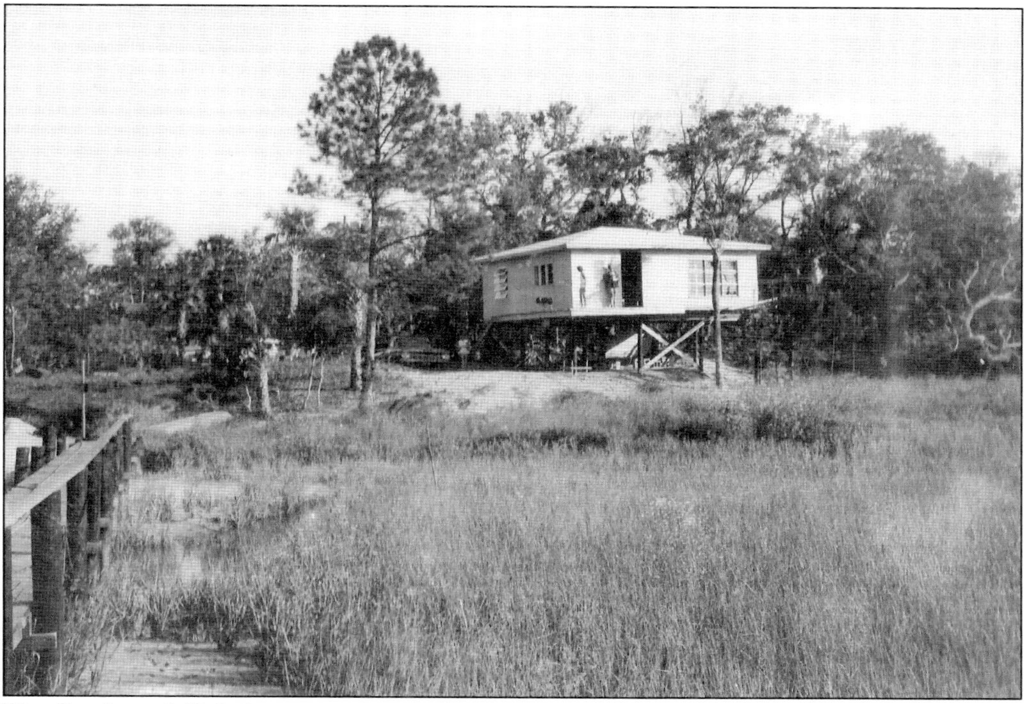

The Southworth/Schultz homestead on East Erie Avenue is seen above in the late 1960s, before the neighbors moved in. (Courtesy of Betty Schultz.)

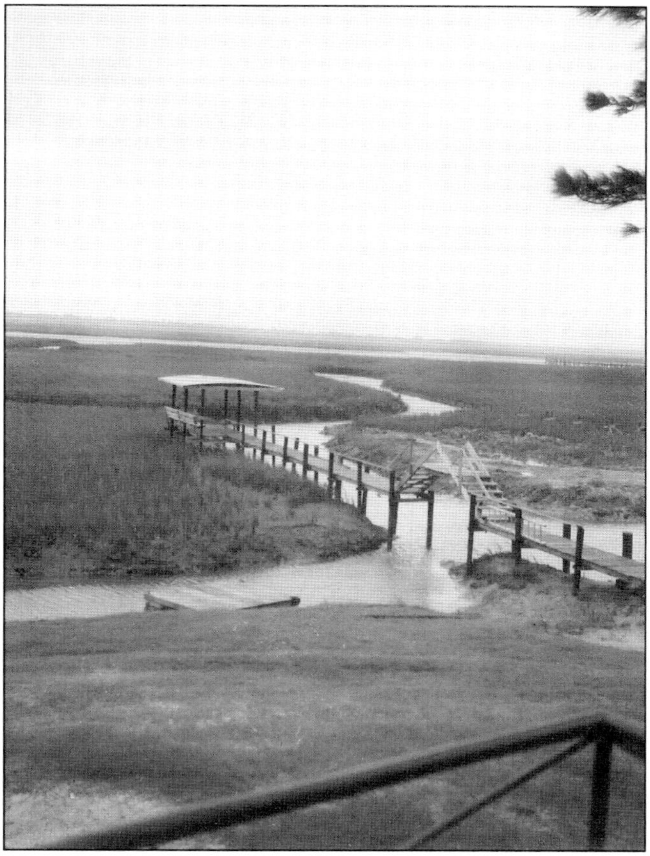

The original Southworth family dock, designed to allow boats to pass underneath, was destroyed by Hurricane David in 1979. Jack Southworth used to do handstands on the dock, claiming, "If I can stand on my head, I'll live 40 more years." (Courtesy of Betty Schultz.)

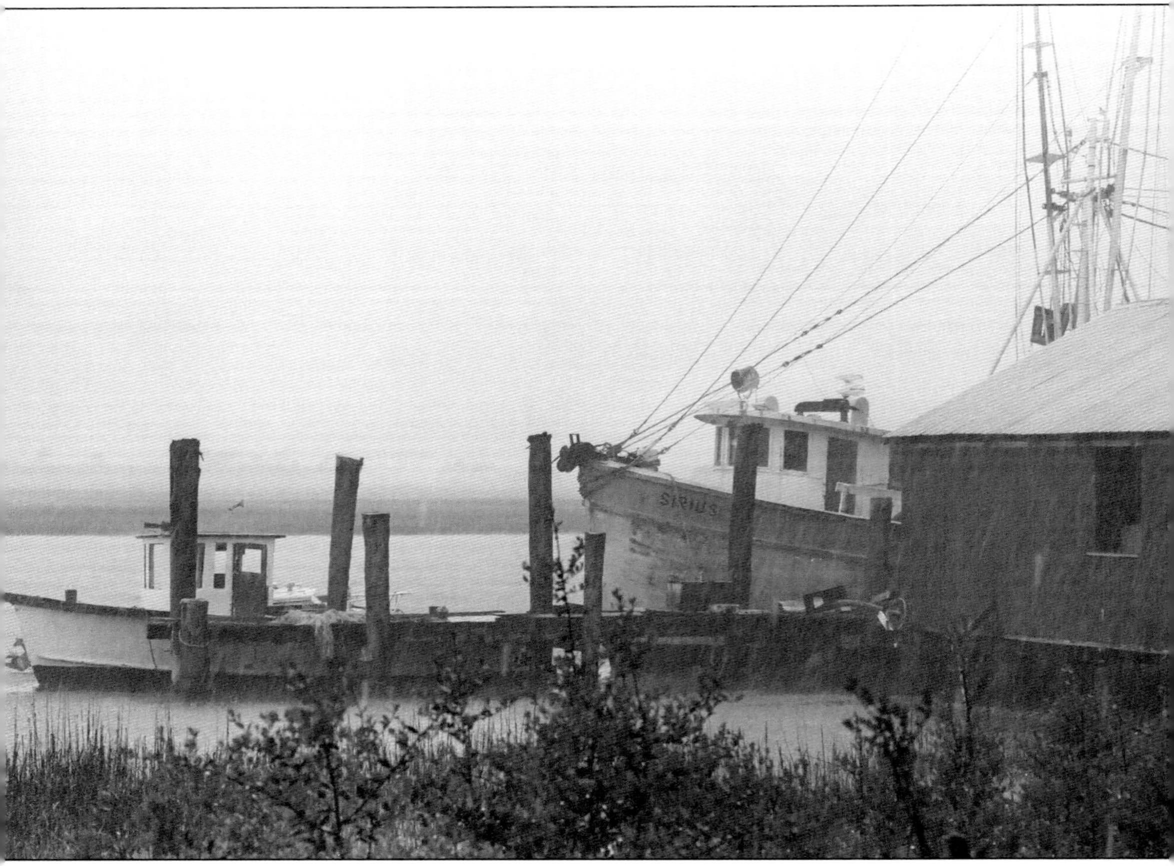

The feeling of the "old Folly Beach" still persists at Bowen's Island. (Courtesy of Cramer Gallimore Photography Studio.)

Four

LIVING ON THE EDGE

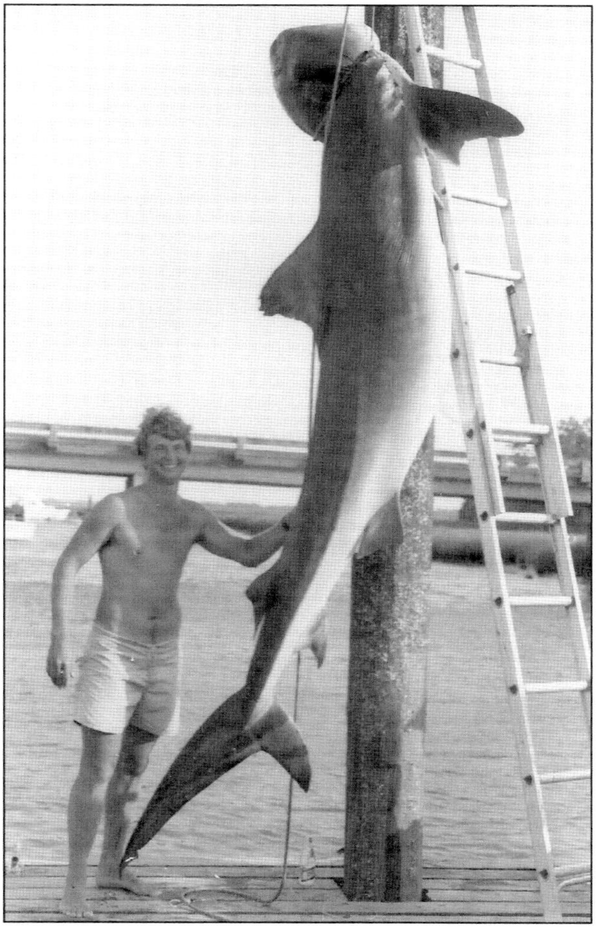

Originally coined as a marketing slogan to promote Oceansports Surf Shop, the phrase The Edge of America carries many connotations. Over the years, both real and perceived dangers occasionally threaten this somewhat isolated community at the terminus of a dead-end road. Although shark attacks are rare, the toothy fish are indeed out there. This 675-pound tiger shark was caught by Capt. Ivan Schultz. (Courtesy of Betty Schultz.)

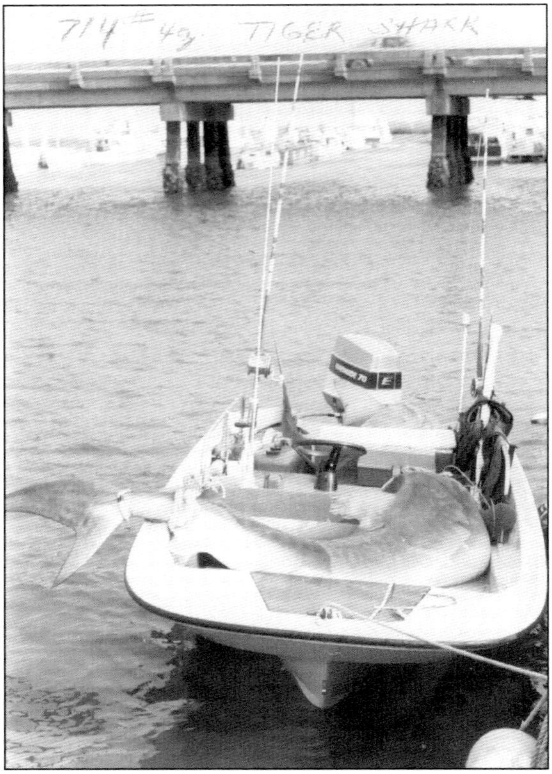

This 714-pound tiger shark took up most of Michael Schultz's fishing boat, but he and his brother Ivan managed to land it and bring it to shore on June 30, 1979. (Courtesy of Betty Schultz.)

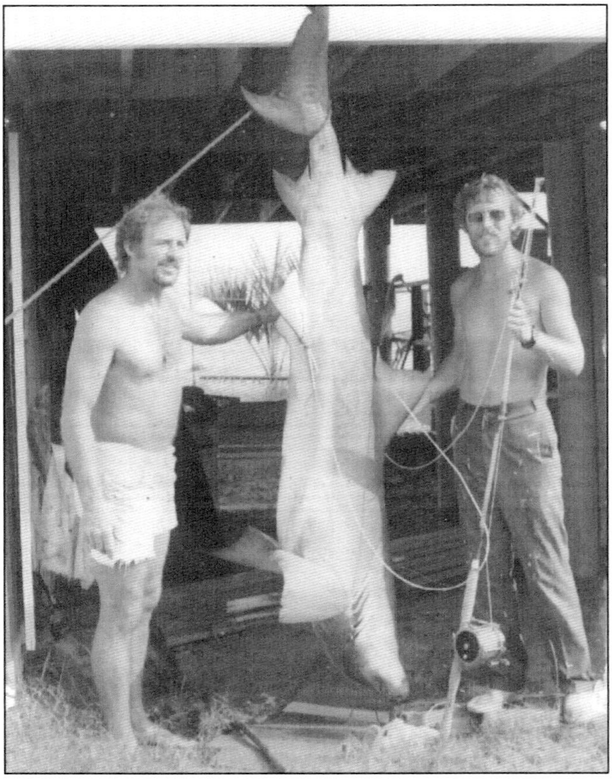

Captains Jack Sheppard and Wallace Benson pose next to a "big 'ol bull shark" reeled in off the coast of Folly Beach in the mid-1970s. Accounts from Union soldiers stationed on Folly Beach mention sharks, including one that attacked a man and nearly took his leg after a group of men prodded the stranded fish on land. (Courtesy of Wallace Benson.)

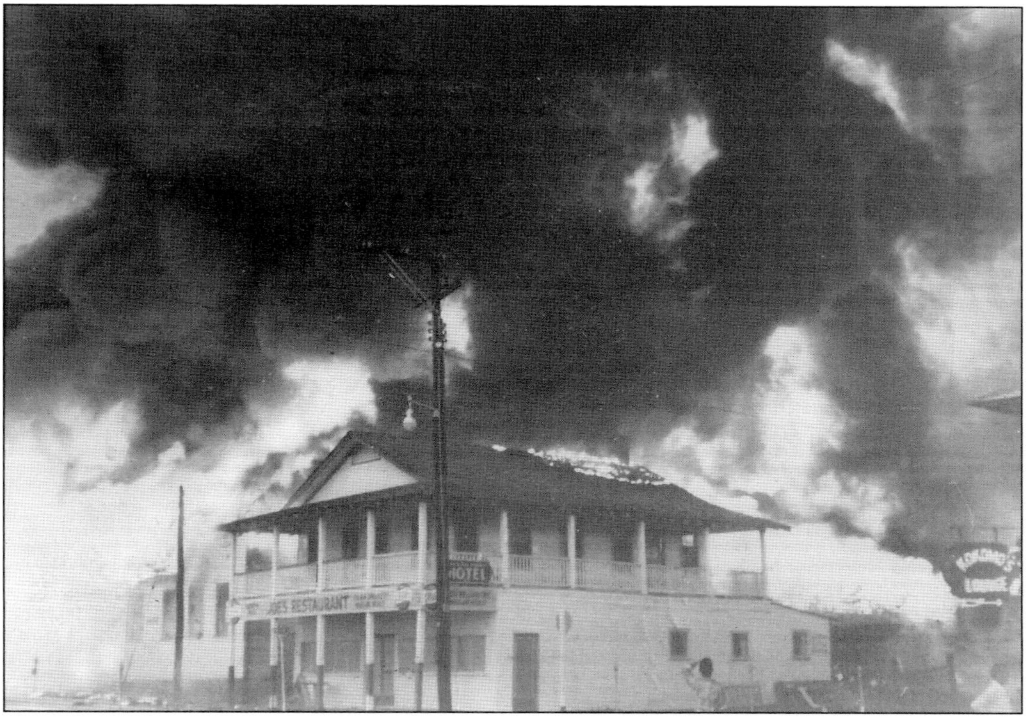

In April 1957, the Atlantic Pavilion and several surrounding buildings, including Joe's Restaurant, burned to the ground. Although the fire ended an era on Folly Beach, the $1.5 million Ocean Plaza opened three years later, including a renovation of the pier designed to accommodate 1,000 people. (Both, photograph by Boss Wilbanks and Henry Castleberry, courtesy of Maebelle Barnett Bazzel.)

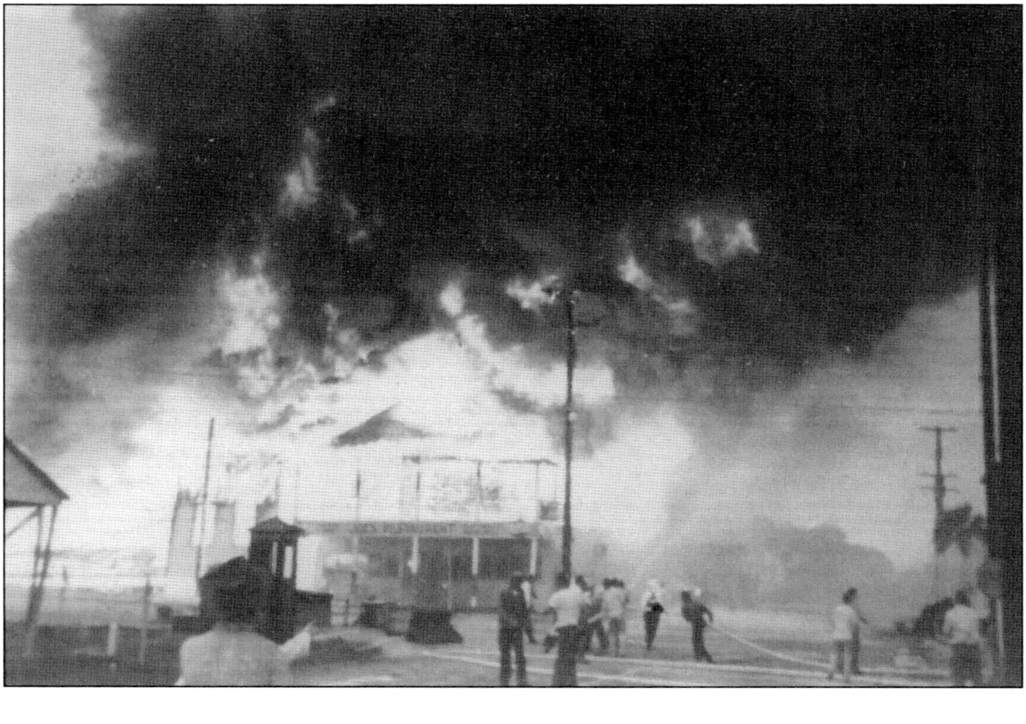

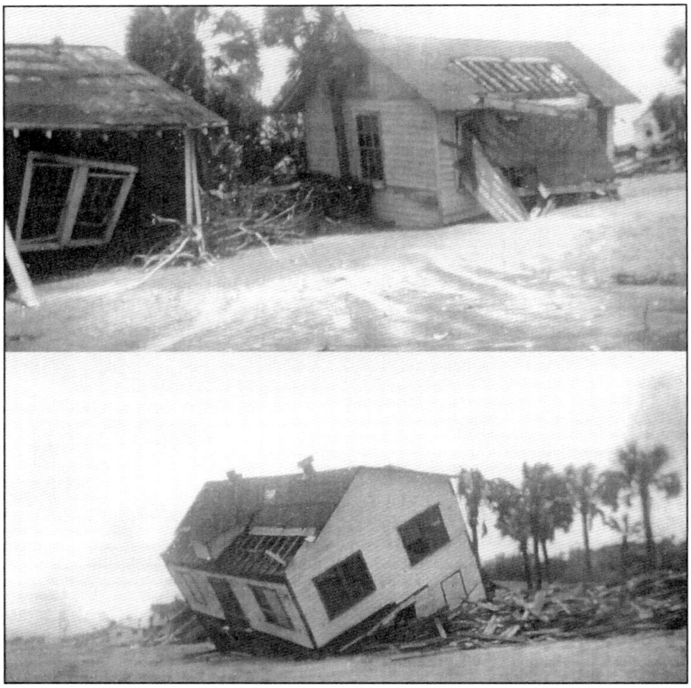

Just as 1989's Hurricane Hugo paved the way for mansions by the sea on Folly Beach, Hurricane Gracie in September 1959 also upended the status quo, ending the days of quaint one- and two-room beach shacks along the front beach. The category-four storm struck near Beaufort and had devastating effects along the southern South Carolina coast, totaling $14 million (in 1959 dollars) in damages across the Southeast. Exactly 20 years later, Hurricane David again wreaked havoc on the island, but the worst was still yet to come. (Courtesy of Karen Stringer via Wallace Benson.)

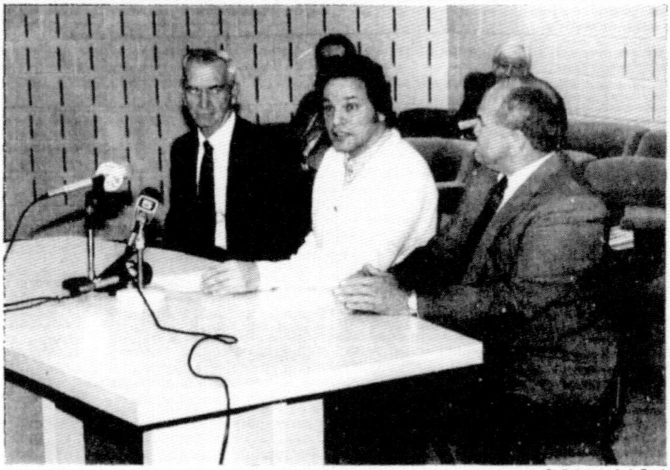

Staff photo by Andy Brack

Richard Valenti, flanked by two ministers, makes a point at his hearing Wednesday.

State board denies parole to murderer of 3 local girls

Far worse than any shark attack story, murderer Richard Valenti terrorized Folly Beach in 1973, killing three teenage girls: Sherri Jan Clark, Alexis Latimer, and Mary Earline Bunch. A Navy sailor, Valenti forced the girls to come from the beach to his house and bound, gagged, and hung them. The girls' bodies were found buried in the sand dunes. Valenti is still serving a life sentence, and petitions to deny his parole appear every two years on Folly Beach. Many of the girls' surviving family members still live on the island. The horrendous crimes left a painful scar on the community, marking a turning point when doors began to be locked at night. (Courtesy of the *News and Courier.*)

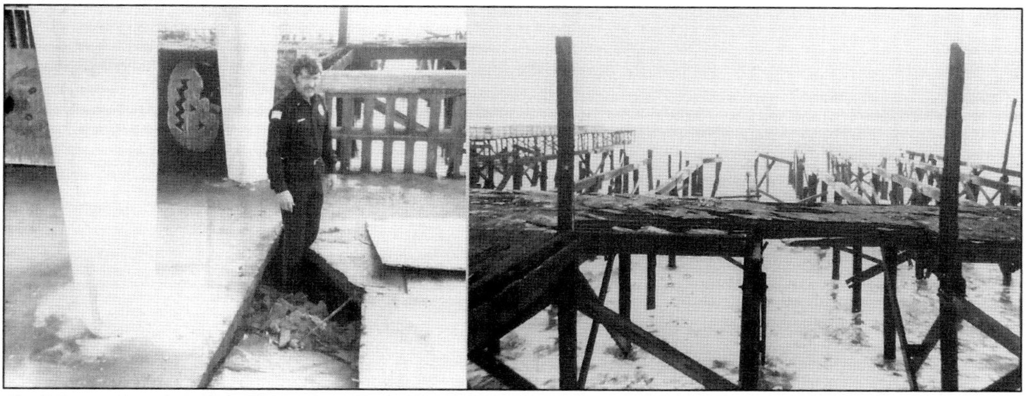

On November 2, 1977, the massive dance pier burned and fell into the ocean. "There is no doubt in my mind that it was arson," says Wallace Benson, the city's chief of police at the time. Benson's suspicions stem from a nearby resident who lived in a trailer and whose wife was known to get "excited" by fire. Facing "sky high" flames, Benson and his team entered the building, but wind swept the fire below the pier, and firefighter Rex Whitcomb fell through a hole that emerged. Benson managed to pull him back to safety just before rushing to escape the inferno. Thus, two local boys who grew up on the island became the last to ever walk on Folly's famous dance pier. Benson is seen on the left in front of the pilings the day after the fire. The shot on the right shows the remains of the pier. Some residents claim the beach was never the same after the pier burned. (Photographs by Robert Grooms, courtesy of Wallace Benson.)

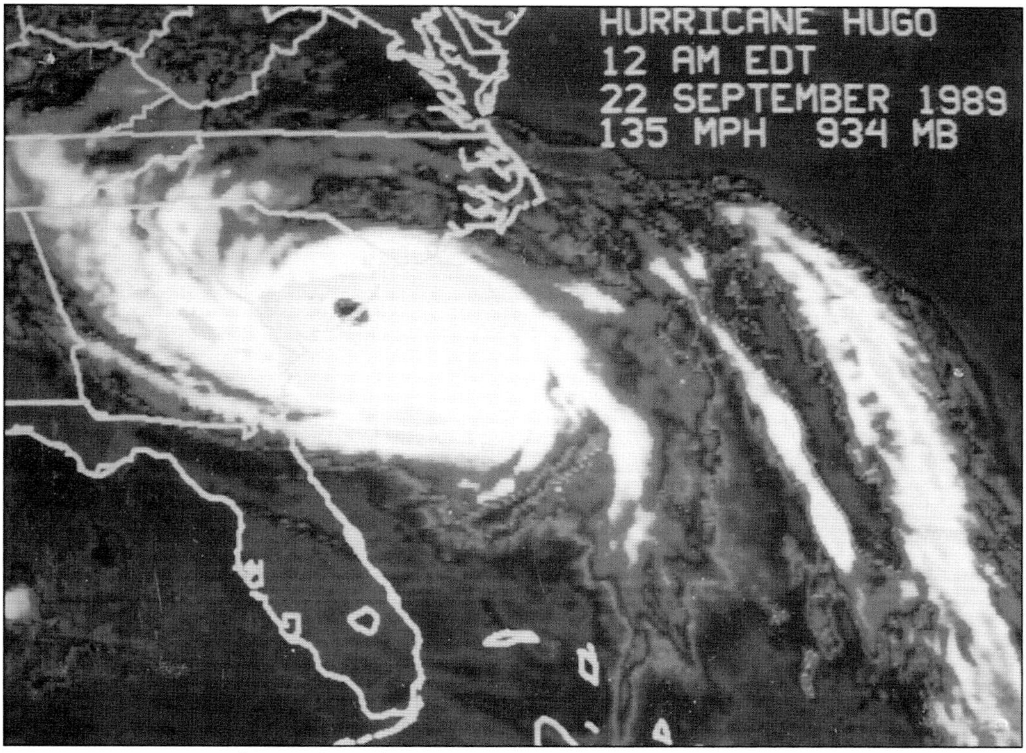

Hurricane Hugo was larger than the entire state of South Carolina. The category-five storm altered Folly Beach forever, making landfall on Isle of Palms on September 22, 1989, wreaking havoc across the Charleston area, and causing damage totaling $10 billion across the United States and the Caribbean. (Courtesy of McKevlin's Surf Shop.)

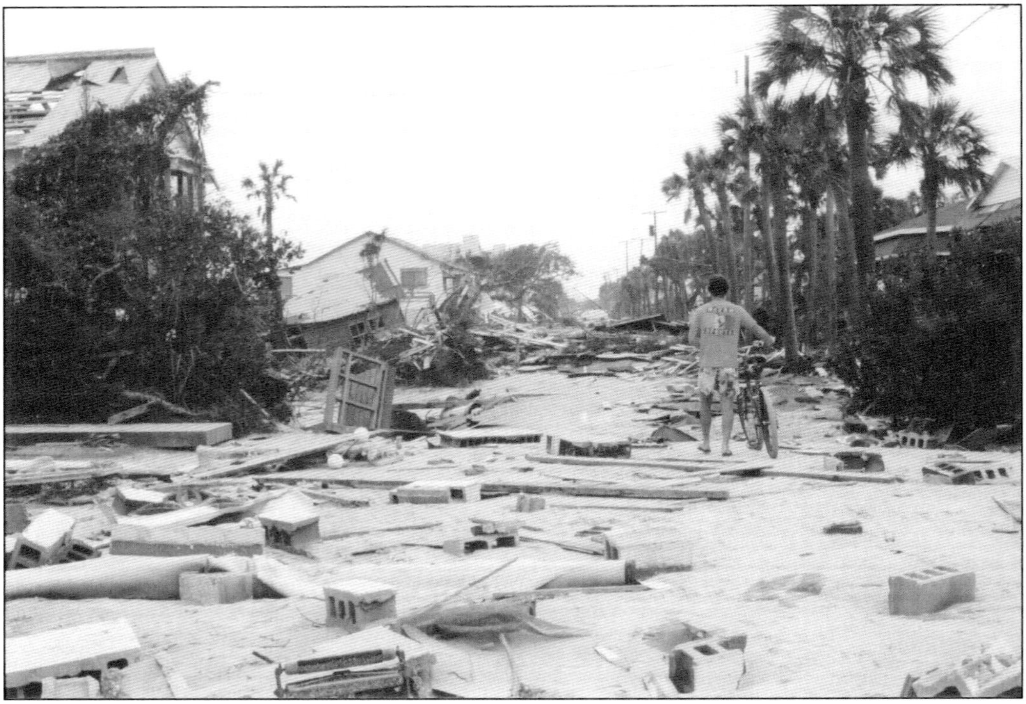

Hugo took the lives of 27 people in South Carolina alone, and 100,000 were left homeless across the storm's path. (Courtesy of Bill Perry and Betty Sue Cowsert.)

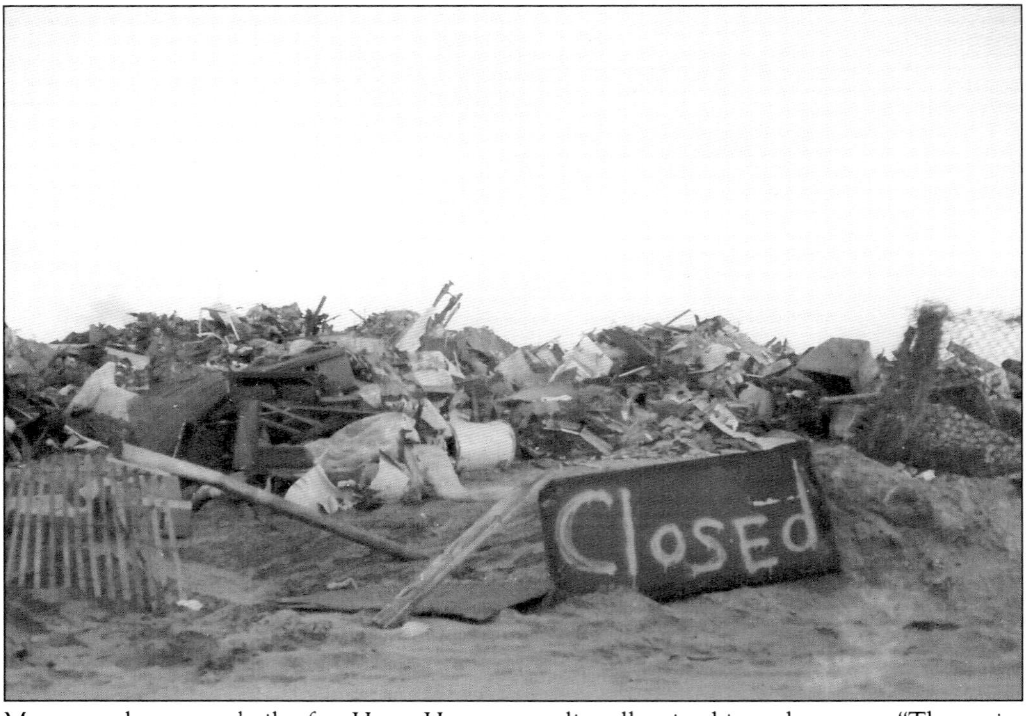

Many people never rebuilt after Hugo. Houses were literally wiped into the ocean. "The entire Mariner's Cay Marina was stuffed underneath the bridge," recalls resident Bill Perry. (Courtesy of Wallace Benson.)

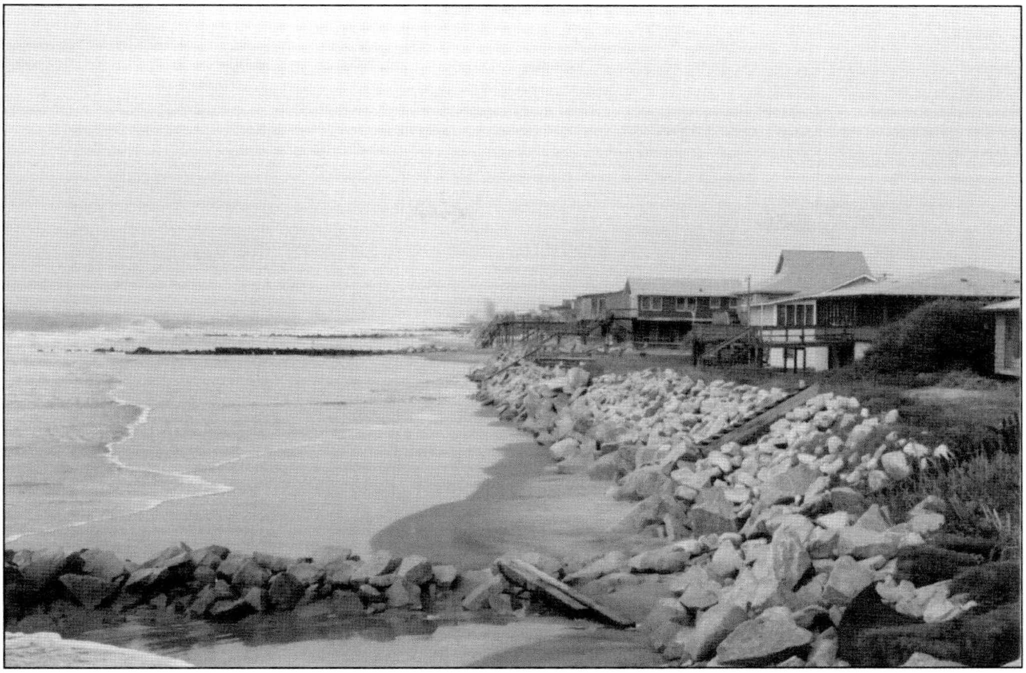

Houses along East Arctic Avenue, from East Tenth Street looking toward Center Street, are seen above the day before Hugo made landfall. Pictured below is the same view on September 23, the day after Hugo passed over. (Both, courtesy of Bill Perry and Betty Sue Cowsert.)

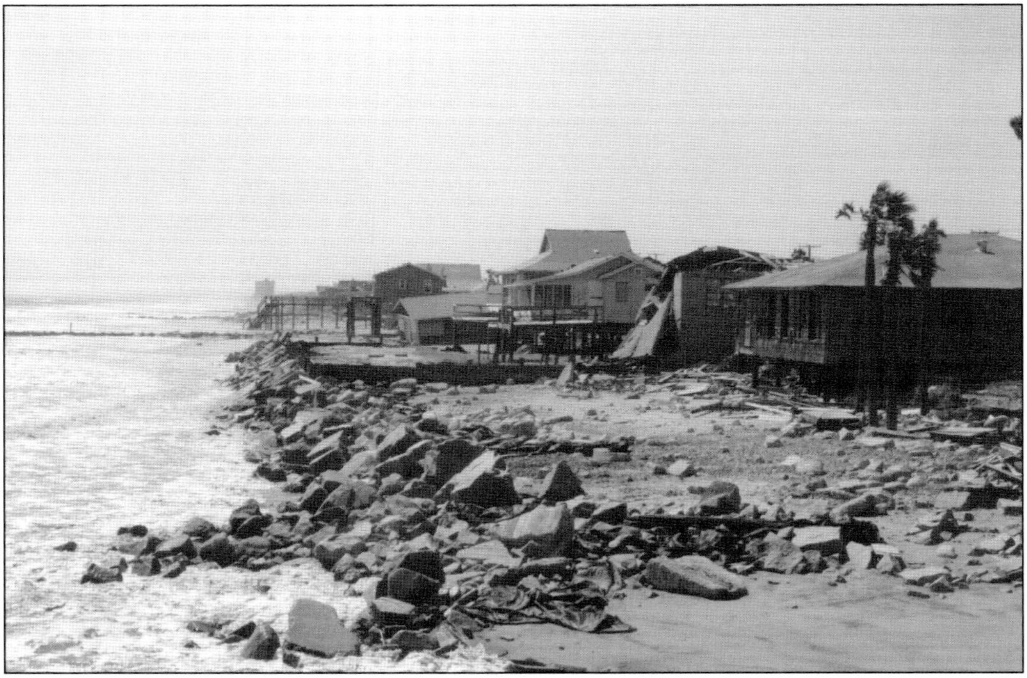

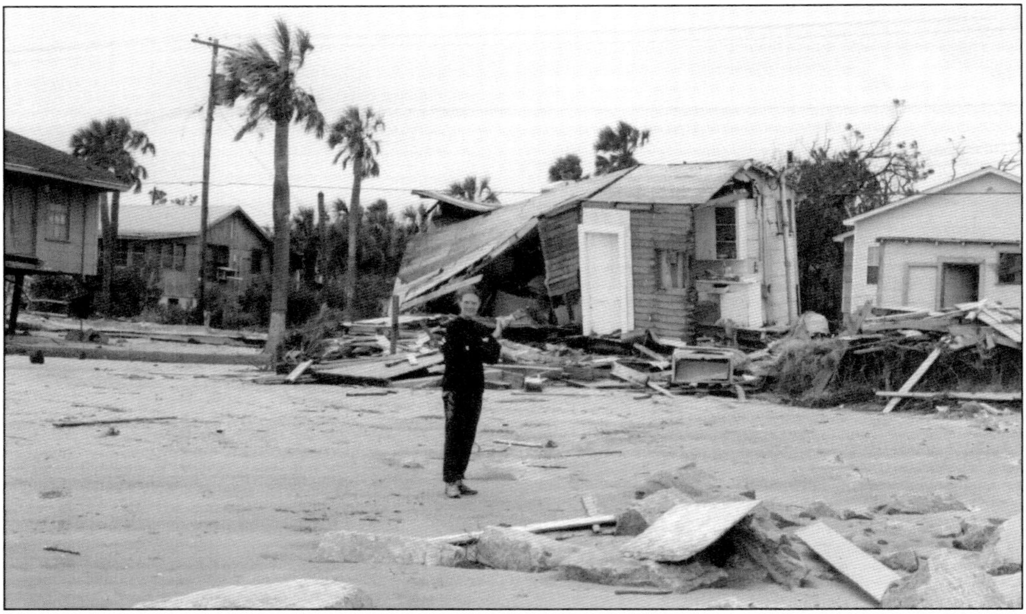

Betty Sue Cowsert stands among the rubble on the beach after Hugo. Many houses literally sat in the middle of the road, and 80 percent of the homes on the beach were severely damaged. (Courtesy of Bill Perry and Betty Sue Cowsert.)

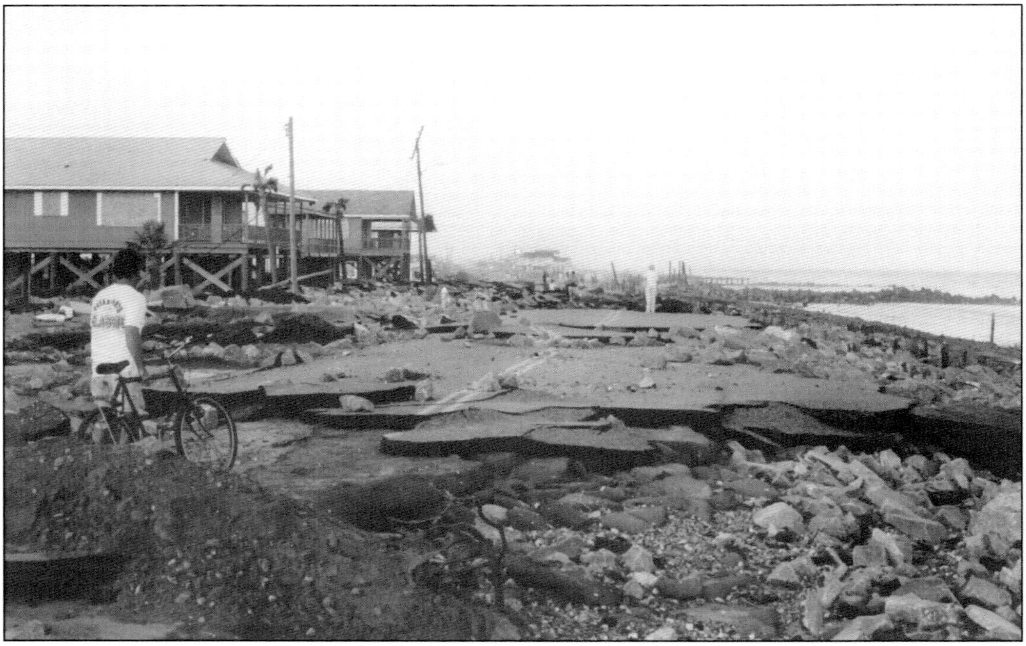

The day after Hugo hit, as councilmember Wallace Benson walked from his brother's home on James Island back to Folly Beach, Mayor Bob Linville spotted him along Folly Road and gave him a lift. The pair arrived back on the beach to discover a 50-foot section of Ashley Avenue completely gone. After replacing enough broken asphalt to make the road passable, they continued to the Washout, only to discover more than 3,000 feet of missing road. In this photograph, Bill Perry walks his bike along East Ashley where the road was literally "washed out." (Courtesy of Bill Perry and Betty Sue Cowsert.)

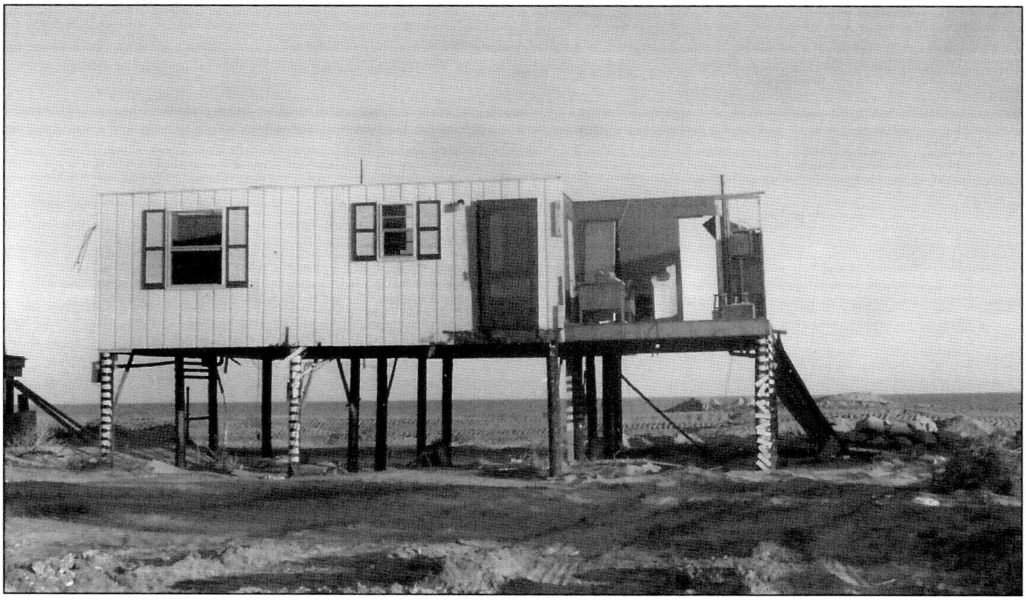

Hugo decimated Folly Beach more severely than any storm before or since. While some beachfront houses were swept completely away, others, like the one at 319 East Arctic seen here, suffered severe structural damage. Others were left mere skeletons of their former selves. The damage from fallen trees, broken roads, and collapsed buildings took years to repair. (Courtesy of Wallace Benson.)

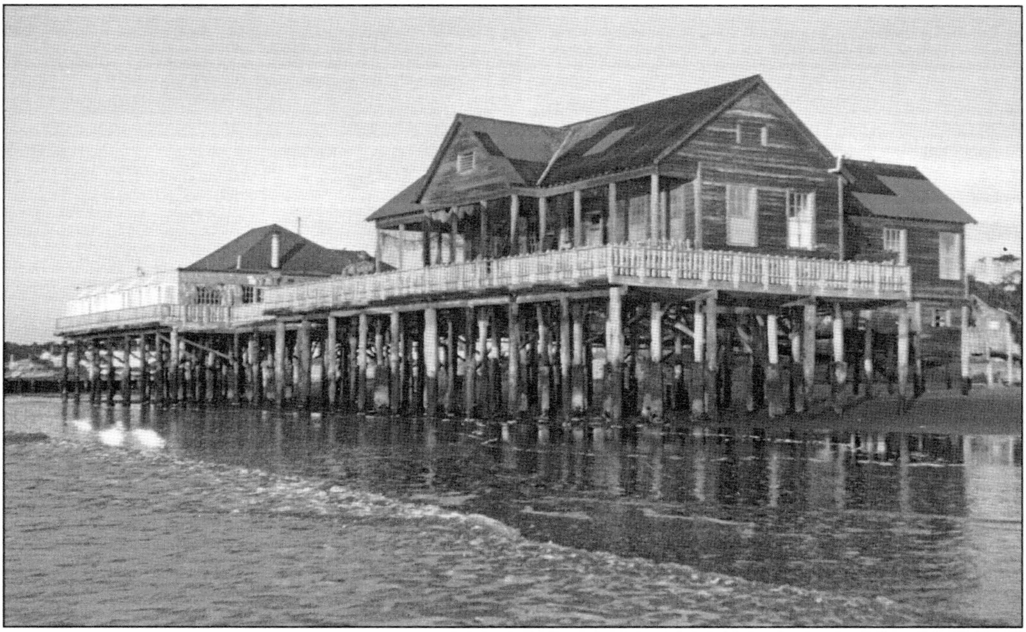

The Atlantic House restaurant and the adjacent OTO (Over the Ocean) bar were favorite local hangouts before Hurricane Hugo swept them into the ocean. Owner Eddie Taylor worked hard to keep the building standing, even earning a few naysayers for foregoing the permitting process when his foundation needed new sand and a bulldozer for re-nourishment. The building stood for years over the ocean as apartments and also as a boarded-up abandoned structure, before finding new life as a popular restaurant under Taylor's guidance. Nothing was left of the structure but a few pilings in the surf after Hugo had its way. (Courtesy of Maebelle Barnett Bazzel.)

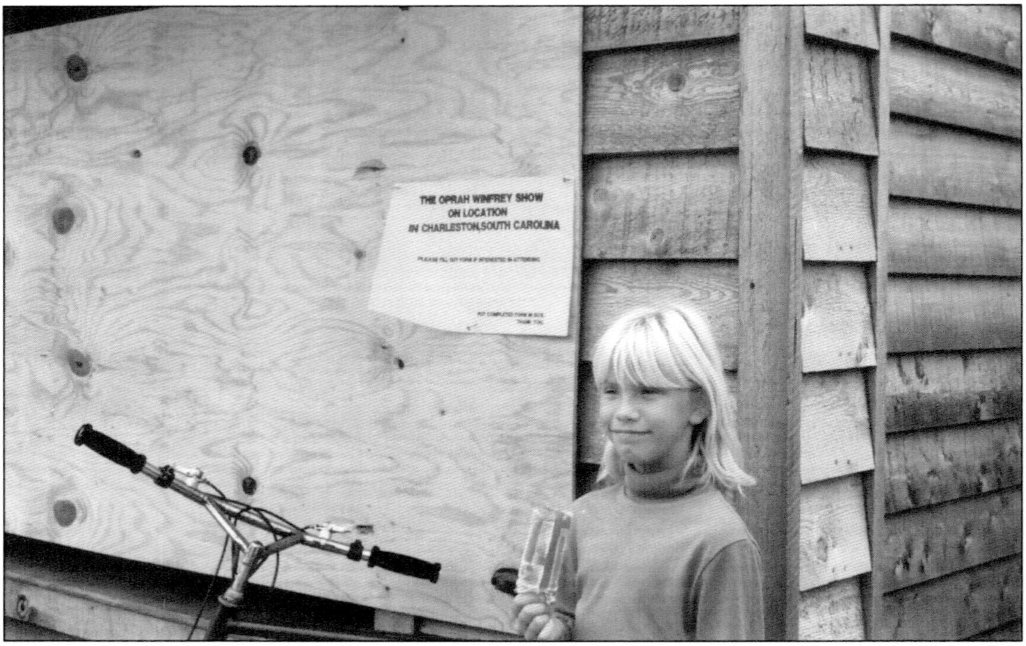

The Oprah Winfrey Show visited Folly Beach soon after the storm. "It was like an event," recalls Betty Sue Cowsert. "Someone from Florida brought popsicles for everyone." Here, Tara Houts enjoys one of those treats amidst the chaos. (Courtesy of Bill Perry and Betty Sue Cowsert.)

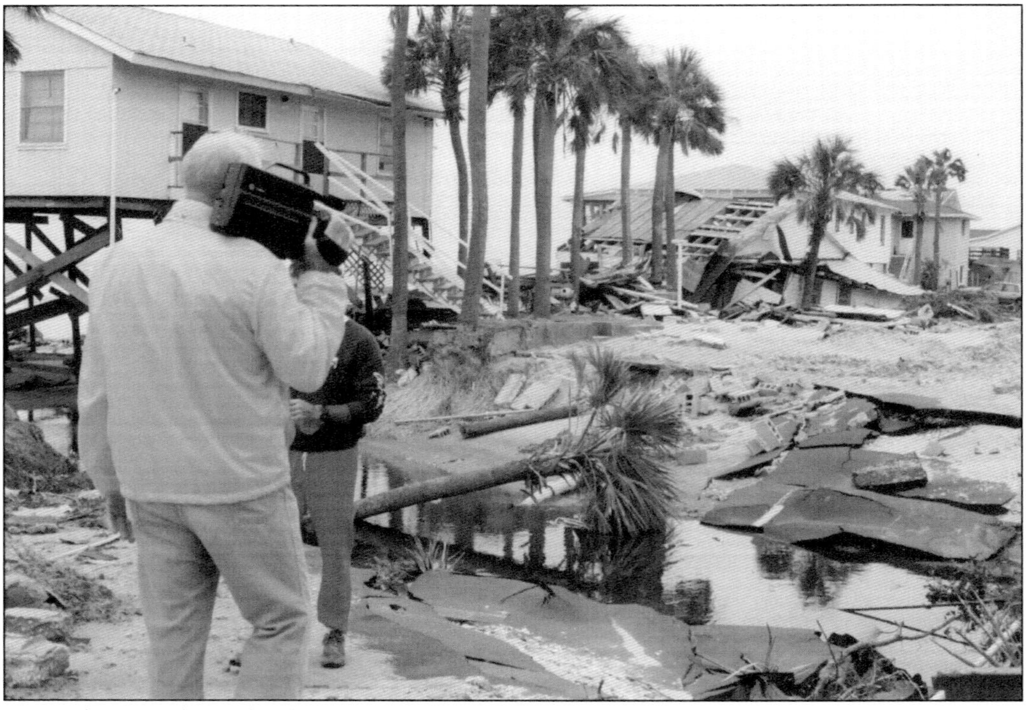

More photographs and video were likely taken on Folly Beach in the weeks after Hugo than at any other time in history. It was a scene of unthinkable destruction. Most residents whose homes survived were without electricity for at least three weeks. (Courtesy of Bill Perry and Betty Sue Cowsert.)

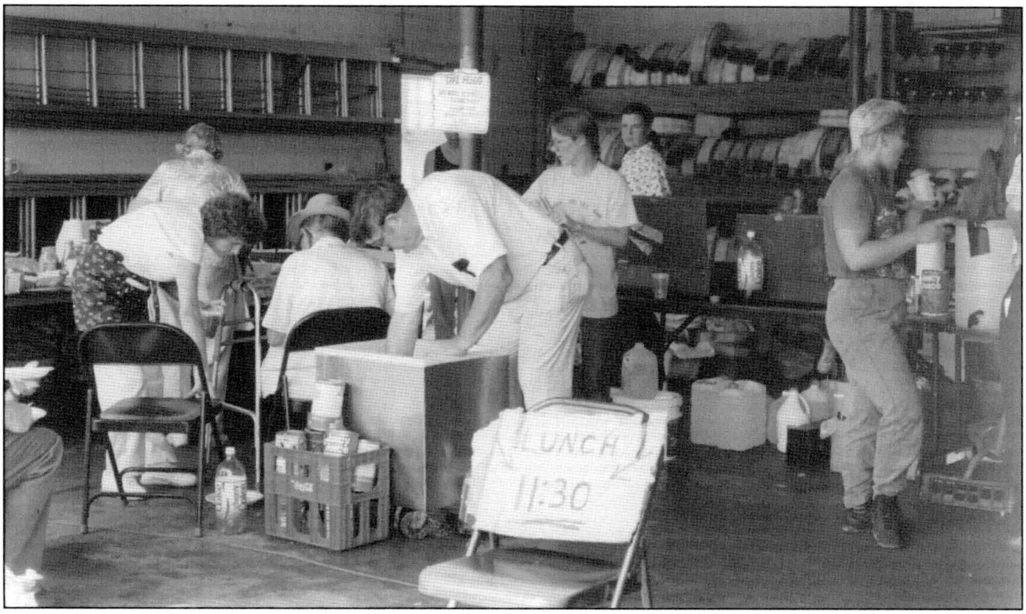

After Hugo, the Folly Beach community came together in an inspiring way. For a few days, residents were entirely self-reliant, filtering water from ponds and toilets and finding cans of food to eat in the mud. Betty Sue Cowsert recalls picking provisions out of the sludge on the ground at the Turtle Corner market (where Planet Follywood stands today) before wiping them off and paying for them. "Cash was king," she says. Many residents took advantage of tetanus booster shots and free meals offered at the fire station. Councilmember Wallace Benson remembers eating very well in the weeks after Hugo, thanks to the generous donations arriving from around the country. (Courtesy of Bill Perry and Betty Sue Cowsert.)

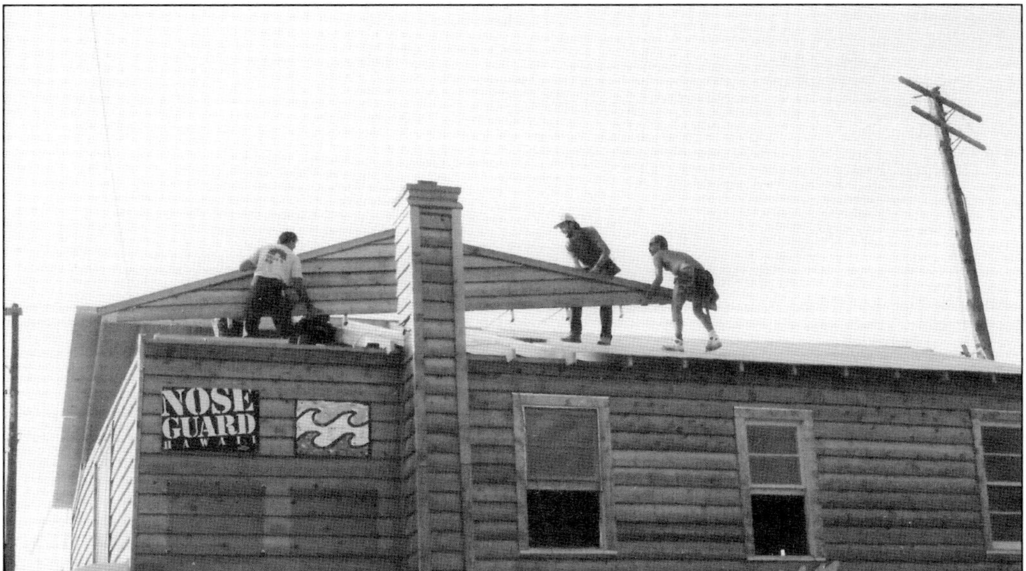

When Hurricane Hugo hit, Oceansports Surf Shop had just been renovated. The storm took the roof and windows with it. Teamwork made for quick repairs in the weeks that followed. (Courtesy of Bill Perry and Betty Sue Cowsert.)

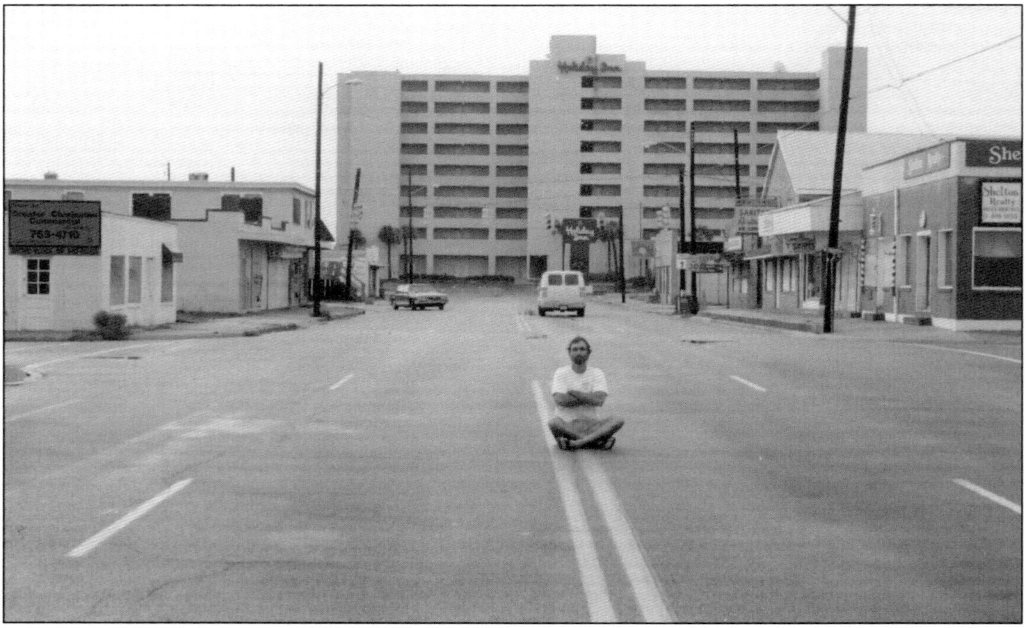

Oceansports Surf Shop owners Bill Perry and Betty Sue Cowsert waited until the last possible minute before deciding to evacuate Folly Beach ahead of Hurricane Hugo. They successfully avoided the traffic and had a smooth drive to Orangeburg and back the following day. Here, Bill sits along a relatively deserted Center Street just before leaving the island. (Courtesy of Bill Perry and Betty Sue Cowsert.)

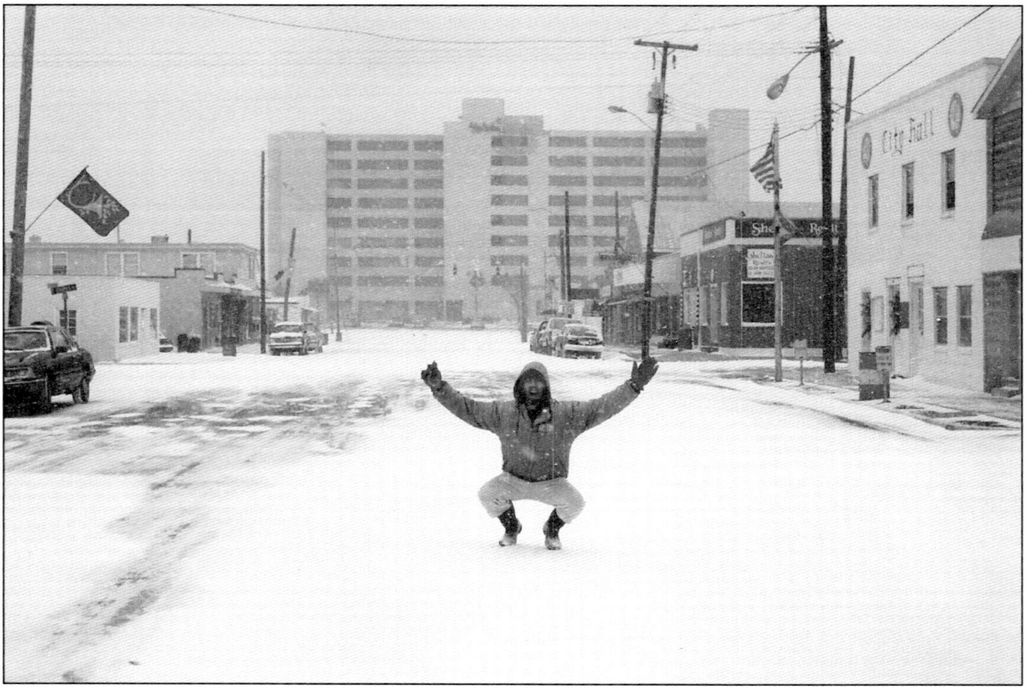

The rare snowfall that came just before Christmas in 1989 helped blanket some of the pain Hugo had caused. Three months after evacuating, nearly to the day, Bill Perry resumed his Center Street pose as the white powder settled in. (Courtesy of Bill Perry and Betty Sue Cowsert.)

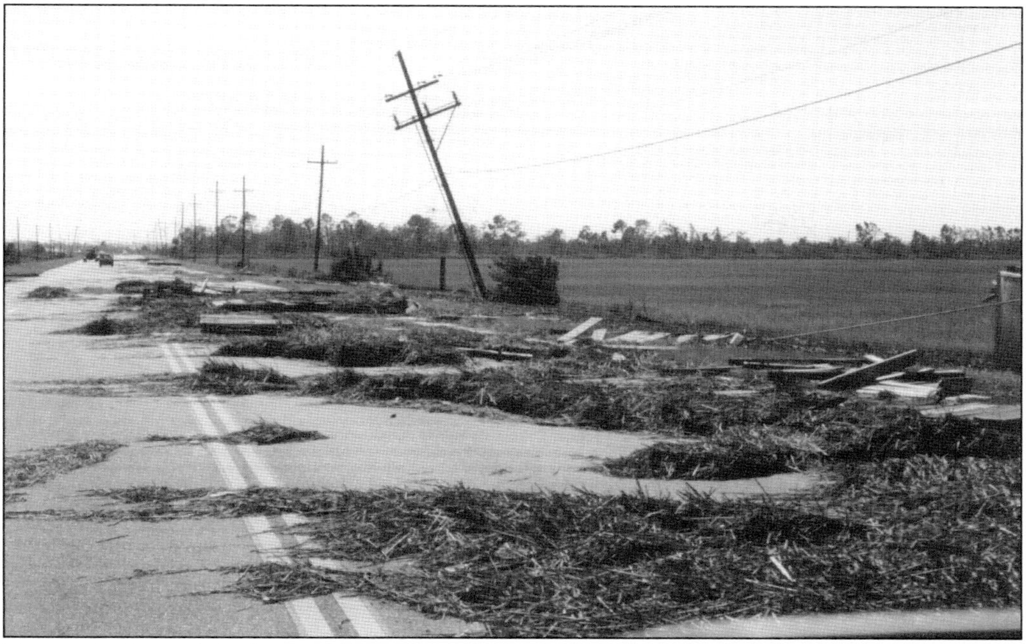

Notice the bow of the boat on the far right edge of this photograph, taken while approaching Folly Beach on the day after Hugo. The boat washed up during the storm and remains there today as the famous Folly Boat, which is painted on an almost-daily basis. (Courtesy of Bill Perry and Betty Sue Cowsert.)

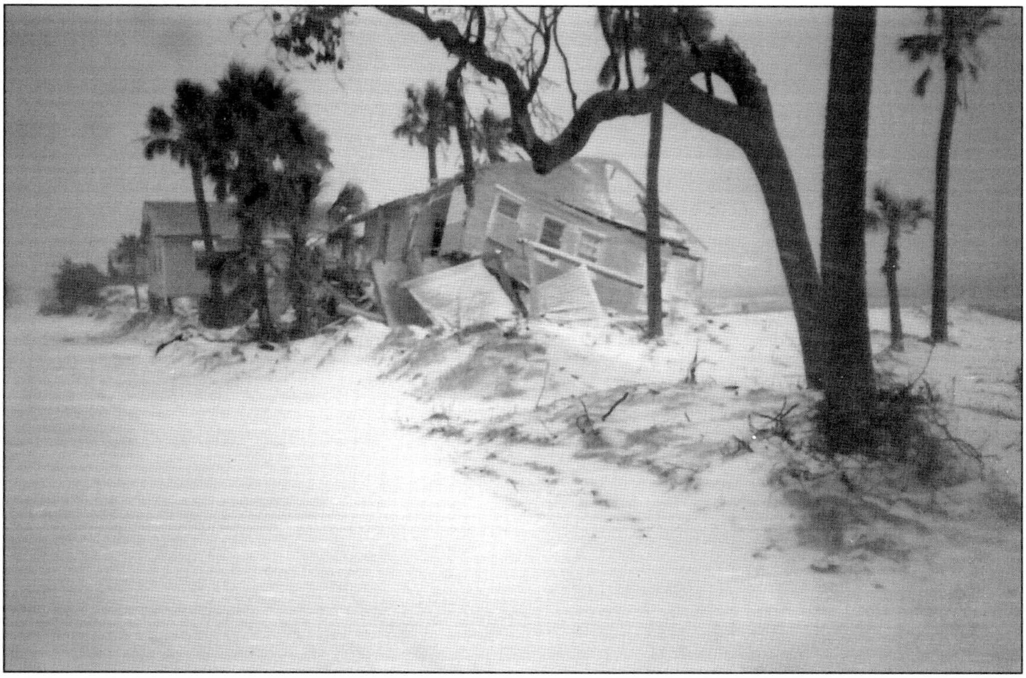

The two-day snowfall in December 1989 was not a complete blessing. Many Folly Beach residents had been without gas service since Hugo, and many collapsed homes remained eerily in place. Pipes froze and burst, leaving some residents with a chilly and frustrating—yet beautiful—white Christmas. (Courtesy of Wallace Benson.)

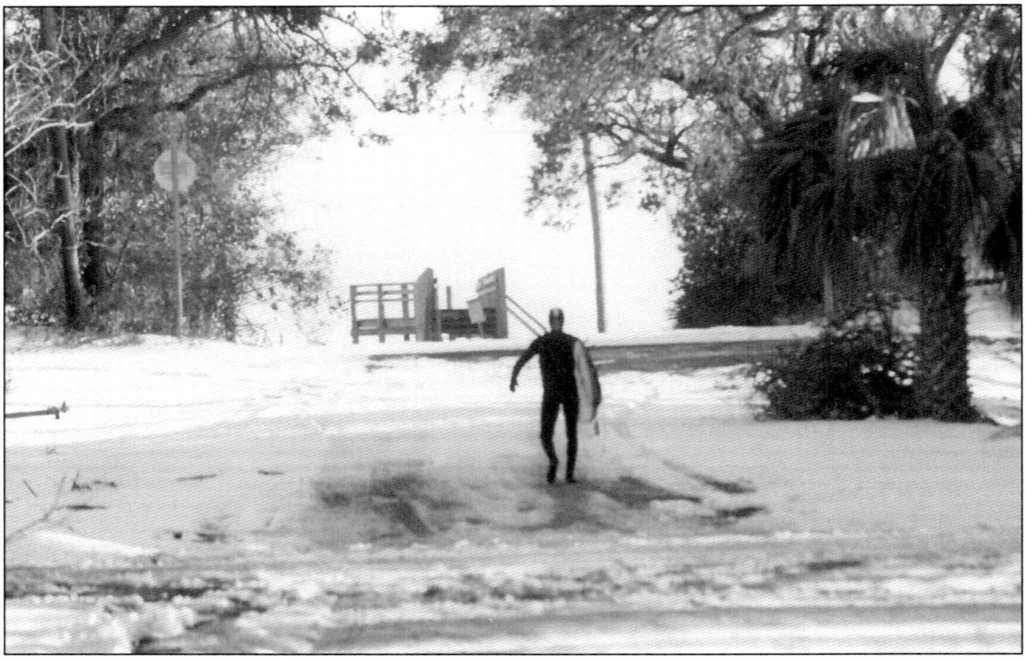

"There were no waves," recalls Betty Sue Cowsert of the snowy day her husband Bill Perry decided to paddle out in December 1989. It is rare that Folly Beach surfers can earn bragging rights about uncomfortable conditions. (Courtesy of Bill Perry and Betty Sue Cowsert.)

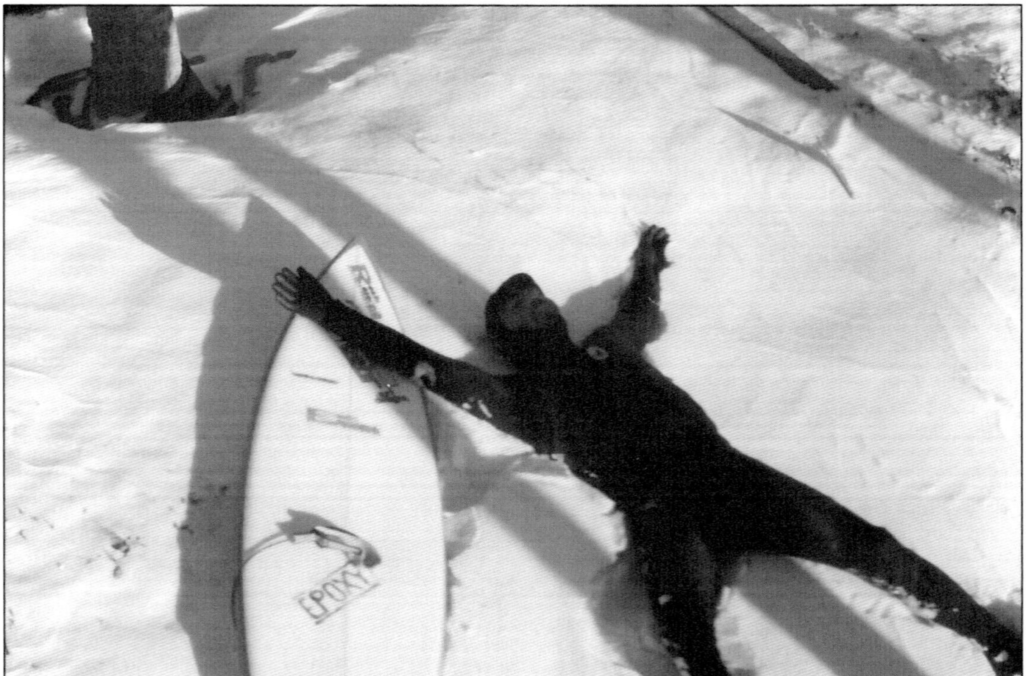

Bill Perry forms a rare snow angel in coastal South Carolina, Folly Beach style. (Courtesy of Bill Perry and Betty Sue Cowsert.)

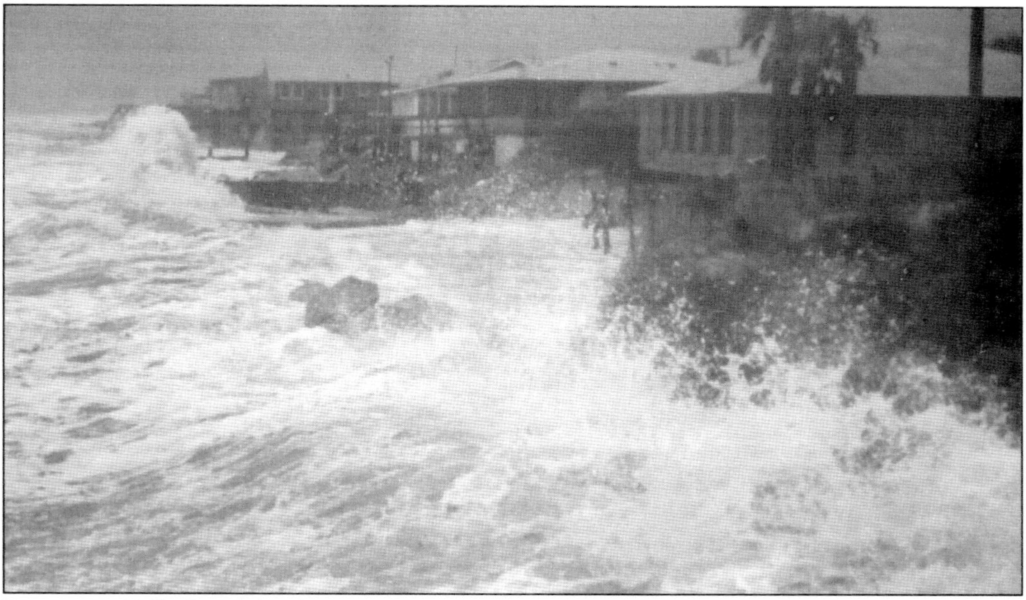

Erosion on Folly Beach has been a major problem for more than a century since the jetties were built leading into Charleston harbor. Despite periodic re-nourishment, the losing battle is most evident when a storm surge pulls defenseless houses with it back into the ocean. (Courtesy of Bill Perry and Betty Sue Cowsert.)

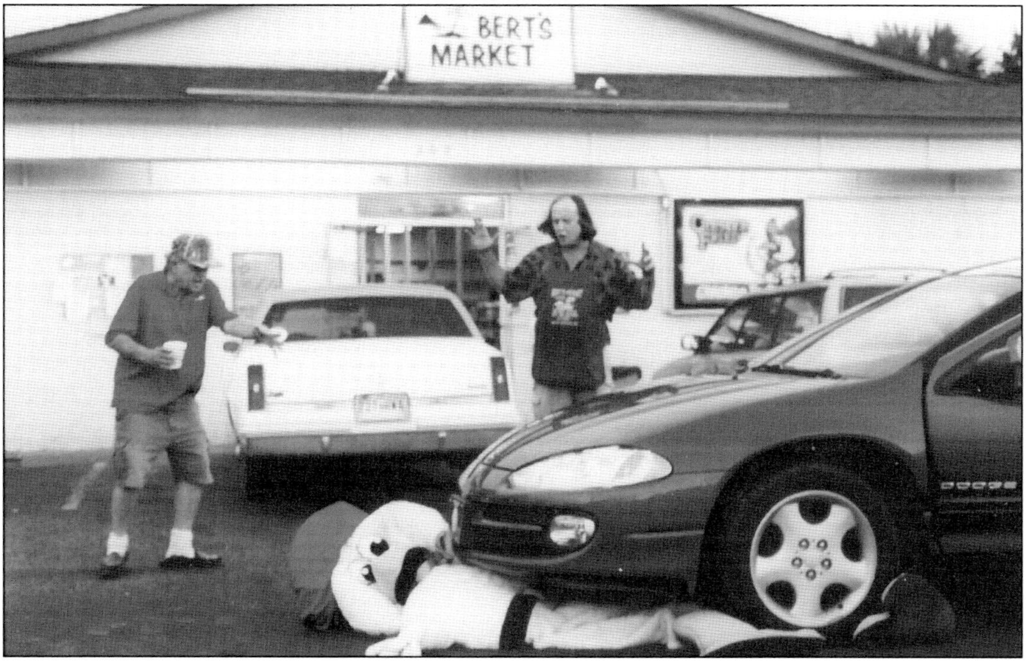

Fire struck Bert's Market in 2004, destroying much of the store's interior. The blaze was believed to have started in their deep fryer, after an employee turned up the heat to compensate for an electricity "brown out." When the power returned, so did flames. Some speculated that the fire was karmic retribution by the Chester Fried Chicken, after Bert and his employees staged the mascot's demise (seen here) during a promotional week when the store had the costume on loan from the supplier. (Courtesy of Bert Hastings.)

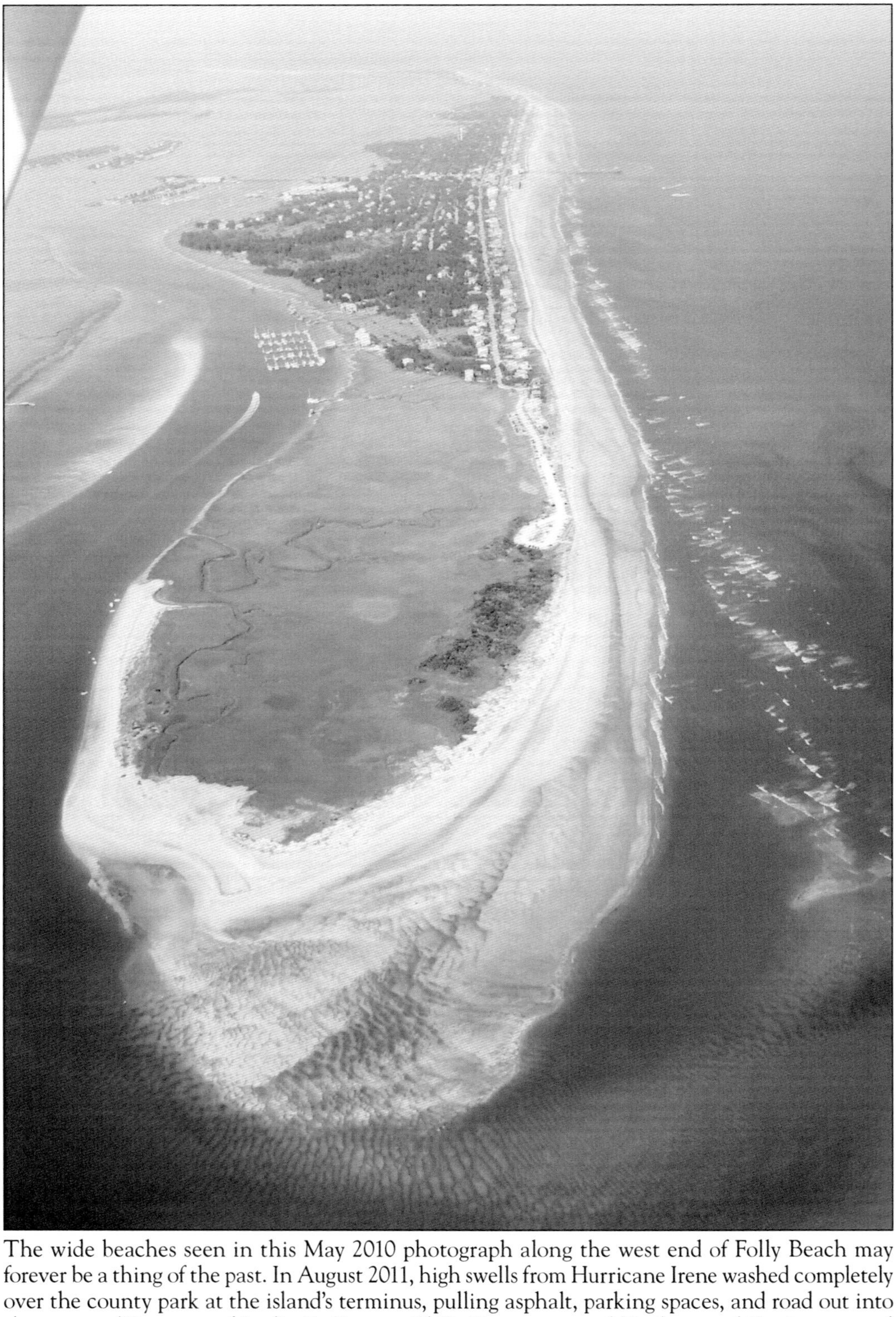

The wide beaches seen in this May 2010 photograph along the west end of Folly Beach may forever be a thing of the past. In August 2011, high swells from Hurricane Irene washed completely over the county park at the island's terminus, pulling asphalt, parking spaces, and road out into the ocean. (Courtesy of Leslie R. Sautter, PhD, Department of Geology and Environmental Geosciences, College of Charleston.)

Five

Fun in the Sun

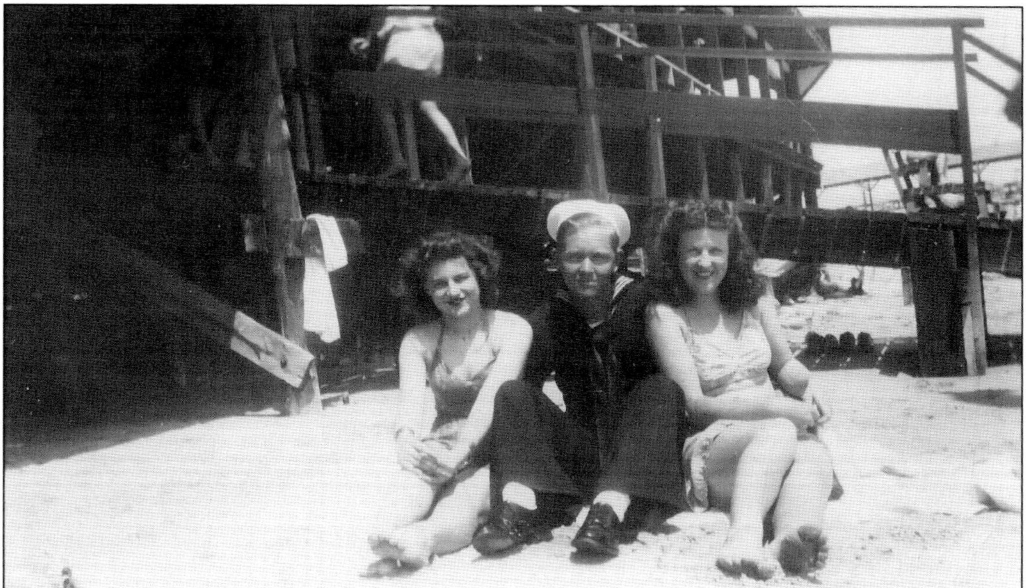

Jeannie Vargo and Wilma Brown (Maherg) sit on the beach near the pier with Jeannie's boyfriend, a Navy sailor named Mac, between them. It was May 1946, and Folly's post–World War II boom was just beginning. Big bands played on the pier at night, while dancers jitterbugged away their worries. Men in uniform were common at the beach, including sailors from the Navy base in North Charleston and Marines who visited from Parris Island. (Courtesy of Greta Anderson.)

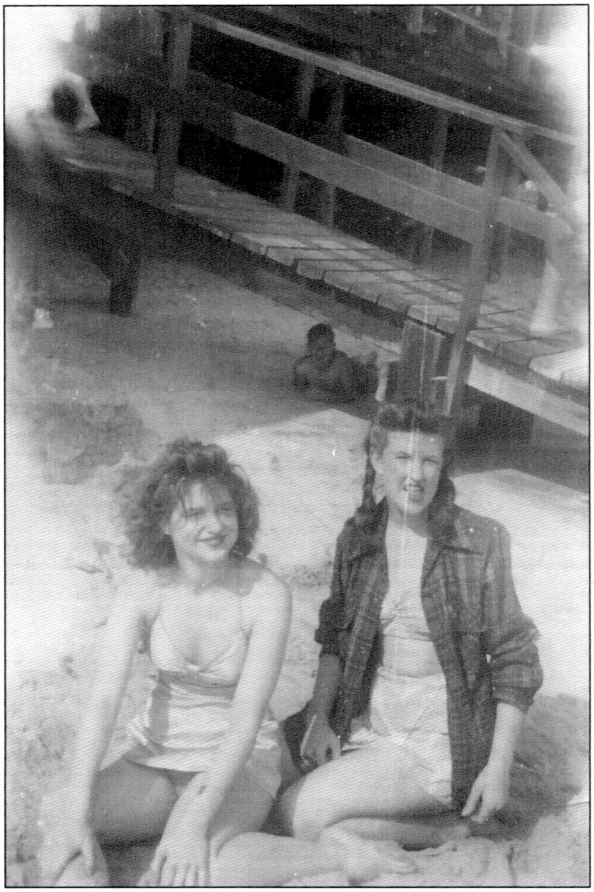

Jeannie Vargo (left) and Wilma Brown relax on Folly Beach in 1946. Brown is sticking her tongue out at a group of sailors behind the cameraman. Note the boy hiding under the pier walkway in the background. (Courtesy of Greta Anderson.)

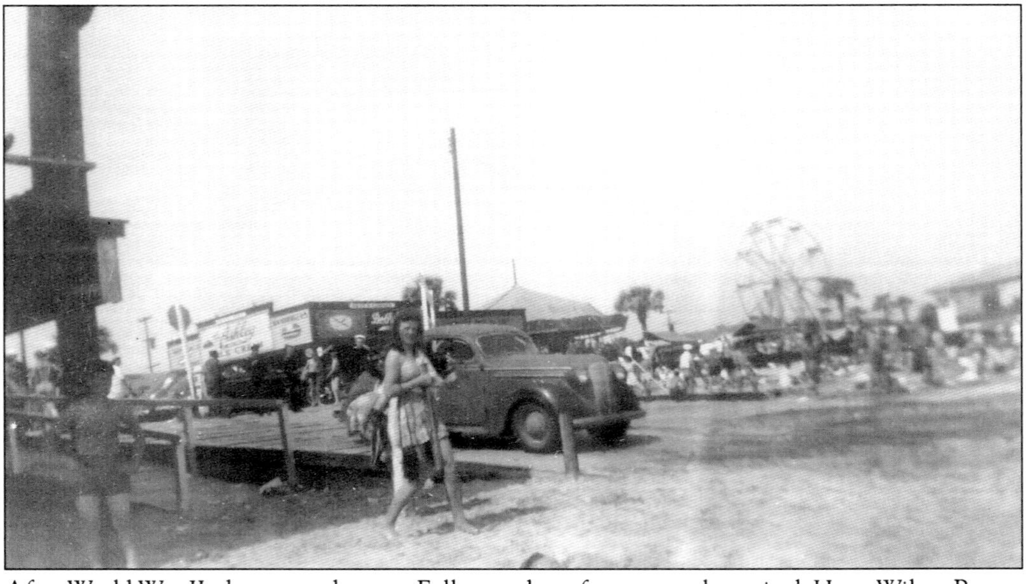

After World War II, the atmosphere on Folly was that of a perpetual carnival. Here, Wilma Brown crosses Arctic Avenue to the beach. An ice cream stand, a merry-go-round, and a Ferris wheel are in the background. (Courtesy of Greta Anderson.)

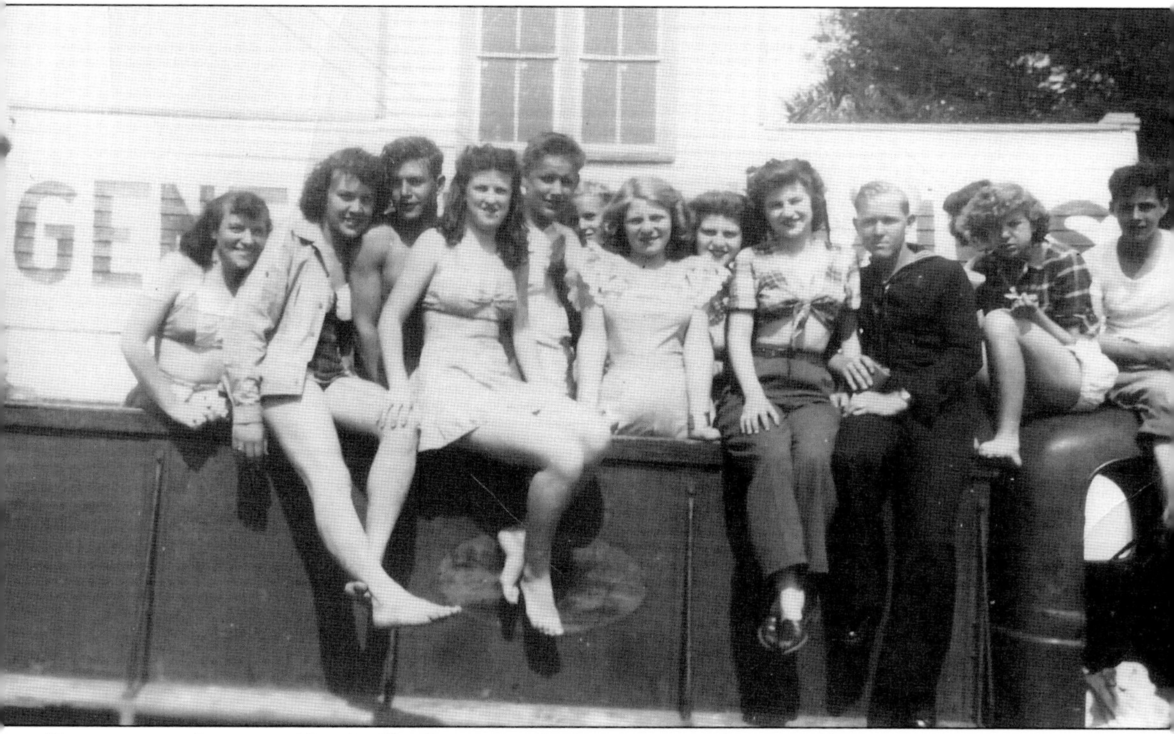

For teenagers living in North Charleston in the late 1940s, a day on Folly Beach was paradise. A neighborhood man, Mr. Tucker, owned an ice truck and offered rides to the beach for youths living in the area around the Navy base. This group is identified as, from left to right, Sissy Davis, Dot Cutrell, Andy, Jack, Shirley, Marilyn, Marcia, Jeannie Vargo, Mac, Delores, and Walter West. West's brother Frank became the sheriff of Charleston County, retiring in 1983. (Courtesy of Greta Anderson.)

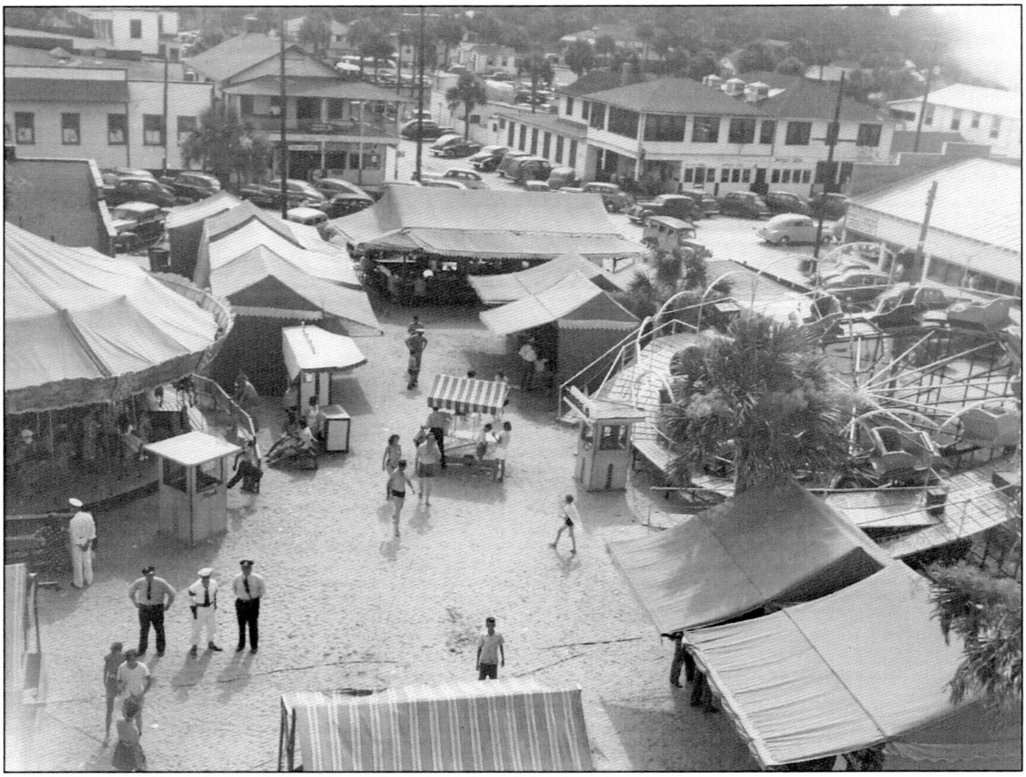

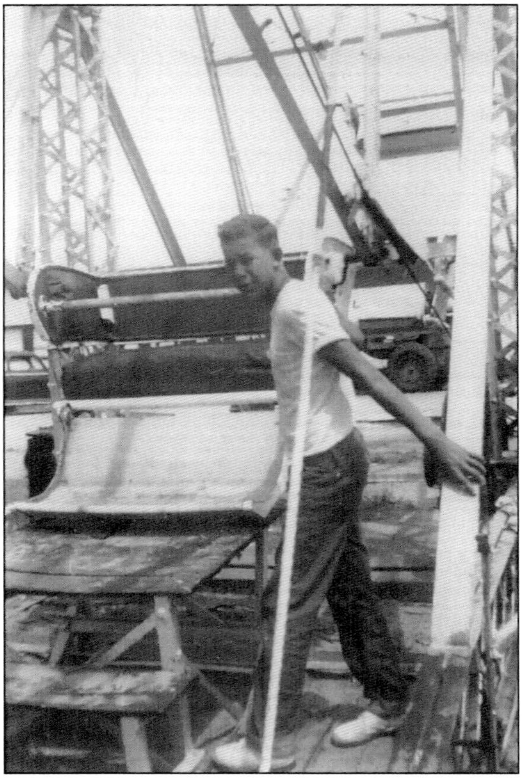

Boss Wilbanks, who owned Folly Drug Sundries with his wife, Florence, took this photograph from atop the Ferris wheel in the 1940s. Note the Little Atlantic concession stand and restaurant on the top left and the bowling alley on the far right. (Courtesy of Patricia Jamison Wilbanks Bragg.)

A young Robert Knight manages the Ferris wheel at the Folly's Playground amusement park. Knight claims he was the youngest person to operate the wheel, a task that required distributing the weight as the chairs were loaded and unloaded. (Courtesy of Maebelle Barnett Bazzel.)

The Folly Beach Civic Club published vacation brochures like this one in the 1950s. Many of the photographs were taken by Boss Wilbanks of Folly Drug Sundries. The pamphlet boasted, "Here you will find ocean bathing, sun bathing, driving on the strand, dancing, bowling, roller skating, fishing and boating. Come to stay—a day, a week, a season. A year-round home." It also promoted Cottage Town, at 208 East Erie Avenue. Those homes remain today. Among the first tourist accommodations on the island, their promotional material touted the island's interior, including its magnolia and cherry laurel trees. Former city councilman Wallace Benson recalls that his parents honeymooned at Cottage Town. (Courtesy of Maebelle Barnett Bazzel.)

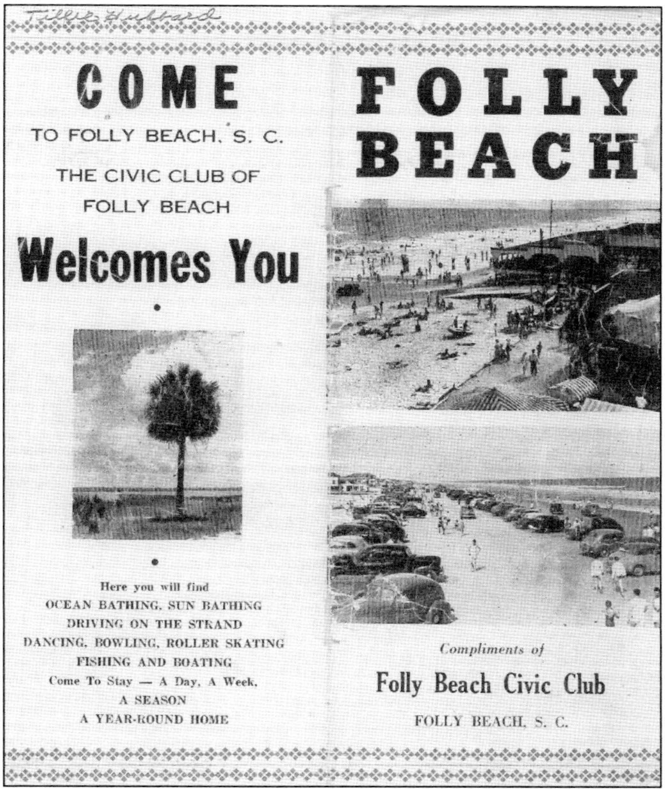

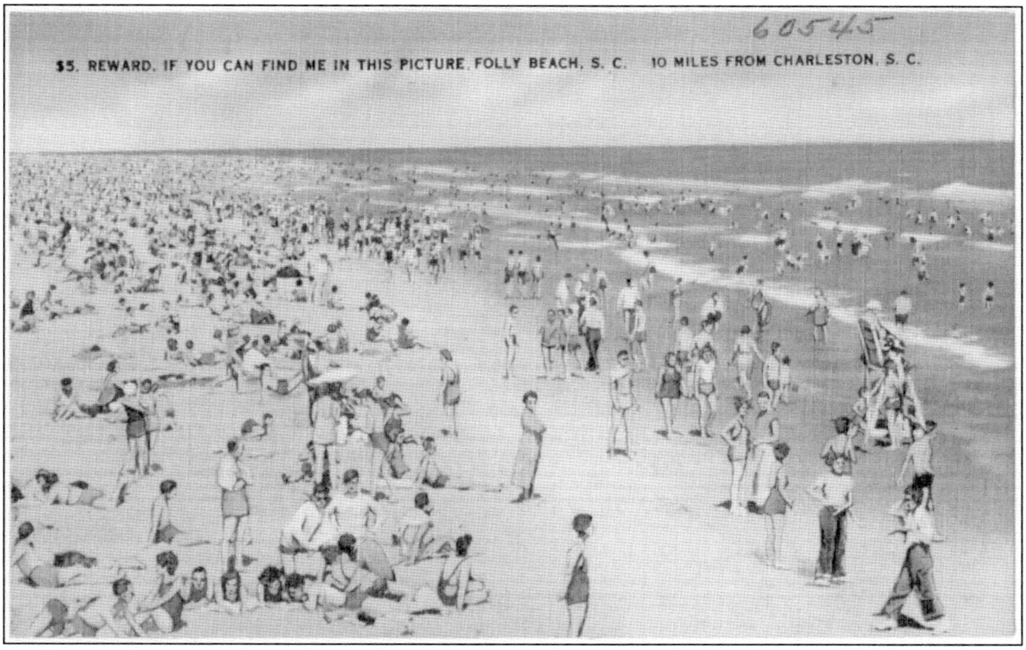

"Folly Beach vies with its sister resorts as one of the finest bathing beaches to be found in America," reads the back of this 1940 postcard. On weekends, the beach would get so crowded that local families arrived as early as 7:00 a.m. to save a spot for a table and chairs. (Courtesy of the Boston Public Library.)

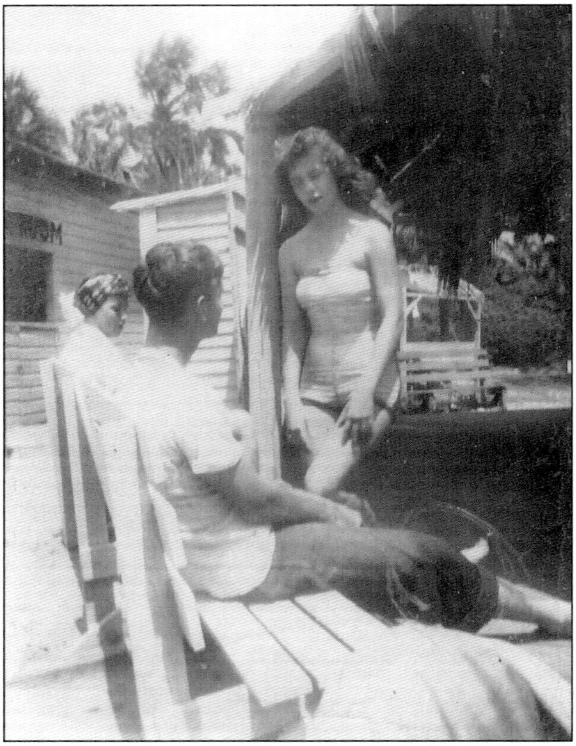

Henry Schultz and Betty Southworth met in 1949 and began flirting when she was 16, after he threw her into the ocean during a Spanish Club gathering on the beach. They are seen here at the beachfront Rainbow Corner hangout, a concession stand with a palm-frond roof and a small dance floor. After being destroyed by Hurricane Gracie in 1959, Rainbow Corner reopened as the Hi-Top. Henry and Betty married in 1952 and recently celebrated 60 years of marriage. They still live on Folly Beach. (Courtesy of Betty Schultz.)

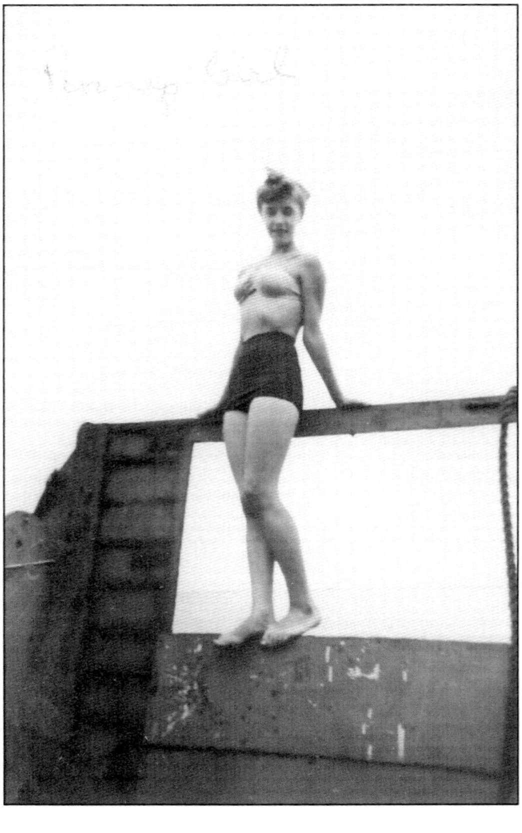

"I agonized over spending $16 for that Jantzen bathing suit," recalls Betty Southworth (Schultz), seen here in the late 1940s. "I only made 50 cents an hour." (Courtesy of Betty Schultz.)

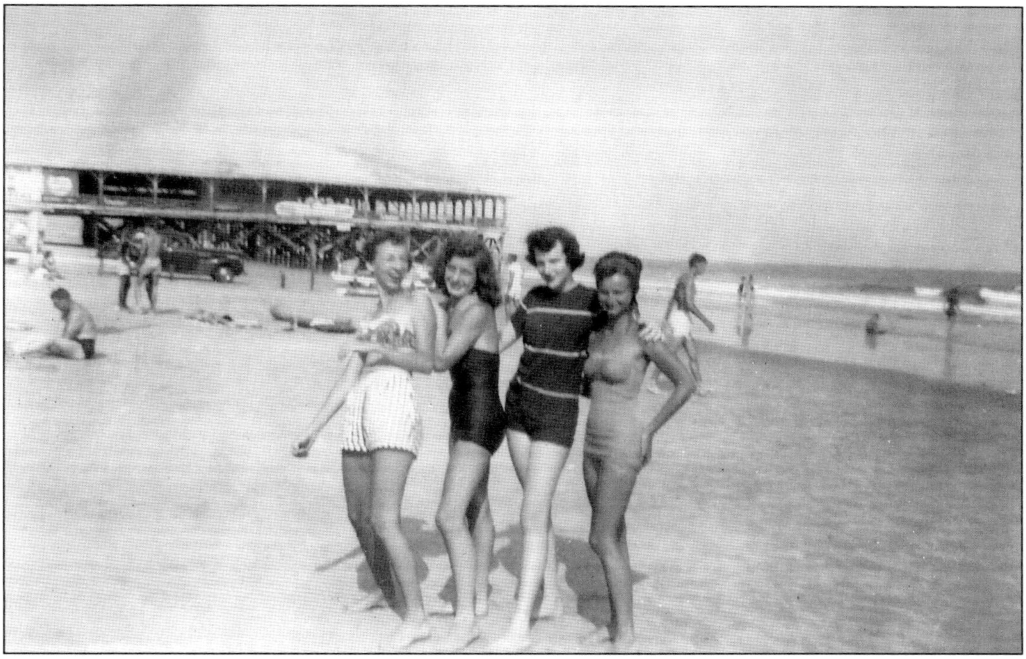

Four "beach bum" friends enjoy a day on the beach in 1950 in front of the pavilion. From left to right, they are Anne Chinnis, Betty Southworth, Patty Palmer, and Edna Joy. (Courtesy of Betty Schultz.)

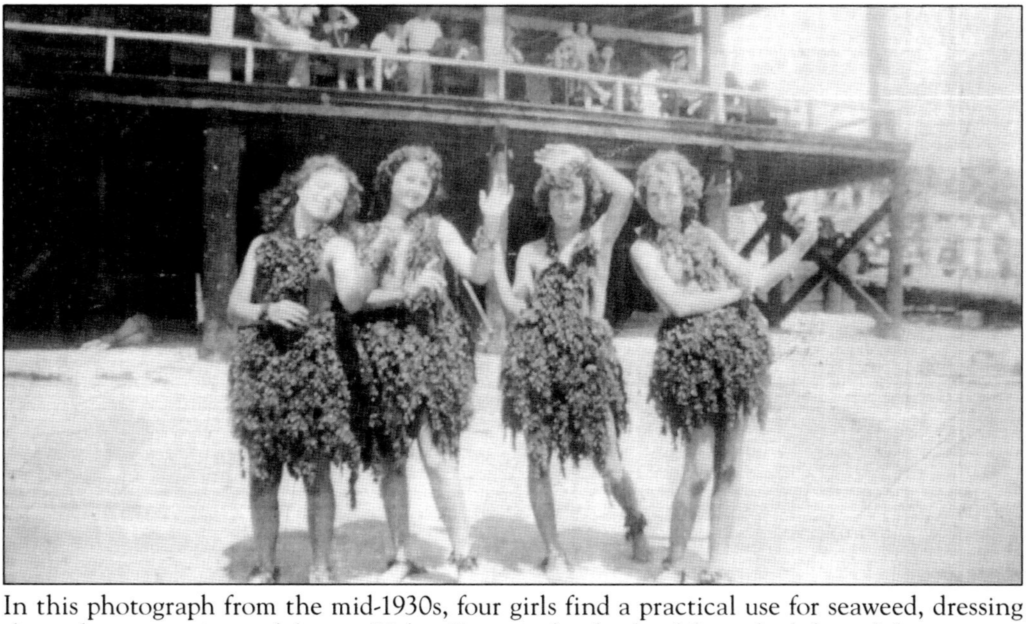

In this photograph from the mid-1930s, four girls find a practical use for seaweed, dressing themselves up as sirens of the sea. Helen Gregg is the third girl from the left, and the pier is in the background. (Courtesy of Marlene Estridge.)

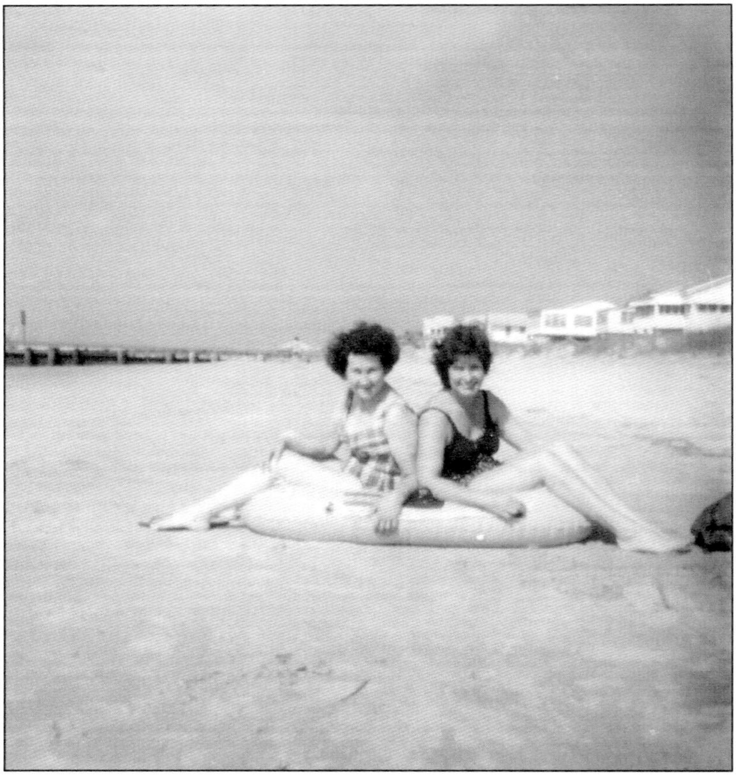

Pals Ellen Selleu (left) and Betty Schultz share a float in August 1975. (Courtesy of Betty Schultz.)

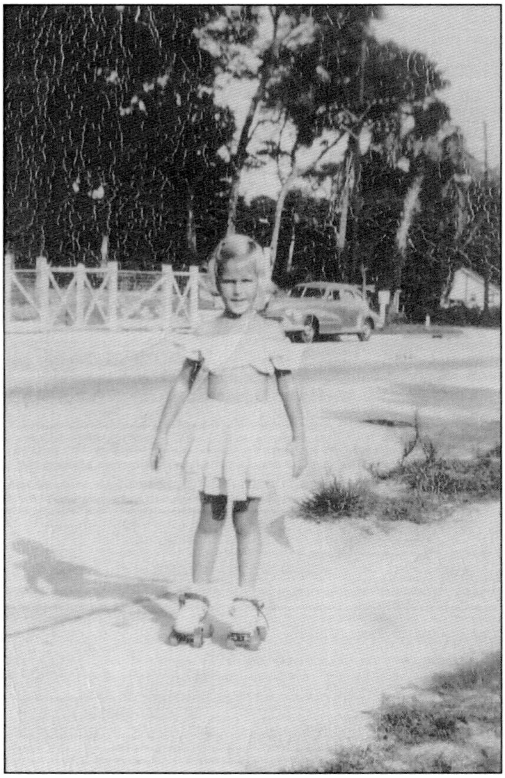

Linda Myers (Dove) rolls down Center Street on her way to the skating rink, her favorite hangout, in 1947 or 1948. Myers's mother ran a restaurant called the Chicken Box from 1947 to 1951. City clerk Marlene Estridge recalls skipping lunch at school as a child and saving the money to go skating when she got home to Folly Beach. (Courtesy of Maebelle Barnett Bazzel.)

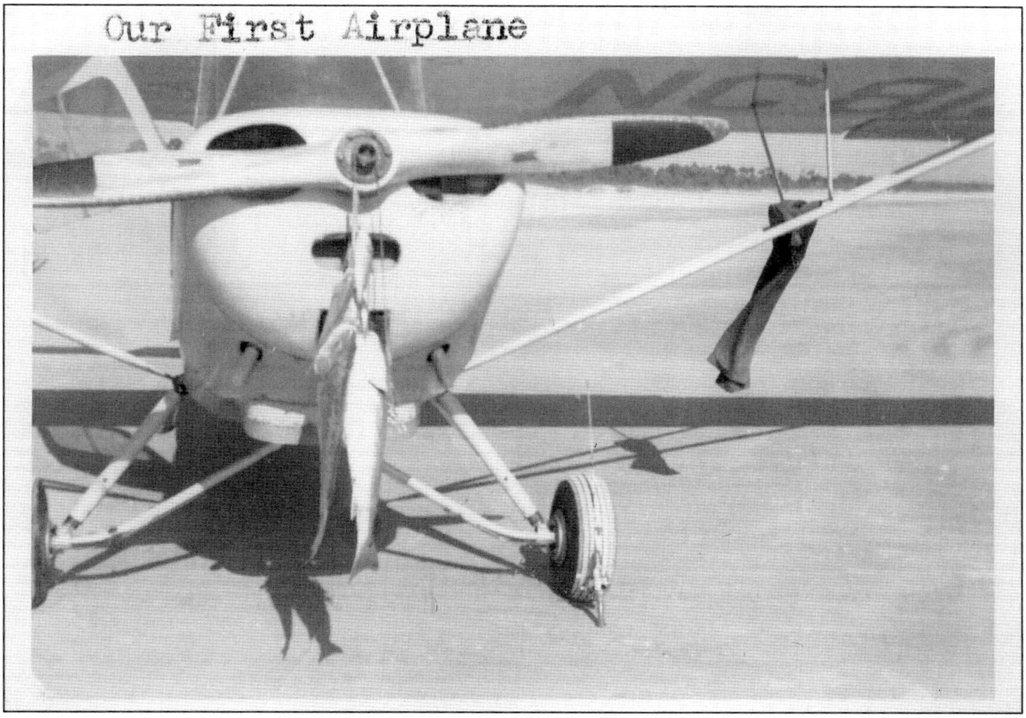

In the days when you could drive on the beachfront, pilots often landed their planes on Morris Island. Folly resident Jack Southworth took advantage of the unparalleled access, showing off a day's catch after an afternoon flight. (Courtesy of Betty Schultz.)

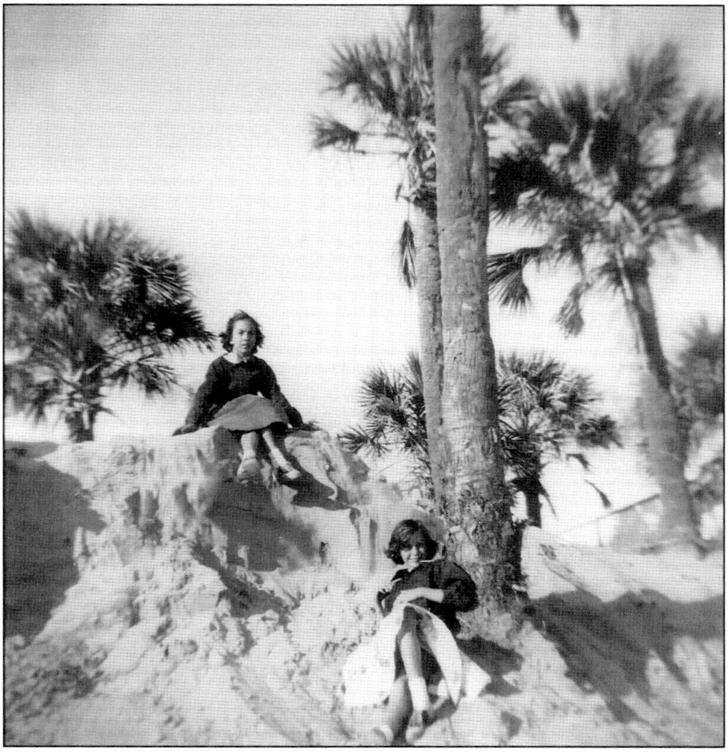

Sis Inabinett and Cookie Jamison play in the dunes. Jamison and her family of five moved to Folly in the summer of 1950, sharing a home with a retired fire chief and a Navy sailor and his wife and child, who lived upstairs, totaling nine people in their one-bathroom home. (Courtesy of Patricia Jamison Wilbanks Bragg.)

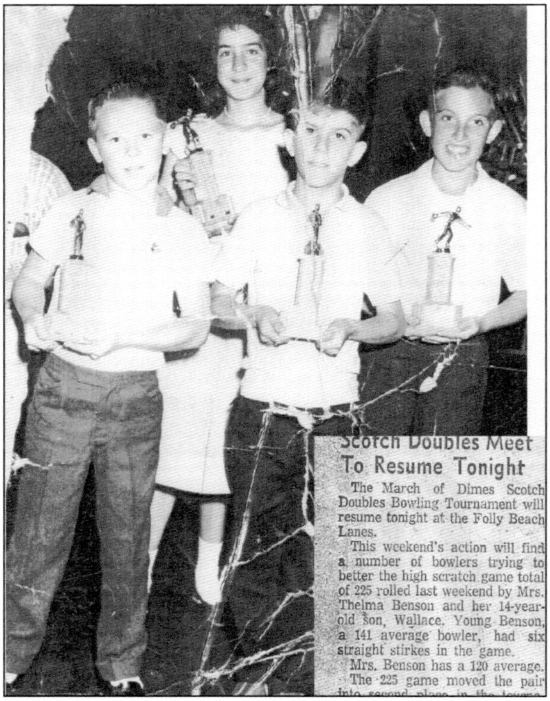

Although many youngsters traveled to James Island to participate in Little League, the eight-lane bowling alley on Folly Beach provided the sole on-island outlet for organized sports for many years. Young Wallace Benson (right) took his bowling seriously. He is seen here with his 1958 championship team, including Jackie McLain (left), Patsy Knight (back center), and Larry McCutchen (second from right). Wallace and his mother also regularly won as a Scotch Doubles team. Games cost 25¢ each, which Benson paid for as a "pin boy," placing the fallen pins back into the semi-automatic machine for 8¢ a game. (Courtesy of Wallace Benson.)

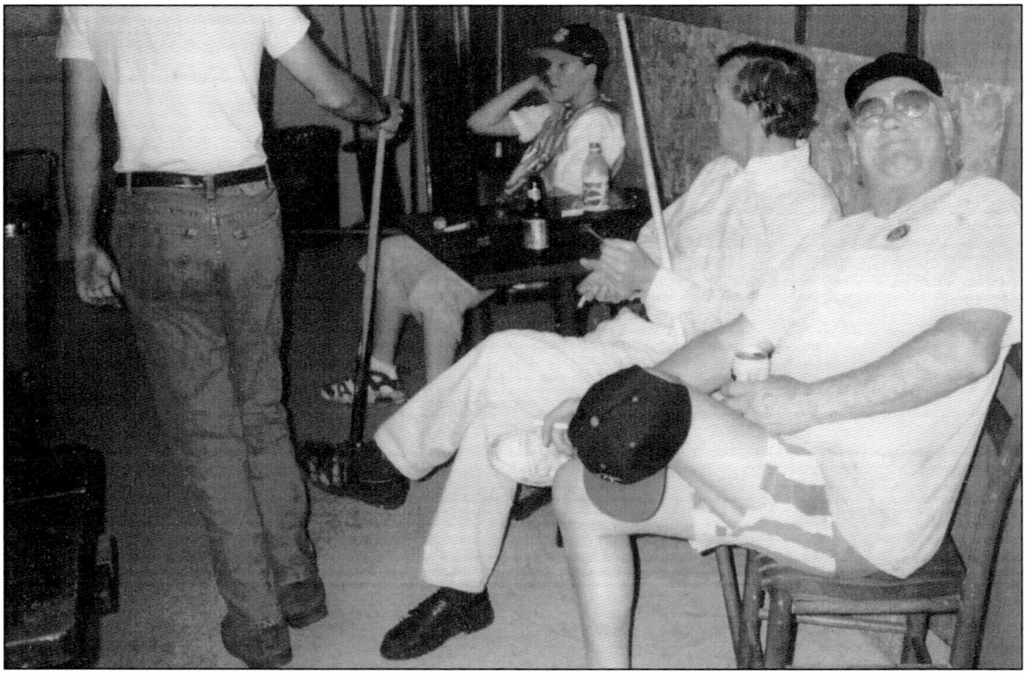

On Folly Beach and throughout the Lowcountry, tackle shops were once synonymous with bars. From 1998 to 2000, former police chief and city councilman Wallace Benson ran the Village Tackle Shop at the site of the former Phillips 66 gas station at Center Street and West Hudson Avenue. A previous tackle shop existed just across the bridge near the current site of Mariners Cay. The tackle shops served as a place to unwind and find level ground between council members and their representatives. And, of course, they also sold bait. (Courtesy of Wallace Benson.)

Mattress surfing was a popular pastime in the 1940s on Folly, before regular surfing caught on. Canvas mattress covers, sometimes acquired from the Coast Guard base at the island's east end, were filled with air by running down the beach while holding the ends open. With the cover full of air, people would immediately throw them down and tie up the ends. In this photograph, Breck Barnett catches his breath after a session catching a few waves. (Courtesy of Maebelle Barnett Bazzel.)

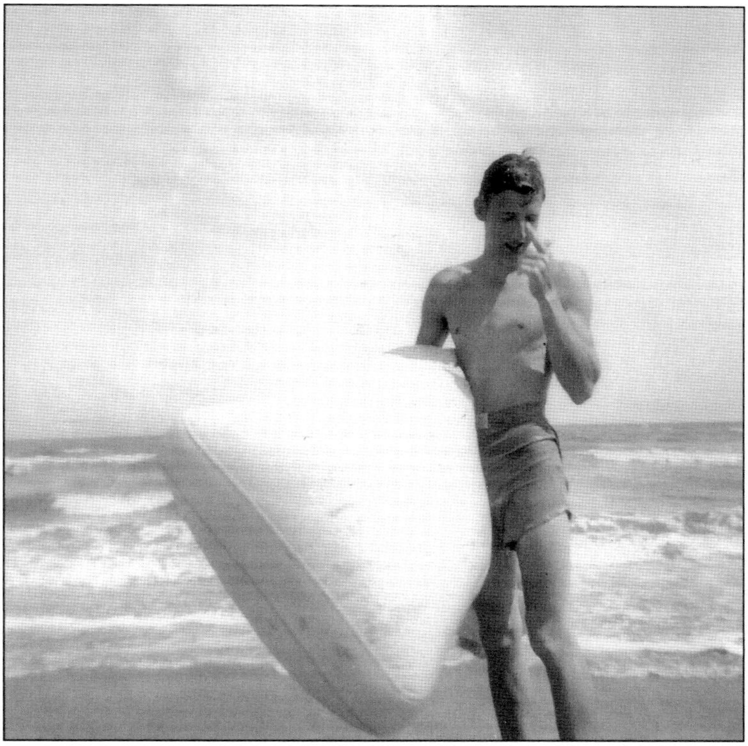

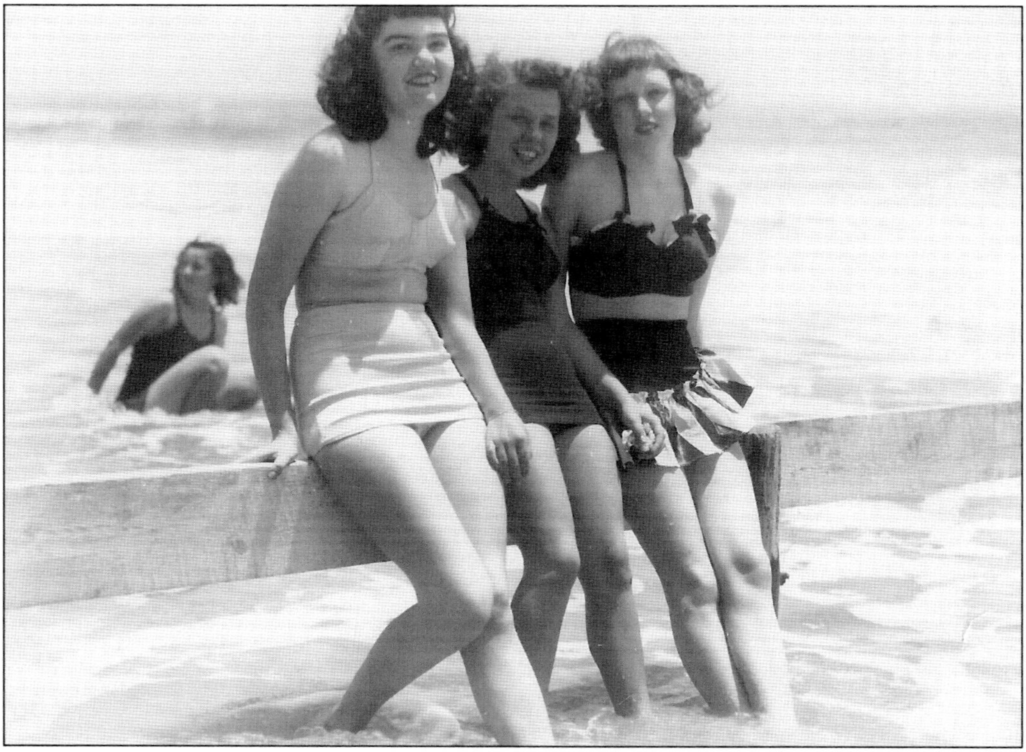

Norma Steele (center) and two friends relax in the surf at Folly Beach in the 1940s. (Courtesy of Patricia Jamison Wilbanks Bragg.)

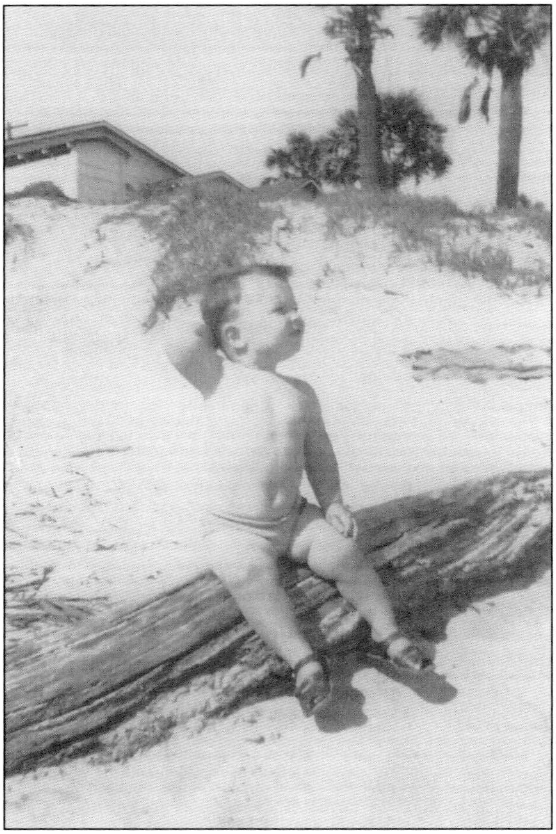

Folks are never too young to enjoy Folly Beach. Here, a young Jimmy Blake strikes a pose. (Courtesy of Maebelle Barnett Bazzel.)

The Jack Wilbanks photograph below was painted and turned into a postcard advertising Folly. "Life Begins at Folly" reads the wall underneath "Welcome to Folly's Playground" at the present-day intersection of Center Street and Arctic Avenue. (Courtesy of Patricia Jamison Wilbanks Bragg.)

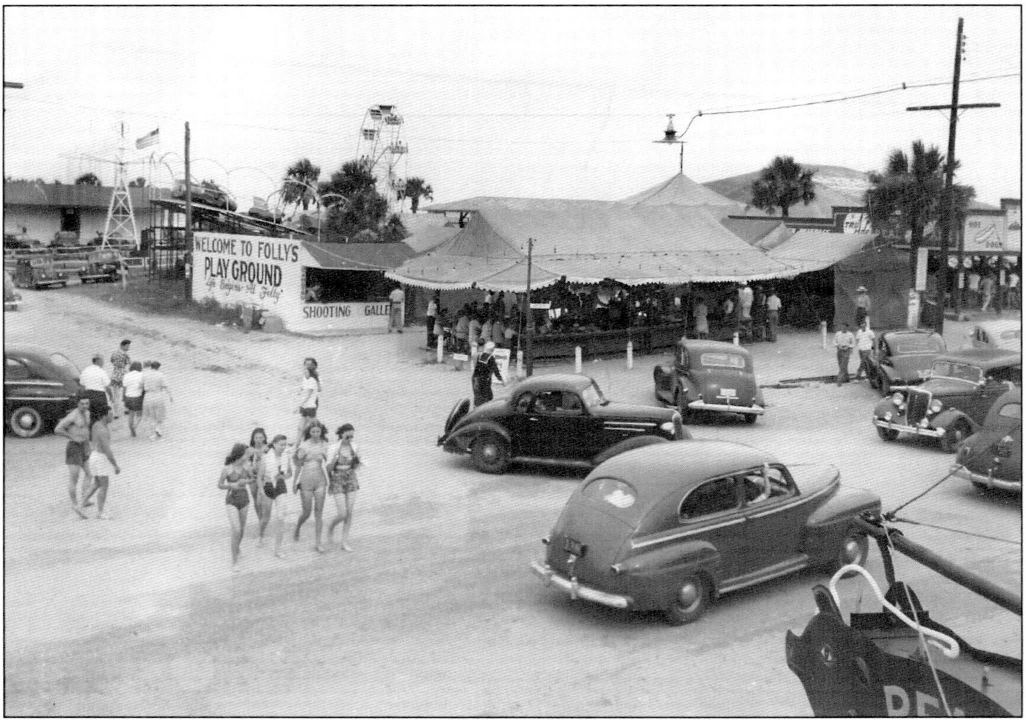

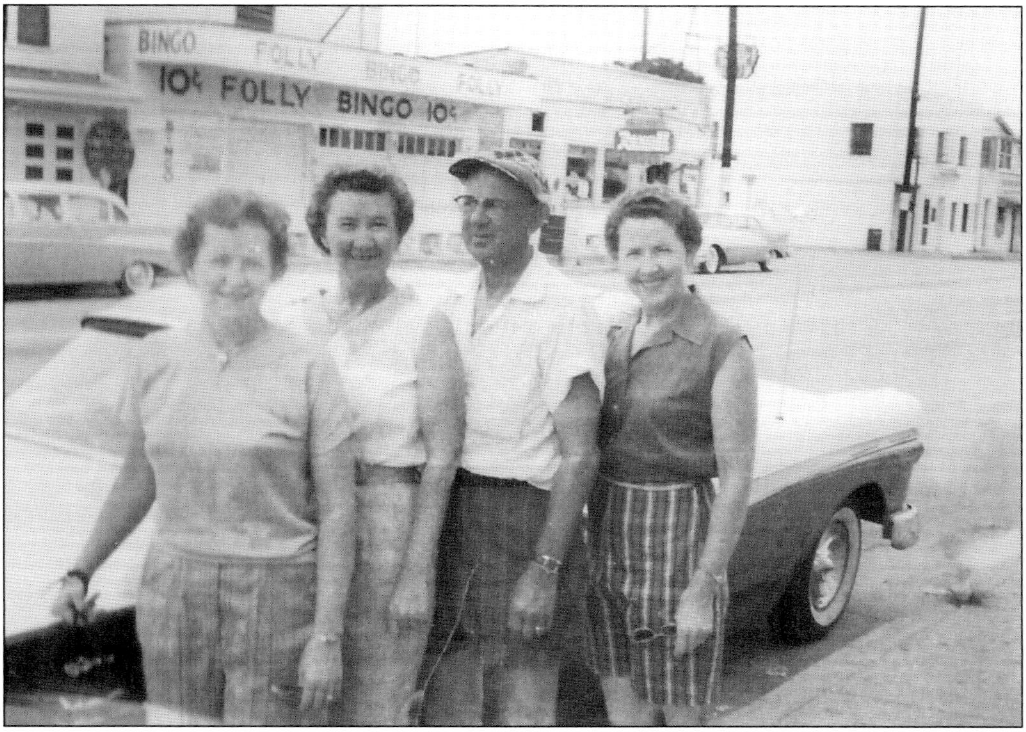

The bingo parlor in the background of this 1960 picture was a major draw on Center Street. Boards were just 10¢, and kernels of corn were used as tokens. (Courtesy of Patricia Jamison Wilbanks Bragg.)

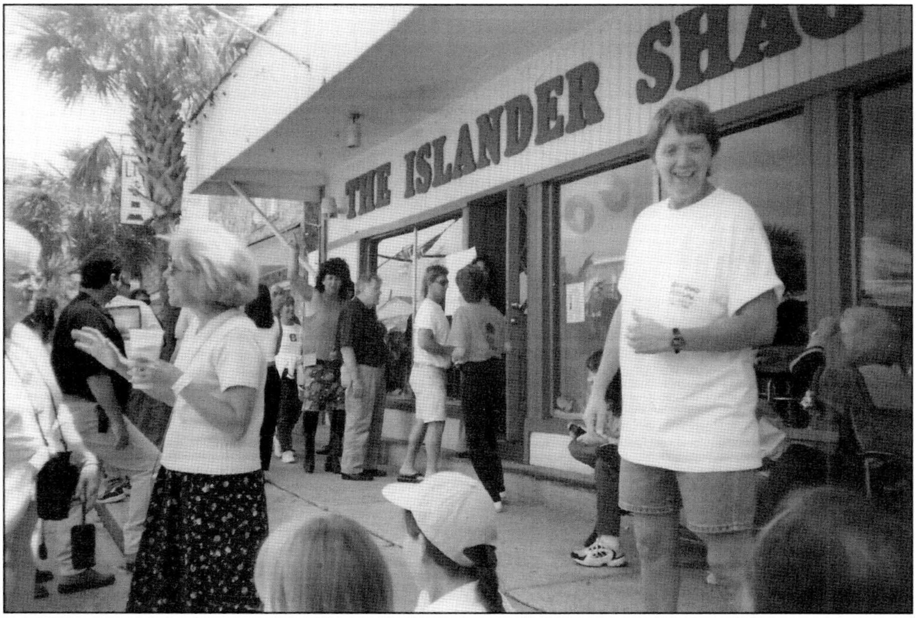

The Islander Shag Club opened in 1997 in the building that once housed the bingo parlor, at West Cooper Avenue and Center Street. Dues were $20 a year. When the club closed nine years later and Taco Boy was built in its place, the original Folly Bingo sign was uncovered beneath the Shag Club facade. (Courtesy of Maebelle Barnett Bazzel.)

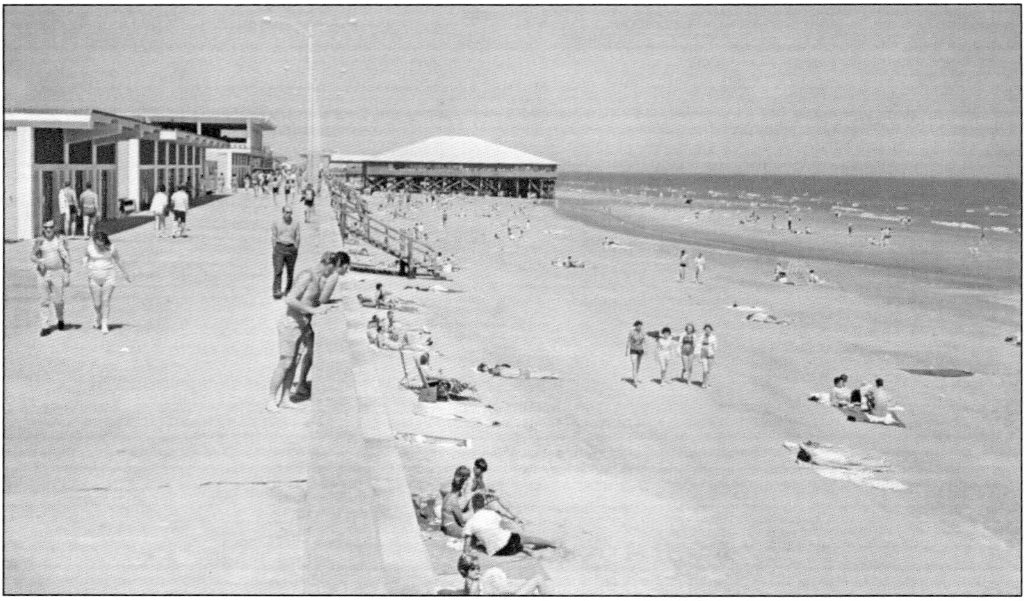

Opened in 1960, the "million-dollar plaza" actually cost $1.5 million to build and was touted as the longest in the South. The 1,700-foot concrete boardwalk's grand opening weekend in July included fireworks and trapeze acts, with advertisements touting the forthcoming four-lane highway to Folly Beach from Charleston. Concessions and fair-style games filled the vendor booths on weekends and summer nights. A go-cart track was at the far end, but it eventually closed after too many carts lost control and drove over the edge onto the beach. (Photograph by Jack Wilbanks, courtesy of Maebelle Barnett Bazzel.)

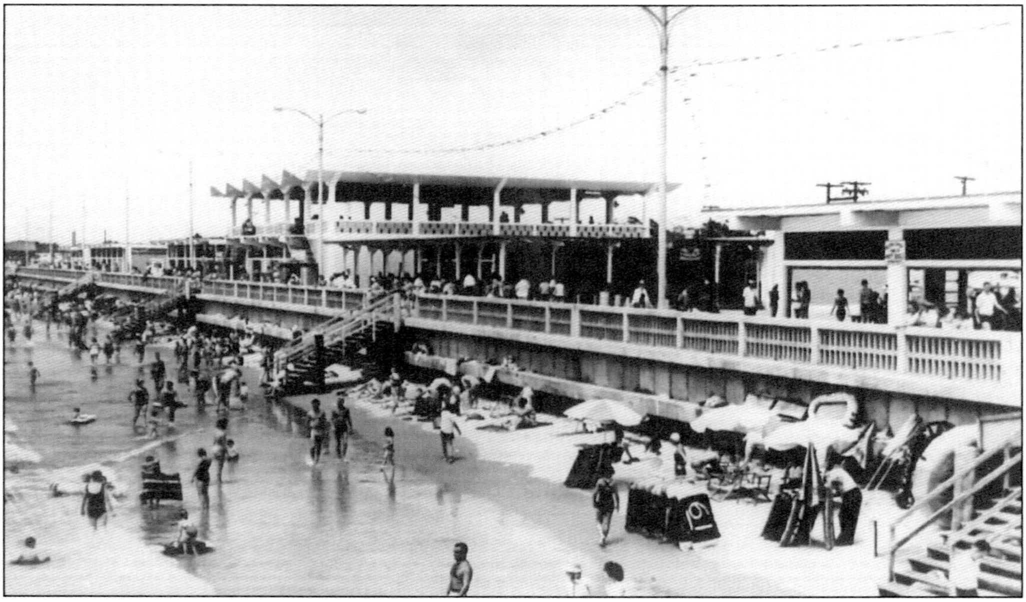

The foundation and bottom floor of the Club Plaza at the boardwalk was incorporated into the construction of the Holiday Inn (now Tides). The downstairs was built as an arcade, with pinball and foosball. The upstairs boasted an open-air putt-putt course on the roof. When that failed to be profitable, the owners walled in the second floor and opened the Sundowner, "a rock café and lounge." (Courtesy of Maebelle Barnett Bazzel.)

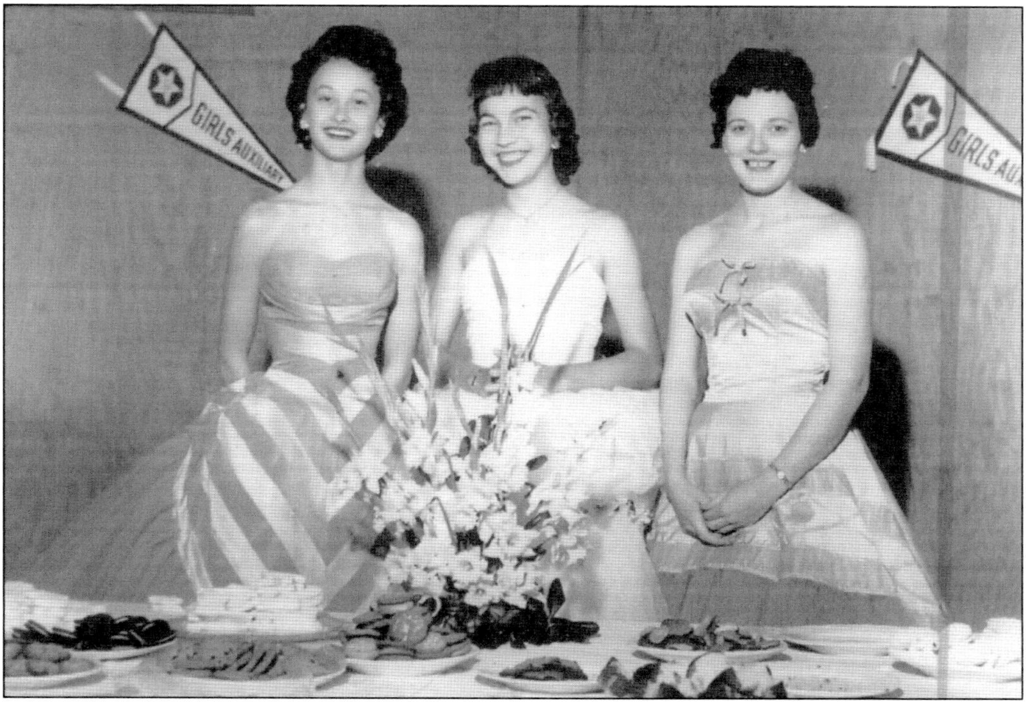

Pageants and beauty contests were more common in the 1950s and 1960s than they are today. Here, from left to right, Pamelia Jowers, Sis Inabinett, and Maebelle Barnett pose in their finest evening gowns at the Girls Auxiliary's Banquet. (Courtesy of Maebelle Barnett Bazelle.)

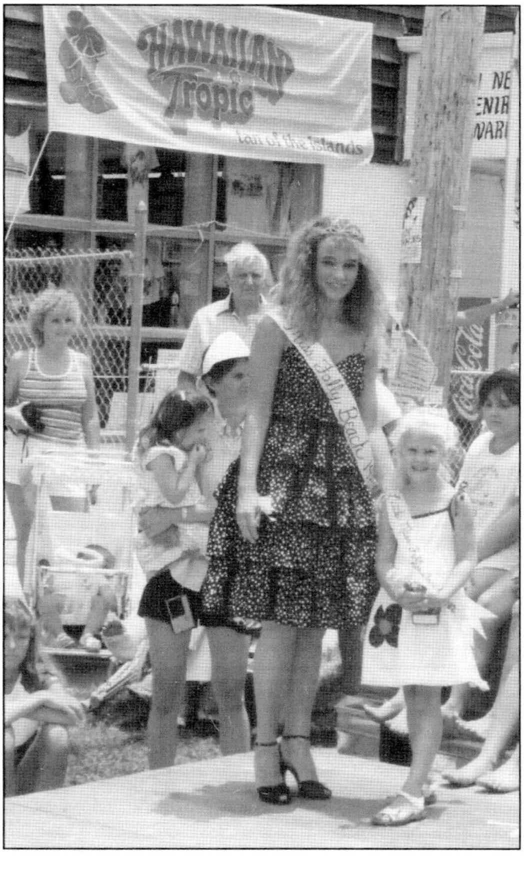

The Miss Folly Beach pageant is a long-standing tradition on the island. Jill Allison Schultz, the daughter of Henry and Betty Schultz, is seen here after winning the honor in 1981, the year she graduated from high school. When George Gershwin visited in 1934, he helped judge a beauty contest on the island. (Courtesy of Betty Schultz.)

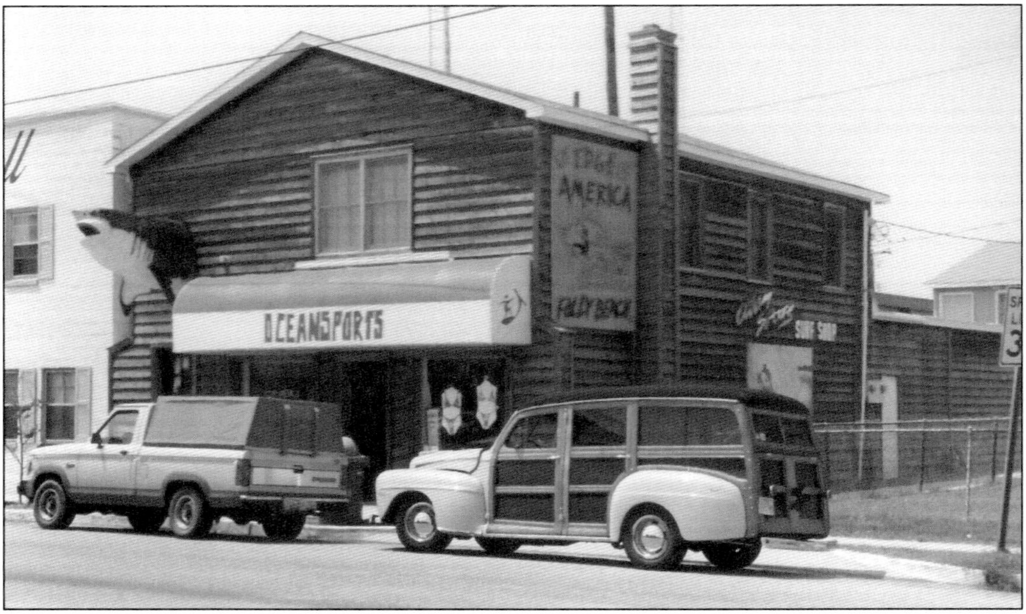

Bill Perry opened his Oceansports Surf Shop (now Ocean Surf Shop) in 1982. It was Perry and his friend Bill Bartlett who together came up with Folly's nickname, "The Edge of America," originally created as a slogan for t-shirts sold at the shop. The logo was modeled after the writing on a U2 album cover, and originally stated, "In God's Waters." Opting to leave religion out of it, they came up with "The Edge of America." They trademarked the phrase and ultimately prevailed against efforts by Wal-Mart to create Edge of America t-shirts for beachside cities across the Atlantic seaboard. "We're truly not the edge, geographically, but it's a state of mind," says Perry. Today, the moniker is Folly's and Folly's alone. (Courtesy of Bill Perry and Betty Sue Cowsert.)

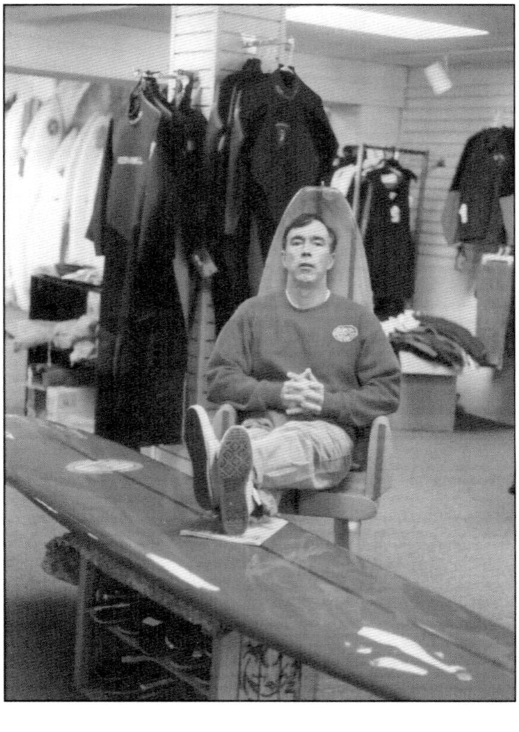

Bill Perry and Betty Sue Cowsert ran Oceansports for nearly 30 years. Bill, a handyman, fashioned the shop's chairs out of old surfboards. They eventually changed the name to Ocean Surf Shop after too many tourists wandered in thinking they were a "damn float store." (Courtesy of Bill Perry and Betty Sue Cowsert.)

In 1965, Dennis McKevlin opened McKevlin's Surf Shop out of a storage room in the back of the Folly Bowling Center. In this 1968 photograph, McKevlin's son Ted stands in the doorway of the store, whose original inventory of boards all exceeded nine feet in length. Note the jar of Penrose pork sausages under his arm and the red, large women's panties hanging in the top right corner. "Slip-Checks" is painted on the wall. This was a spray-on, gritty adhesive used to replace board wax that ultimately failed because it made people bleed. The shop grew through several buildings on Folly Beach and locations on Sullivan's Island, Isle of Palms, and in Mount Pleasant. Today, the 3,300-square-foot flagship store on Folly Beach is the sole McKevlin's location, run by Dennis's son Tim. (Courtesy of McKevlin's Surf Shop.)

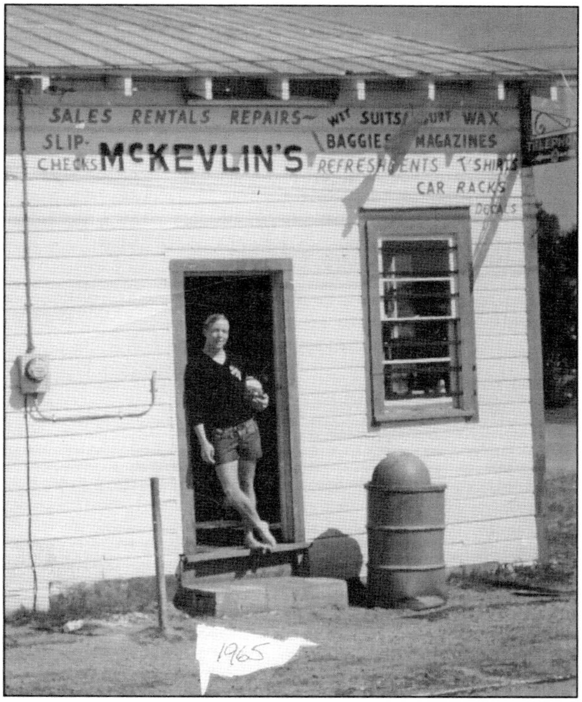

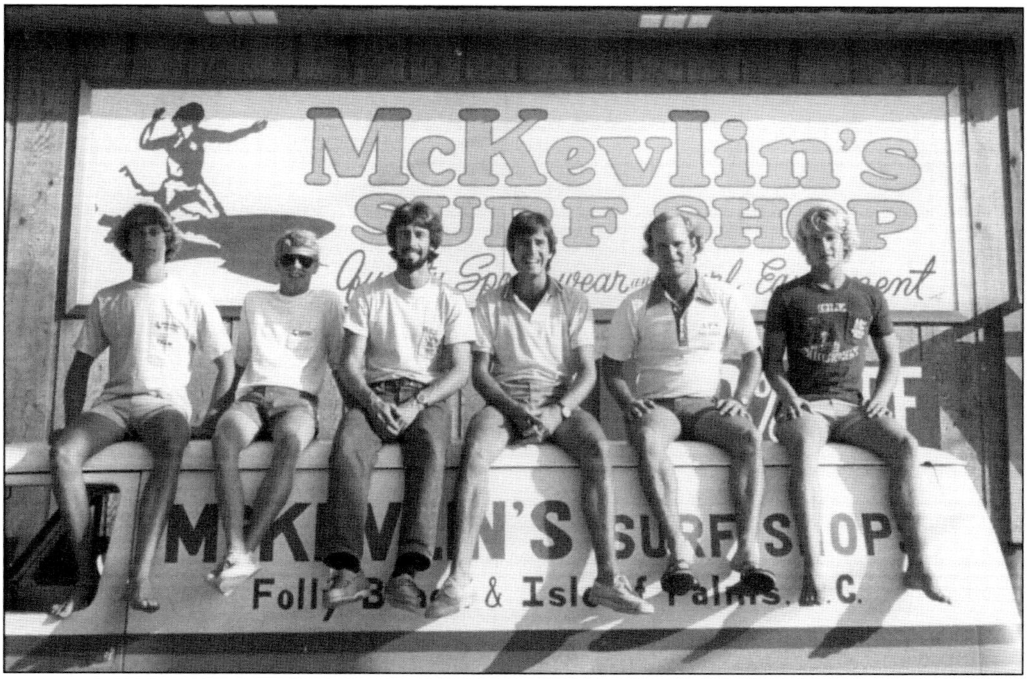

Although styles and trends change—the 1980s were a big time for neon wetsuits—the general surf ethos and lifestyle remains much the same. In 1981, members of the McKevlin's team who had qualified to surf in the Eastern Surfing Association Championships in Cape Hatteras, North Carolina, pose atop the shop's rainbow-colored van. The team included, from left to right, Jace Boozer, Champ Smith, Norman Godley, Al Logan, Tommy Anderson, and Andy Nettles. McKevlin's has the longest established surf team in South Carolina. (Courtesy of McKevlin's Surf Shop.)

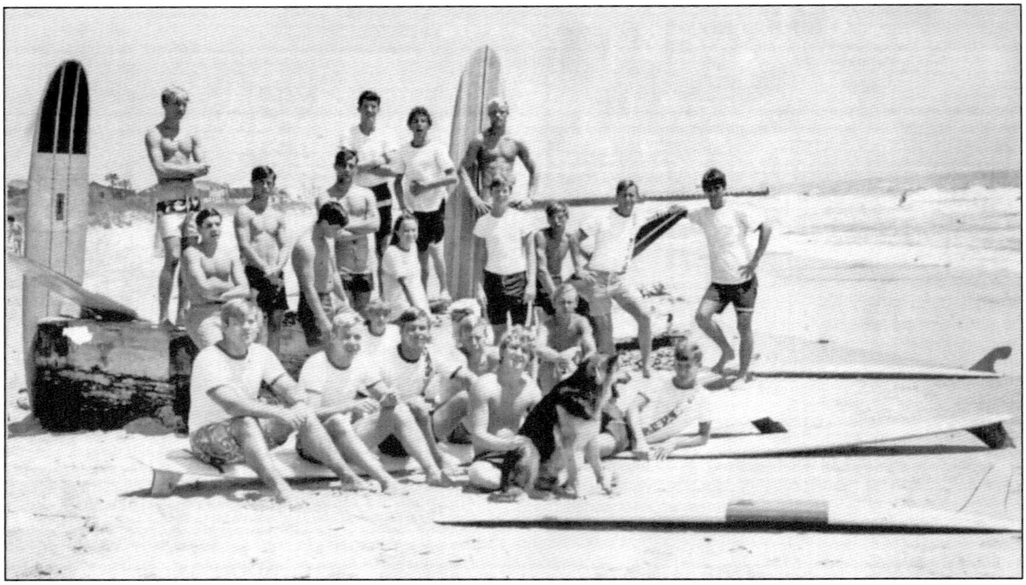

By the late 1960s, Folly Beach had a dedicated group of surfers. Early contests took place in front of the boardwalk plaza. The surfers in this photograph include, in no particular order, Dean Monk, Teddy McKevlin, Ronnie Shepherd, and the future mayor of Folly, Carl Beckmann. The dog's name was Chief. (Courtesy of McKevlin's Surf Shop and the Folly Beach Civic Club.)

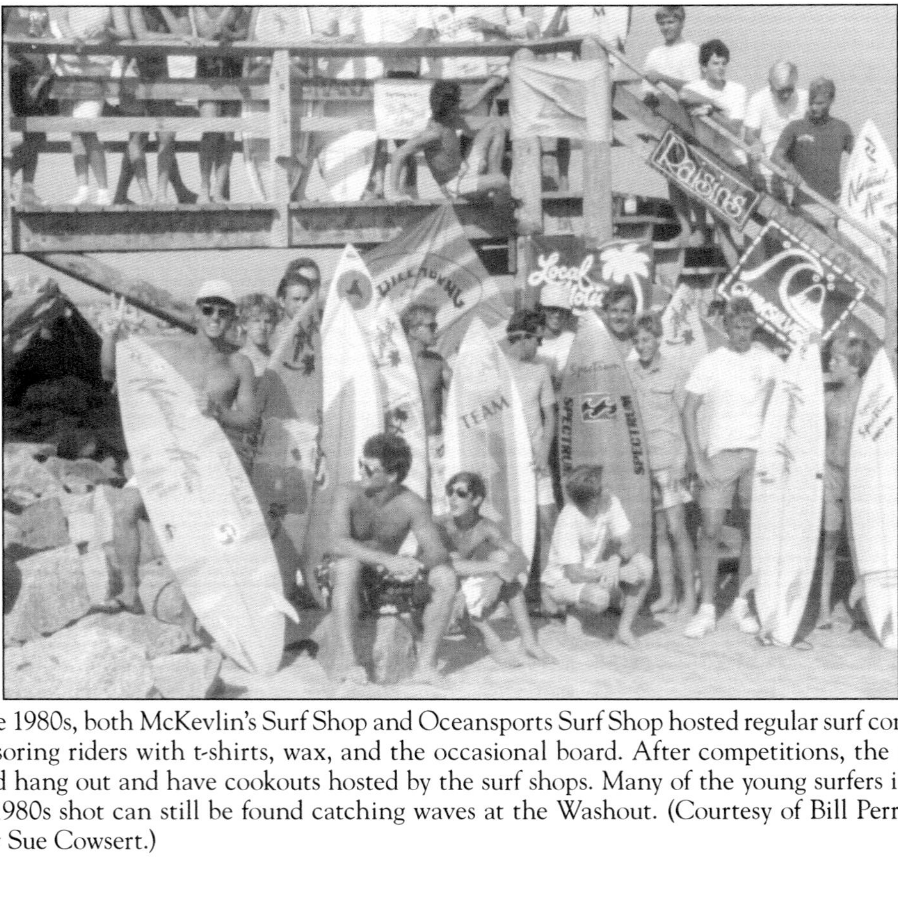

In the 1980s, both McKevlin's Surf Shop and Oceansports Surf Shop hosted regular surf contests, sponsoring riders with t-shirts, wax, and the occasional board. After competitions, the teams would hang out and have cookouts hosted by the surf shops. Many of the young surfers in this late 1980s shot can still be found catching waves at the Washout. (Courtesy of Bill Perry and Betty Sue Cowsert.)

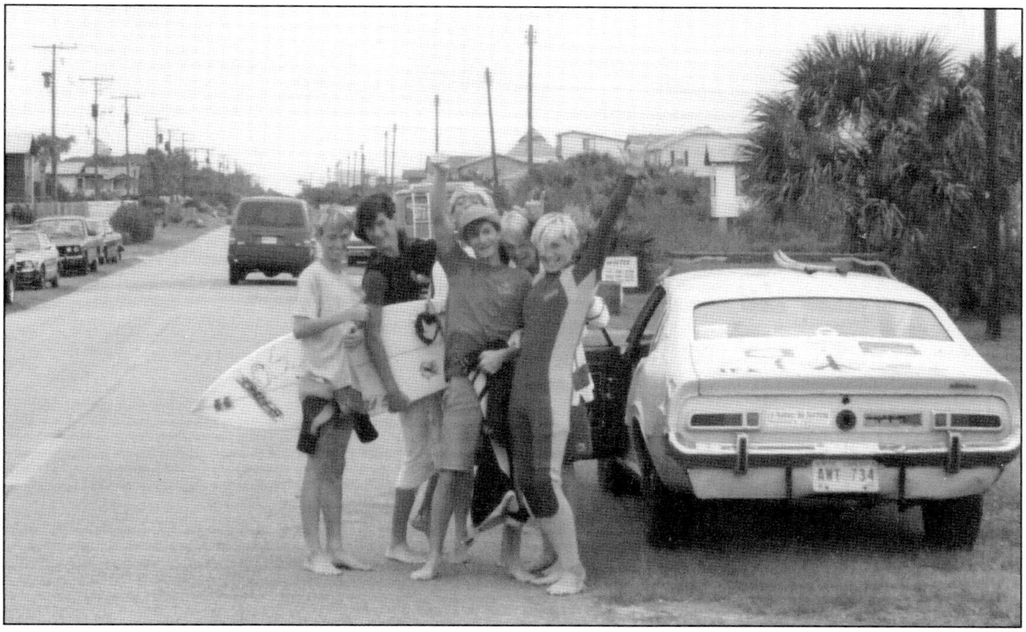

Young Folly surfers exit Scott Quattlebaum's car, the "Blue Bomb." Quattlebaum (center) now owns the Ocean Surf Shop on Center Street. Keeping the Washout open to surfers required a fight in the early 1970s. Due to safety concerns and misperceptions about the type of people who surf, the city banned surfing except for two blocks of the beach. Tommy Bolus, Dennis McKevlin, and Betty Sue Cowsert were among the organizers of a surfers' march down the beach in protest. Ultimately, the surfers won out—after the issue went to federal court—and with some restrictions, surfing is now allowed across most of Folly. (Courtesy of Bill Perry and Betty Sue Cowsert.)

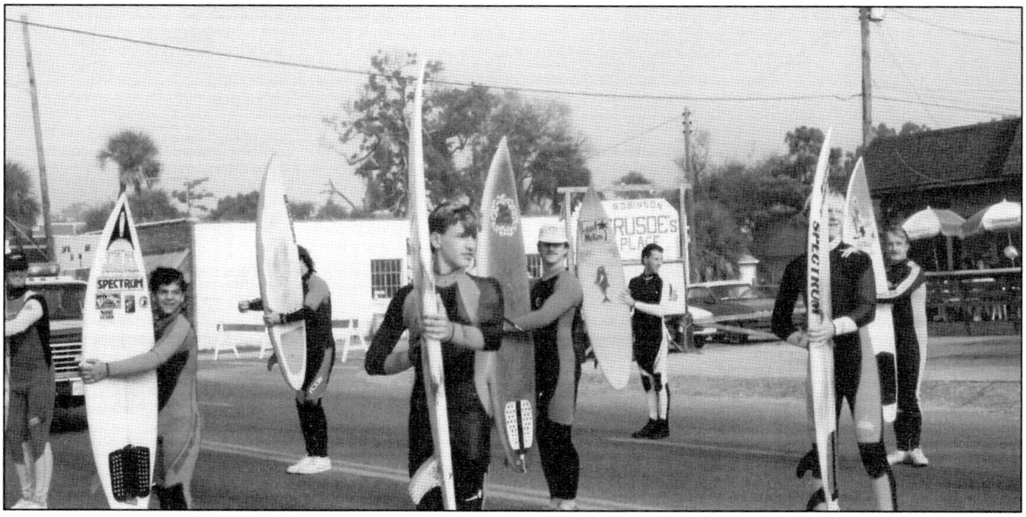

After watching a Folly Beach Christmas parade that included "nothing but wreckers" (tow trucks), Oceansports Surf Shop recruited a "drill team" to march in the next year's event. These young cadets include Chris John (left front) and Lee Hollingsworth (center front). The group spun their boards like rifles and stood at attention. Eventually, the young surfers "became so cool they wouldn't wear a wetsuit and march down Center Street," recalls Perry. After surfing had very nearly been banned on Folly, however, the parade showed how far acceptance of the sport had come in the public eye. (Courtesy of Bill Perry and Betty Sue Cowsert.)

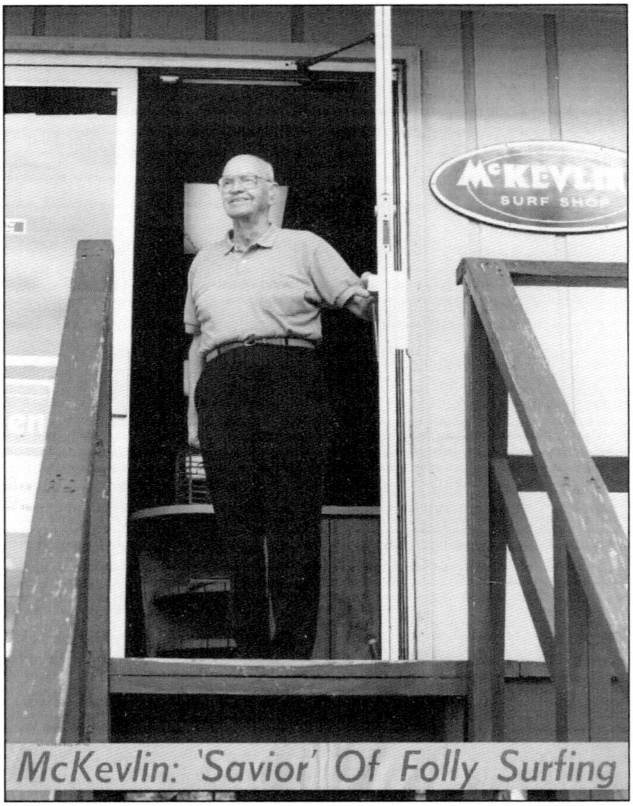

Dennis "Mr. Mac" McKevlin served as a spokesman for Folly Beach surfers, both as a business owner and as a representative on city council for 10 years. He is seen here outside his flagship store in 1997. (Courtesy of McKevlin's Surf Shop.)

Surfer dudes have all the luck. McKevlin's encouraged Folly's "wahines" through regular bathing suit fashion shows, including the one below in 1985. The shows were promoted by local radio stations and included both men and women, including the shop's team and employees. (Courtesy of McKevlin's Surf Shop.)

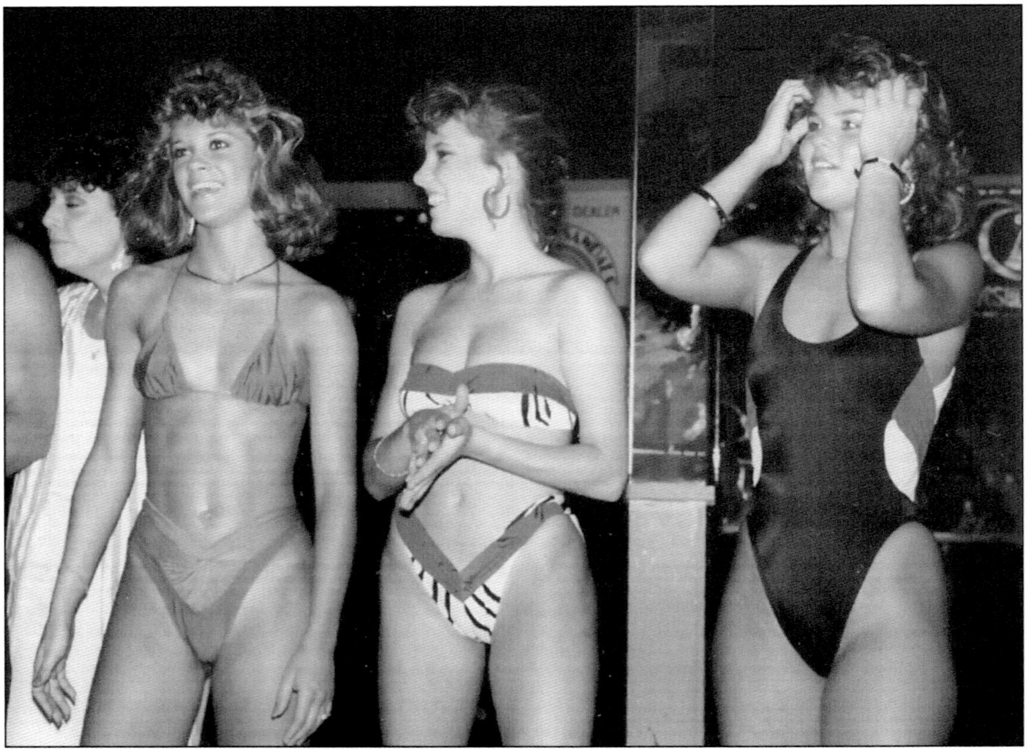

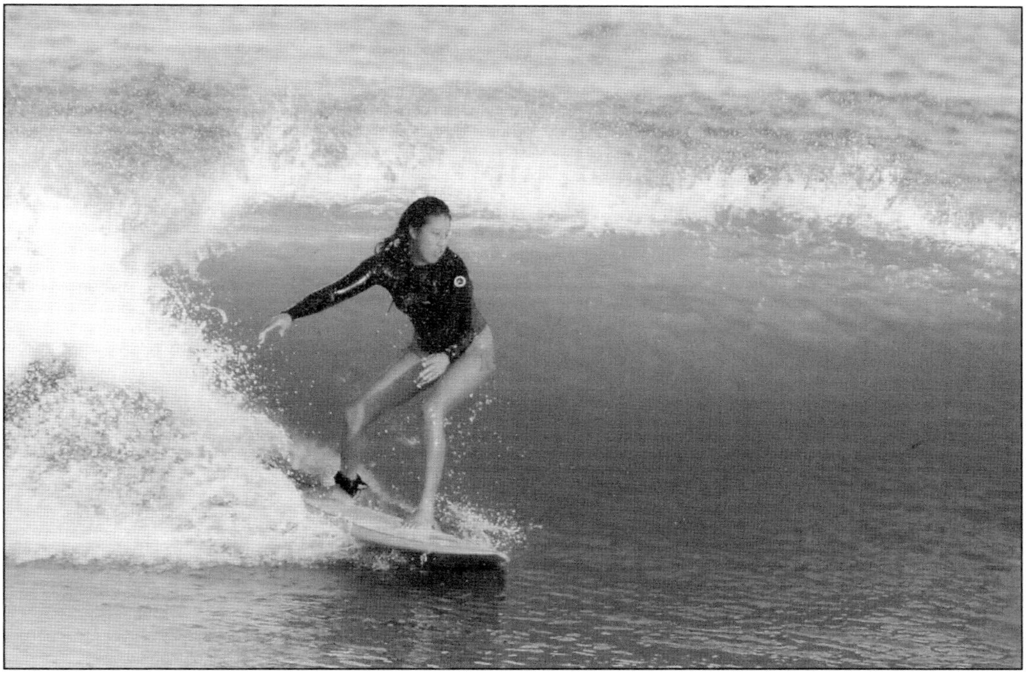

When the waves roll in clean, one can count hundreds of surfers out past the break along Folly's six miles of shore. Here, local surfer Perng Chen takes advantage of good conditions for a nice left. (Courtesy of McKevlin's Surf Shop.)

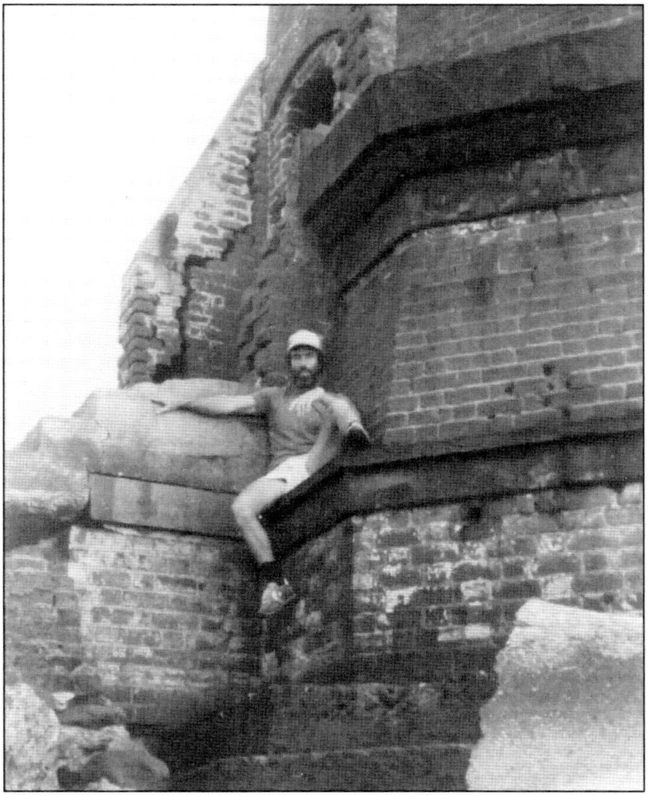

Many of those who grew up on Folly Beach remember when the Morris Island Lighthouse was unlocked. Visitors frequently anchored near the rocks and rebar that surrounded the structure, then climbed to the entrance to make their way to the top. "Their was no door; no locks—you just pulled your boat right up to the base," recalls Bill Perry. Here, Perry sits at the base in July 1983 after a climb. (Courtesy of Bill Perry and Betty Sue Cowsert.)

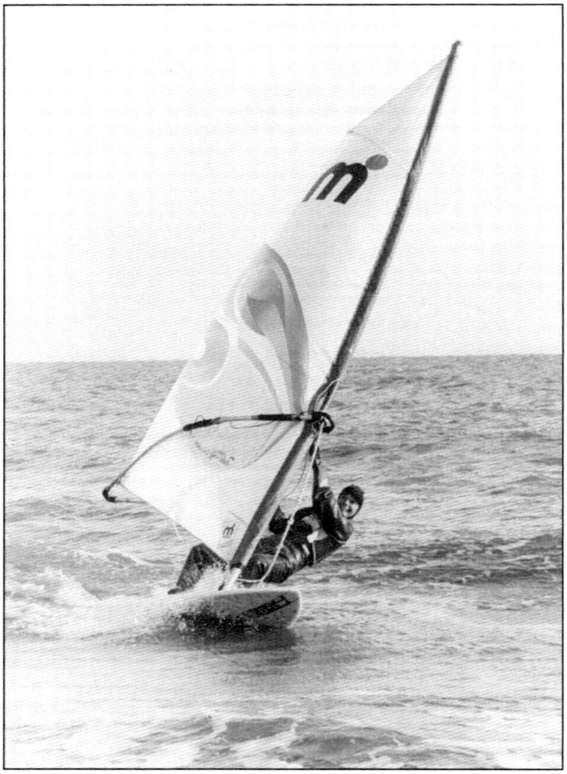

In the 1980s, windsurfing caught on as an adventure sport on Folly Beach. In this shot, Oceansports Surf Shop co-owner Betty Sue Cowsert rides toward the camera in July 1983, wearing a "dry suit," designed to be put on over street clothes for quick access to the water. Although they did not catch on for water sports, the suits proved popular for clamming—just put on your white rubber boots and hit the mud. (Courtesy of Bill Perry and Betty Sue Cowsert.)

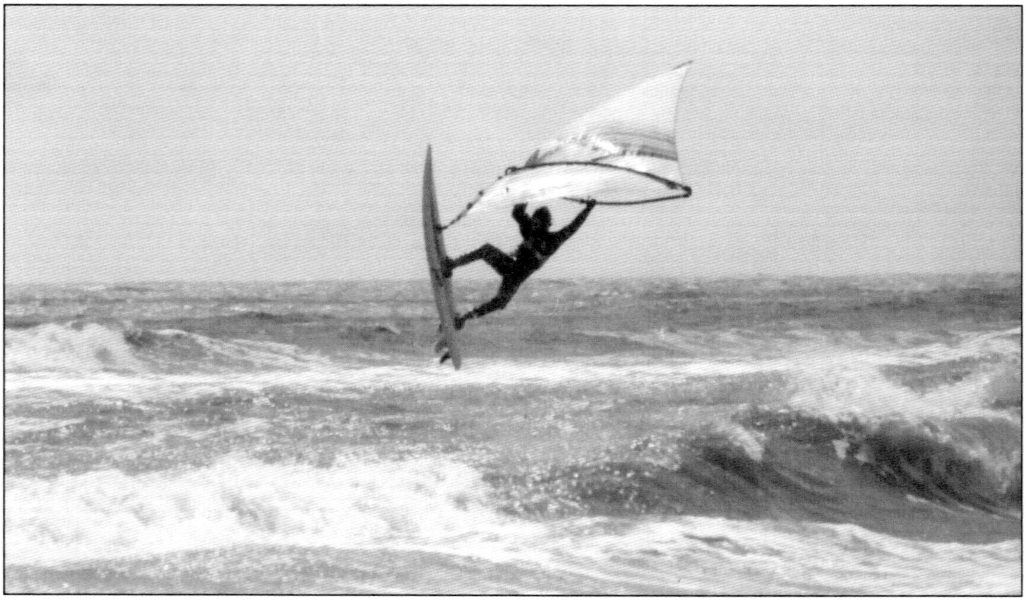

Although kiteboarding has largely usurped windsurfing as the adventure sport of choice on Folly Beach, modern-day wind-catching board riders should not forget that windsurf pioneers were the first to catch serious air off the lip of a wave. The pursuit of new heights led to rapid innovations in board size and shape, with several backyard shapers on Folly Beach at the forefront of the movement. Oceansports Surf Shop even hosted an annual regatta that attracted windsurfers from around the Southeast. (Courtesy of Bill Perry and Betty Sue Cowsert.)

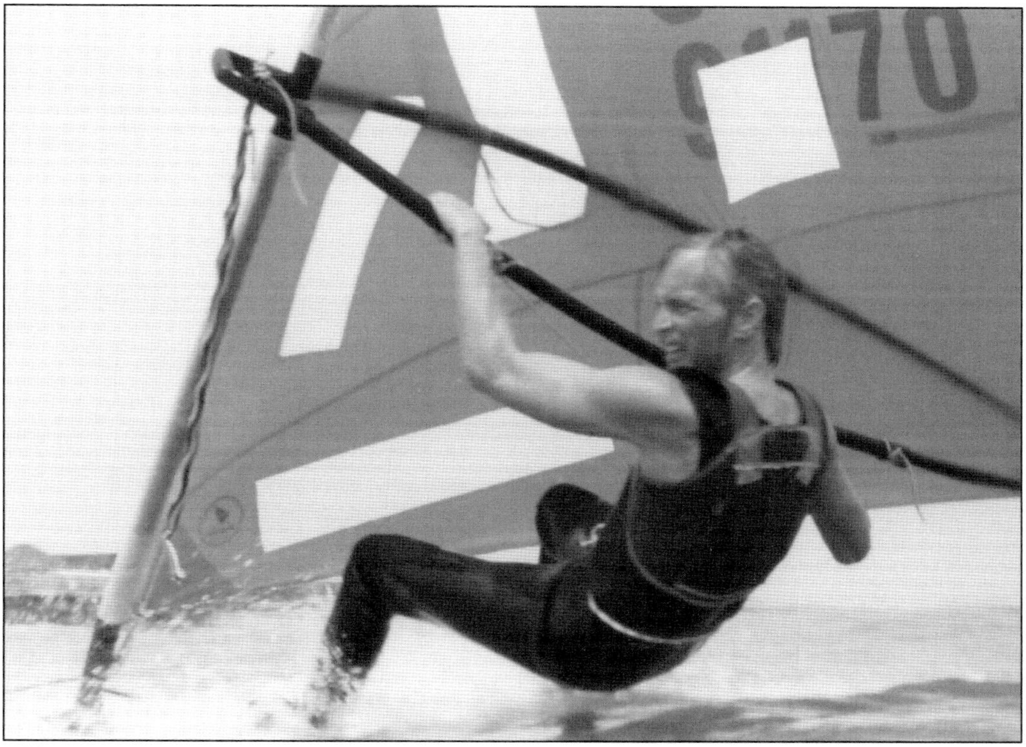

Old-school wave rider Gene Marie grabs some wind in August 1982. Marie went on to become a pioneering kitesurfer on Folly Beach. An engineer by trade, he worked occasional shifts at Ocean Surf Shop as recently as 2012. (Courtesy of Bill Perry and Betty Sue Cowsert.)

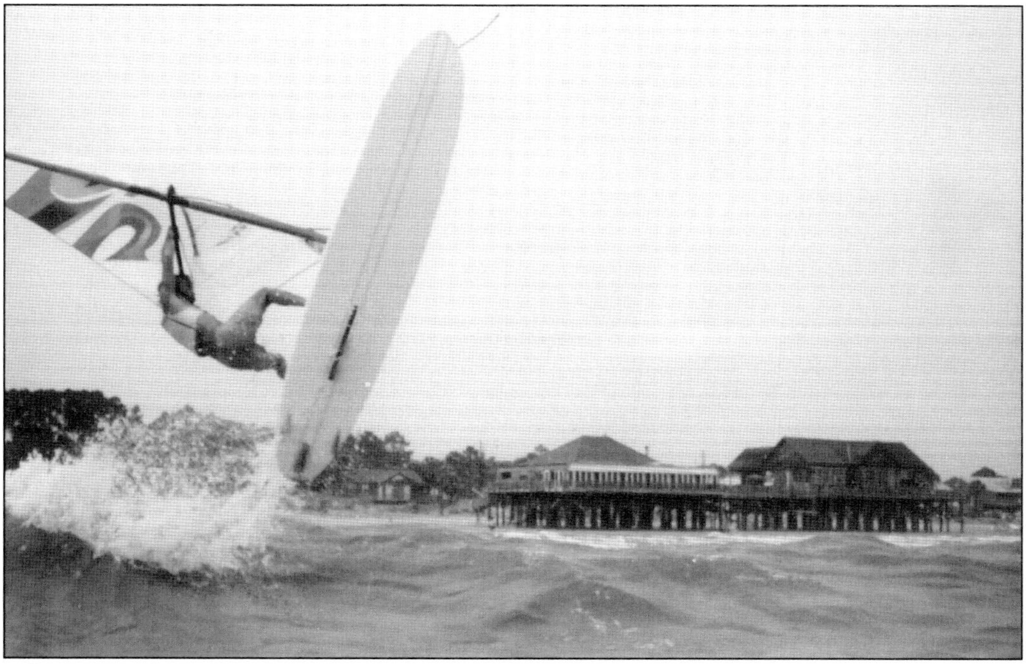

Bill Perry catches some serious air on a big board, with the Atlantic House in the background. His wife, Betty Sue, took this picture from a boat. (Courtesy of Bill Perry and Betty Sue Cowsert.)

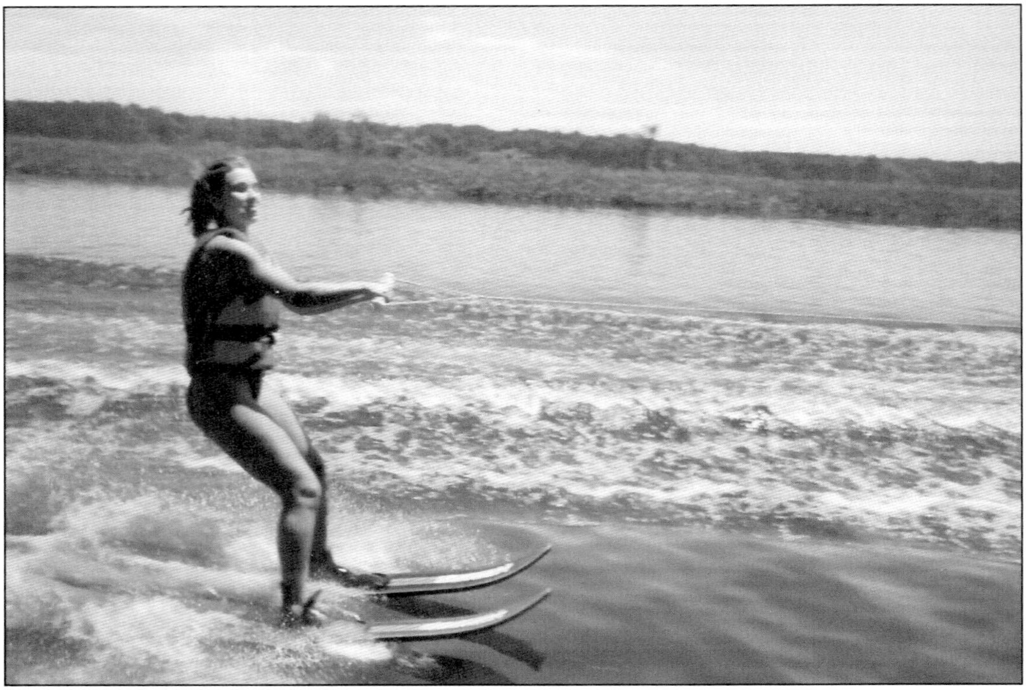

Waterskiing, although now less common than wakeboarding, is still a popular activity on days when the wind dies down and the creeks behind Folly Beach are clear and glassy. Here, Jill Schultz enjoys a particularly smooth ride. (Courtesy of Betty Schultz.)

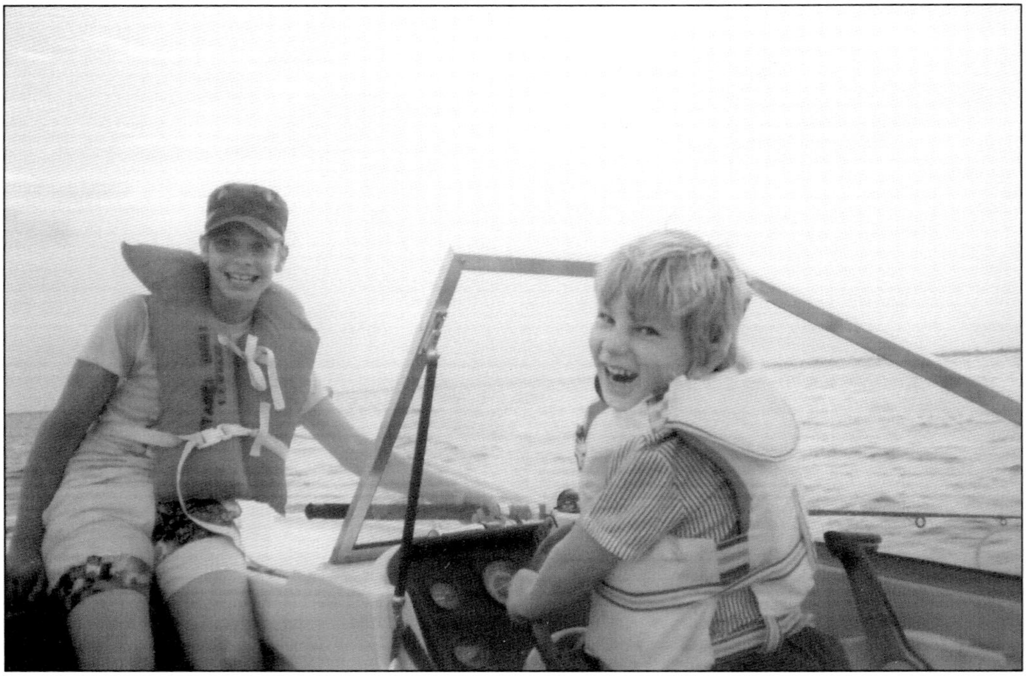

Chad Carter (left) and Austin Schultz, the grandchildren of Henry and Betty Schultz, enjoy a day on the water in 1990. Chad went on to serve multiple tours in Afghanistan and Iraq. Austin lives on James Island with his family. (Courtesy of Betty Schultz.)

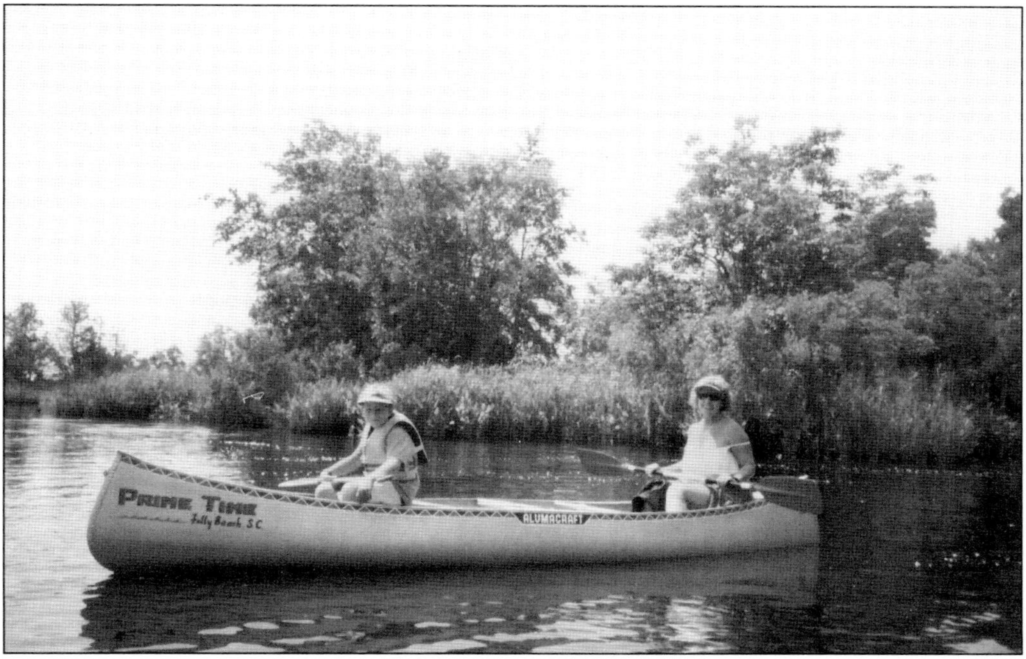

Betty Schultz's favorite pastime with her grandson Austin was to explore the waterways of the Folly River in their canoe, *Prime Time*. On an early trip in the late 1980s, Austin asked, "Grandma, where is your motor?" showing off the growing generation gap. Betty Schultz served as the treasurer of the Lowcountry Paddlers club. (Courtesy of Betty Schultz.)

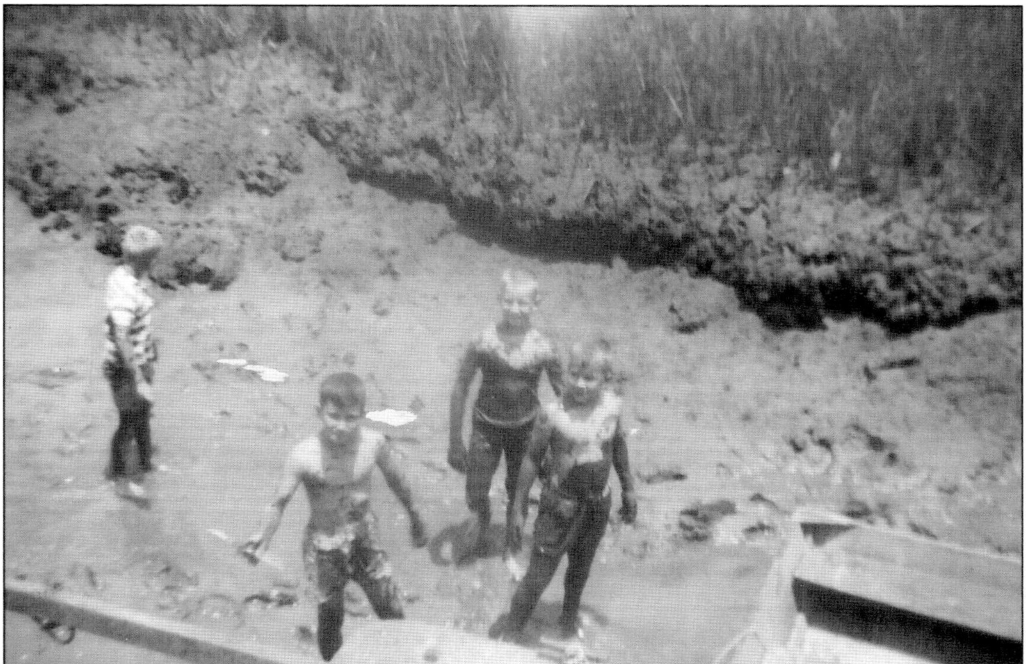

With friends from Mobile, Alabama, in town for a visit in 1964, Ivan (far left) and Michael (back middle) Schultz took advantage of mom's blessing to roll in the mud. Their mother, Betty Schultz, remembers being spanked as a child for the same infraction. (Courtesy of Betty Schultz.)

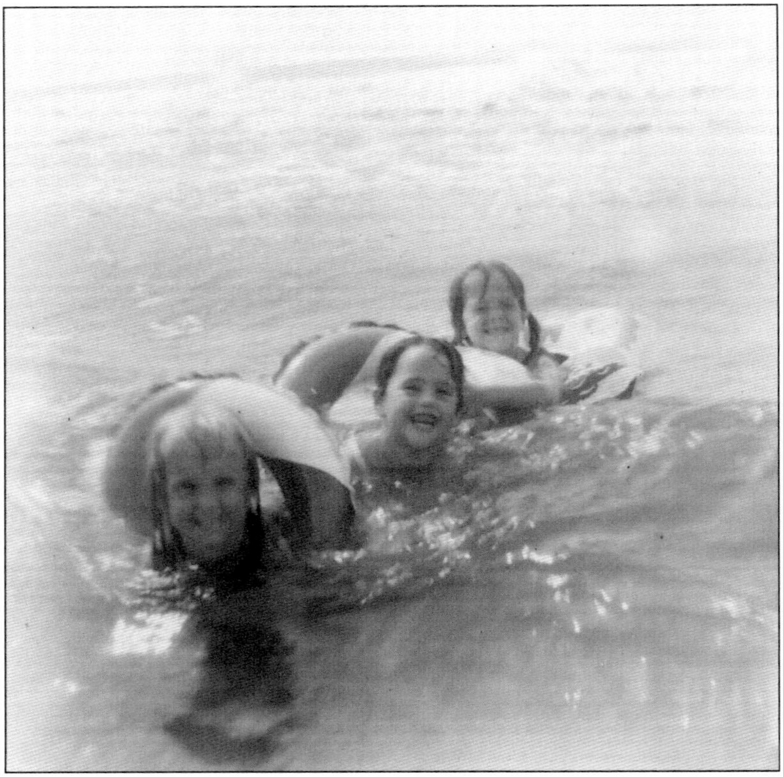

Five-year-old twins Greta Anderson (left) and Glenda Szad (right) play in the ocean in August 1969 with pal Robin Maxwell (center). (Courtesy of Greta Anderson.)

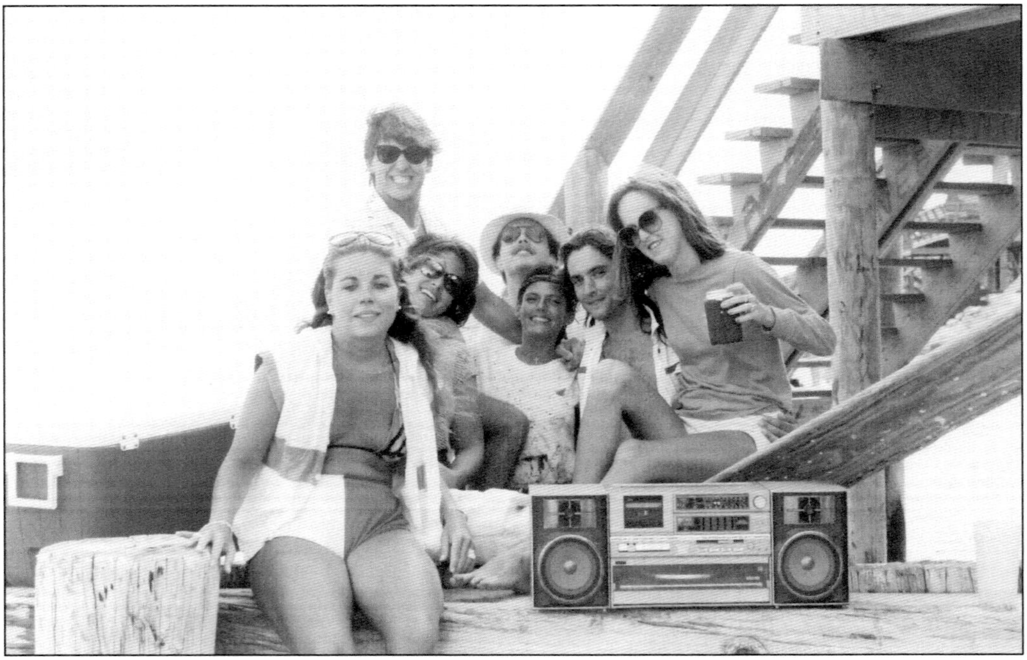

A young Greta Anderson (far right) hangs out on the beach with friends who worked with her on King Street at merchants like Jackson Davenport and M. Dumas and Son. Every weekend, the group met at sixth block to listen to music, have a few beers, and relax away from work. (Courtesy of Greta Anderson.)

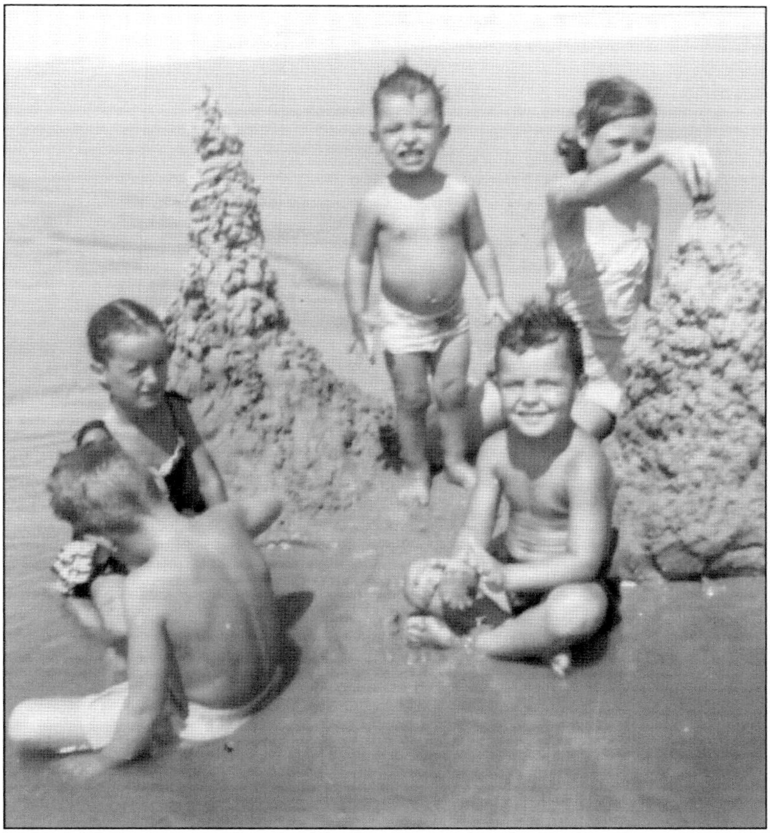

On every day of every summer for nearly a century, the incoming tide has washed away the hard work of countless children building sandcastles on Folly Beach. Here, in the early 1950s, Maebelle Barnett (back right) perfects her drip castle while her friends and relatives look on, including her nephews Michael and Jimmy Blake (center), her sister Cynthia (left), and her friend Chip Yarnell (back to camera). "I burned and peeled all summer," recalls Maebelle. (Courtesy of Maebelle Barnett Blake.)

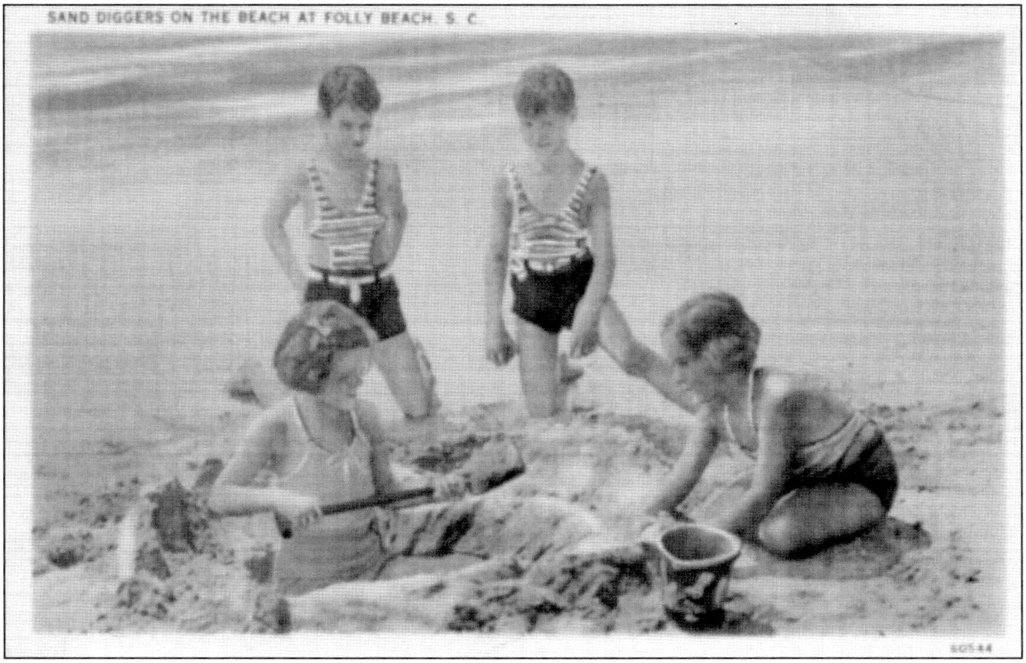

Children enjoy the age-old labor of castle building on this 1940 postcard from Folly. (Courtesy of Carol McLendon Porter.)

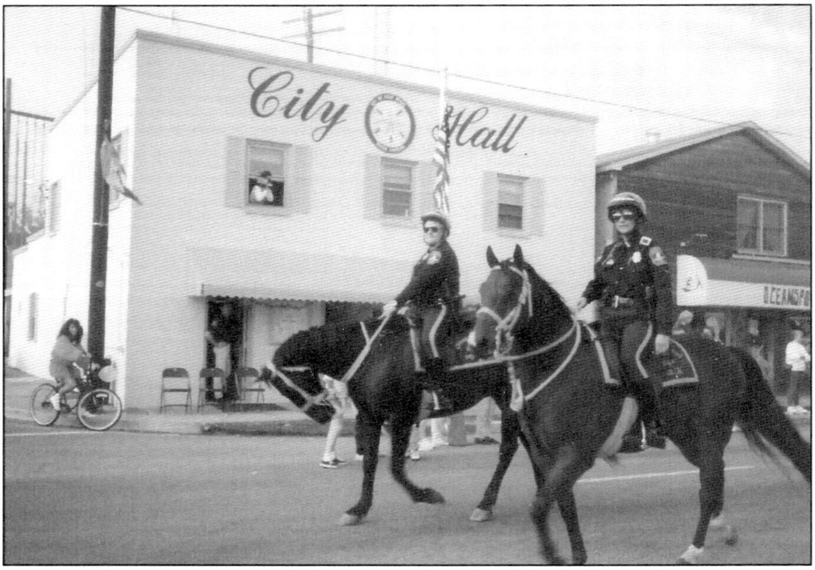

During a city parade in the late 1980s, the City of Charleston mounted patrol trots past the old pink city hall at Center Street and Cooper Avenue. When the current city hall was constructed in 1997, councilman Allen Boyd wrote to the *Post and Courier*, "Folly Beach is a small fishing type community and most of us live in modest homes. Obviously, this is not a modest building." (Courtesy of Wallace Benson.)

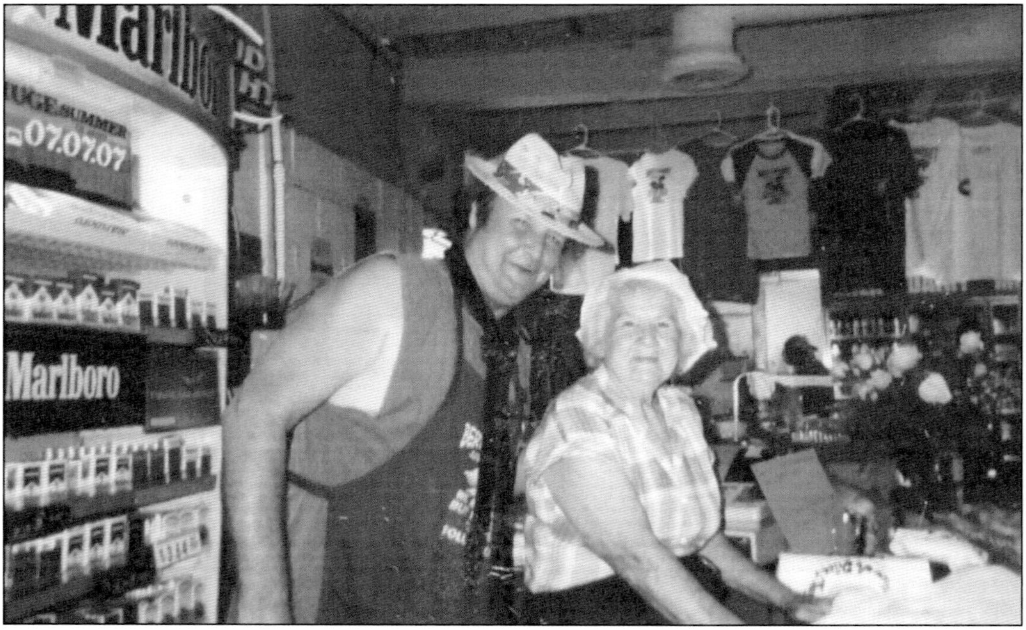

Norman Albert Hastings opened Bert's Market in 1993 at the corner of East Ashley Avenue and Second Street. The all-purpose grocery took over the space formerly held by Chris and Jerry's convenience store. Offering 50¢ hot dogs and plenty of cold beer, Bert's quickly became an institution on the island, selling thousands of t-shirts and koozies sporting the always-open store's motto: "We may doze, but we never close." "Miss Emily" Erickson worked at the store from 1997 until 2004, when the store suffered a major fire. Bert rebuilt, and Miss Emily still visits Bert's each morning to buy a cheeseburger for her dog. (Courtesy of Bert Hastings.)

In 1991, the staff at Oceansports Surf Shop was struggling to find a way to get patrons down the street from the beach to their store. When owners Bill Perry and Betty Sue Cowsert spotted a giant fiberglass shark on its way to a delivery in Myrtle Beach, they made an offer for their own "half shark," knowing it was just what the store needed to attract attention. (Courtesy of Bill Perry and Betty Sue Cowsert.)

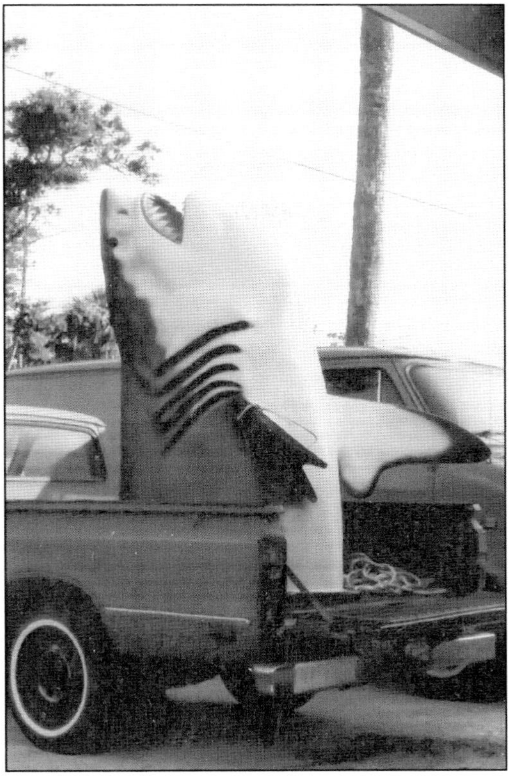

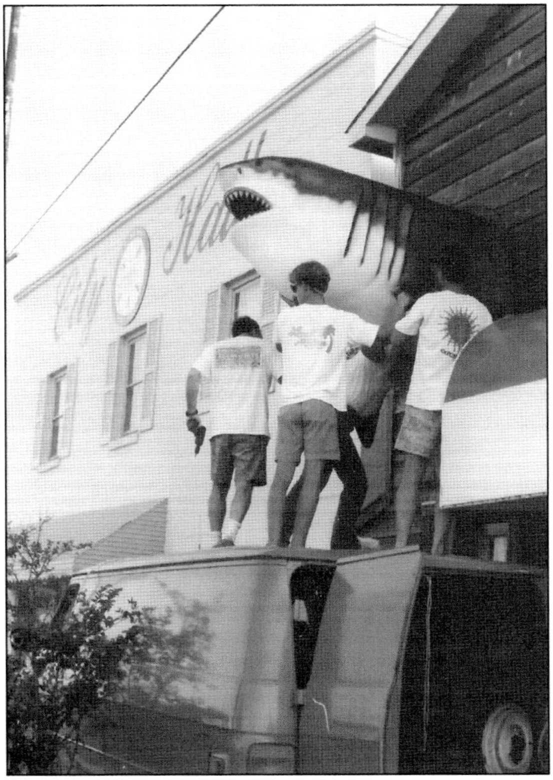

On a Sunday evening in 1991, Bill Perry, his friend Ed Hollingsworth, and Ed's two sons, Charles and Lee, arrived at Oceansports Surf Shop with a covert mission. Taking advantage of the building inspector's day off, they stood atop a van backed onto the sidewalk to mount a shark head on the shop's exterior wall, mere inches from city hall. "The next morning, we all showed up and said, 'Well, look at that,'" recalls Perry. "Nobody from the city ever said anything about it." The shark remains in place above the Bolus Law Firm. (Courtesy of Bill Perry and Betty Sue Cowsert.)

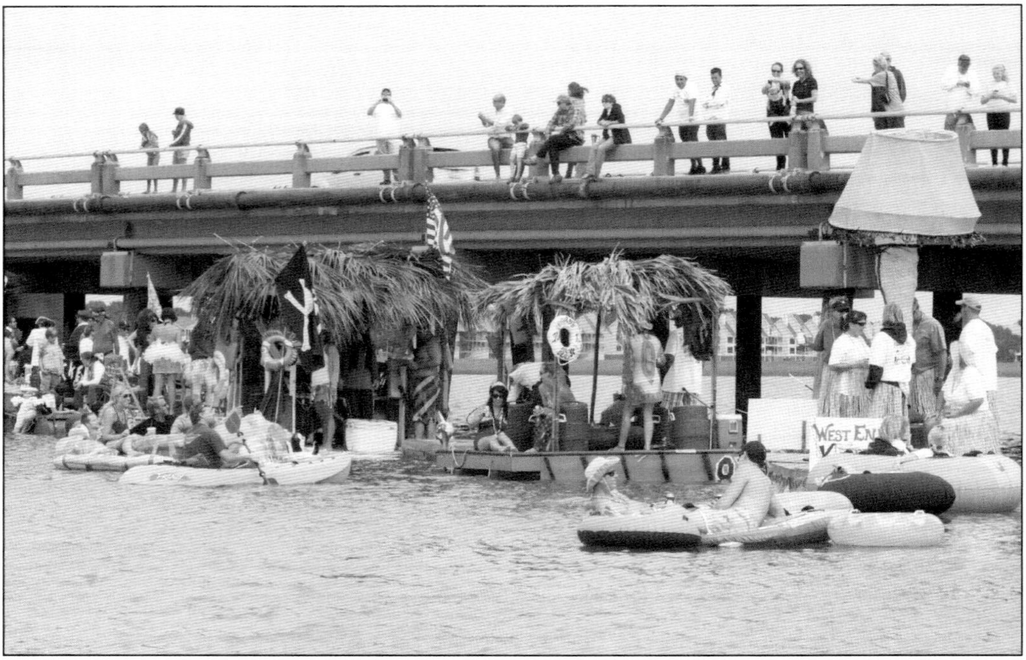

Since the 1980s, with a few gap years in between, residents have built outlandish "boats" each year for the Folly Float Frenzy, constructing sea-worthy barges out of anything that floats and setting sail down the Folly River. (Courtesy of Bonne Isenhour and the *Folly Current*.)

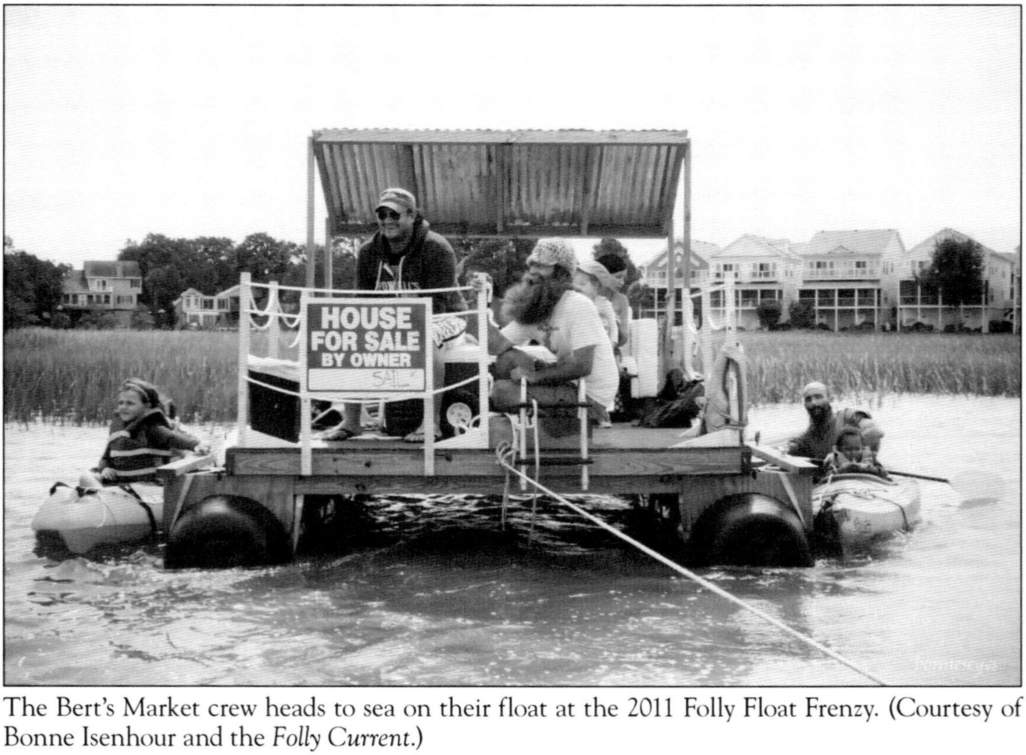

The Bert's Market crew heads to sea on their float at the 2011 Folly Float Frenzy. (Courtesy of Bonne Isenhour and the *Folly Current*.)

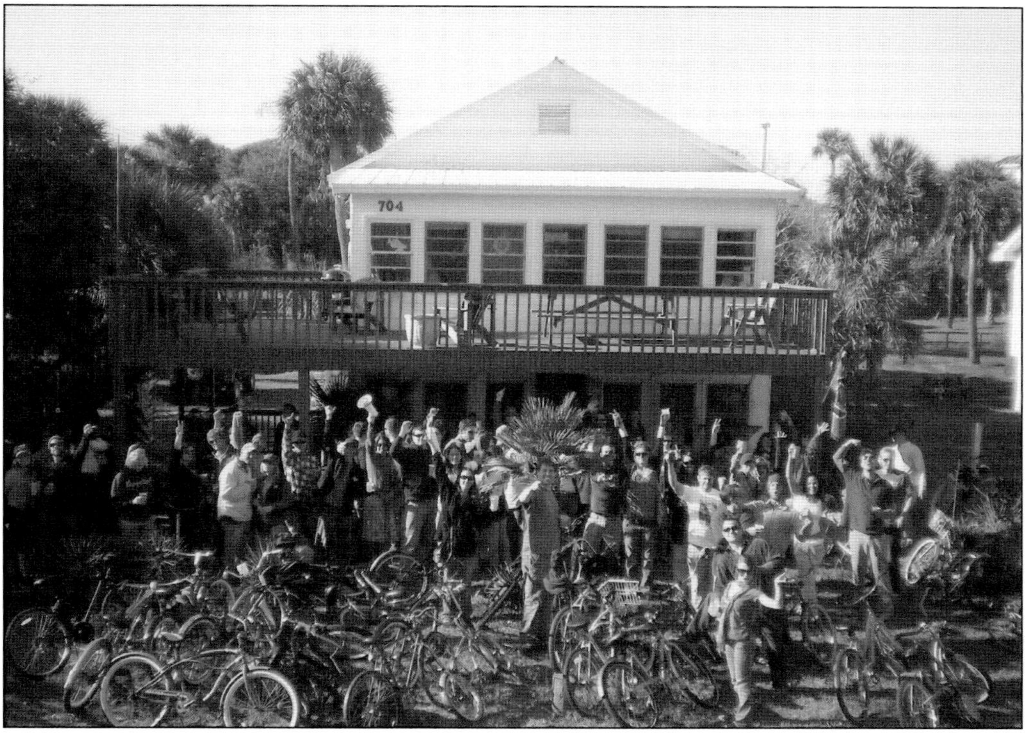

In the 1990s, the Bicycle Beach Bonanza grew into an annual February event for free spirits living on the island year-round. (Provided by the author.)

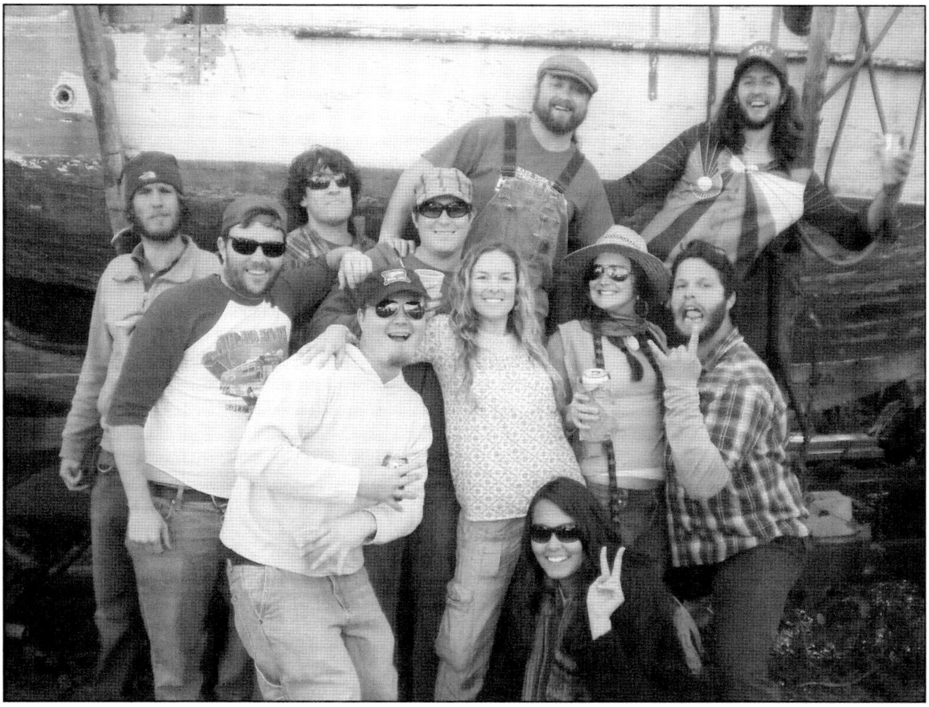
Folly still fosters a community of young people, many of whom go on to become business owners and professionals with successful careers based on the island. (Provided by the author.)

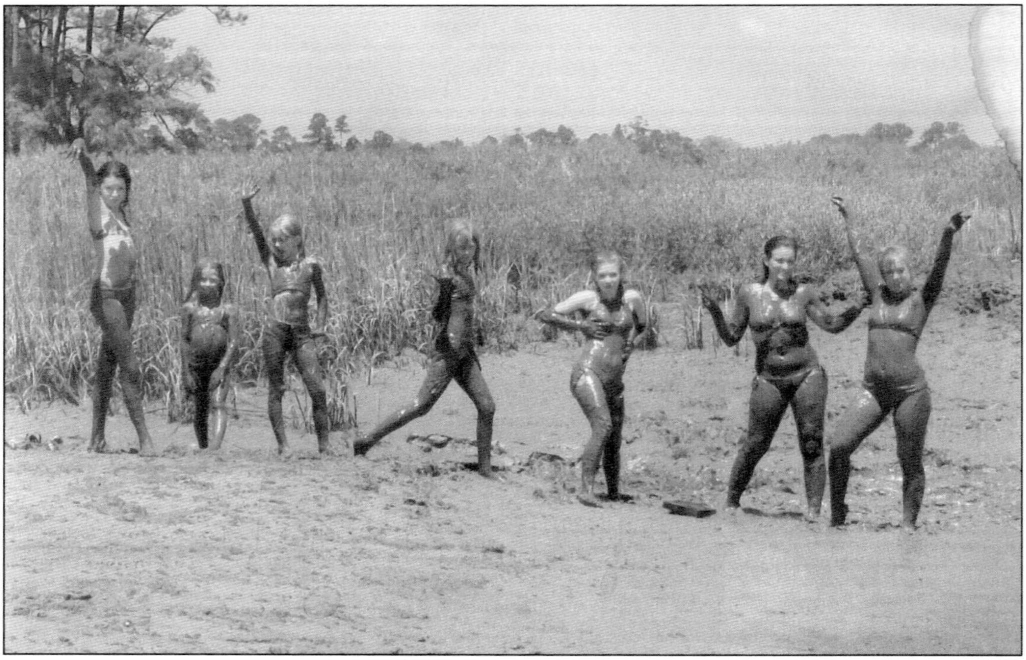

The true essence of Folly Beach—its vast expanses of salt marsh, wide-open beaches, and dramatic sunrises and sunsets—cares not what occurs in city hall. Exploring the myriad waterways separating Folly from the "mainland" is a pastime that will never go out of style. Here, local girls enjoy some "good clean fun" and show that pluff mud is nothing to be afraid of. (Courtesy of Wallace Benson.)

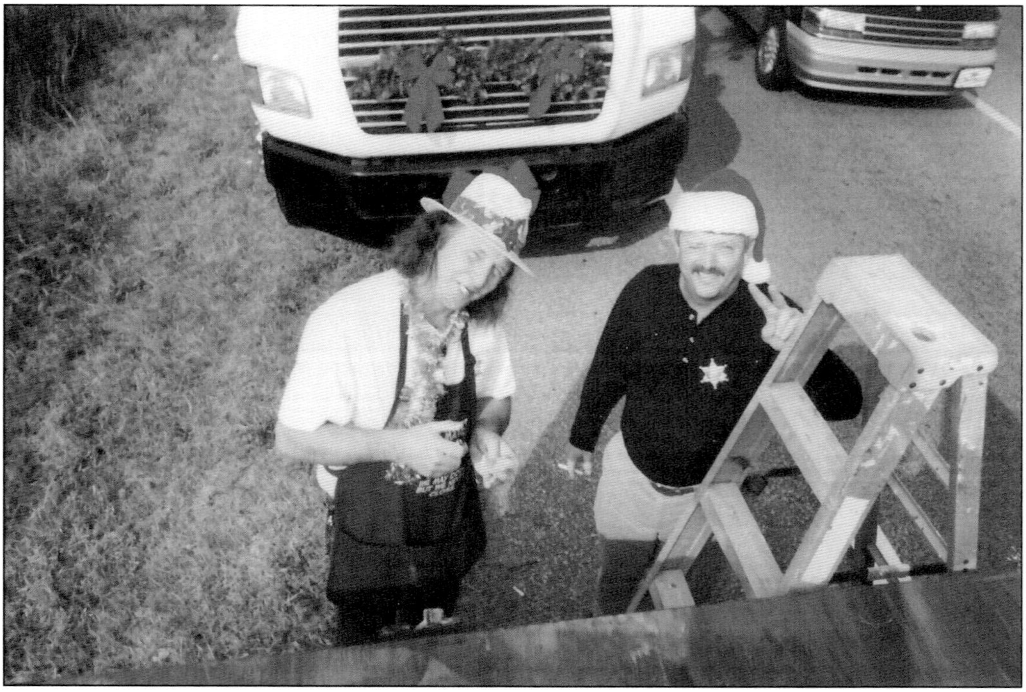

Bert Hastings (left) and Alfred Tiedemann are pictured here getting into the holiday spirit. (Courtesy of Bert Hastings.)

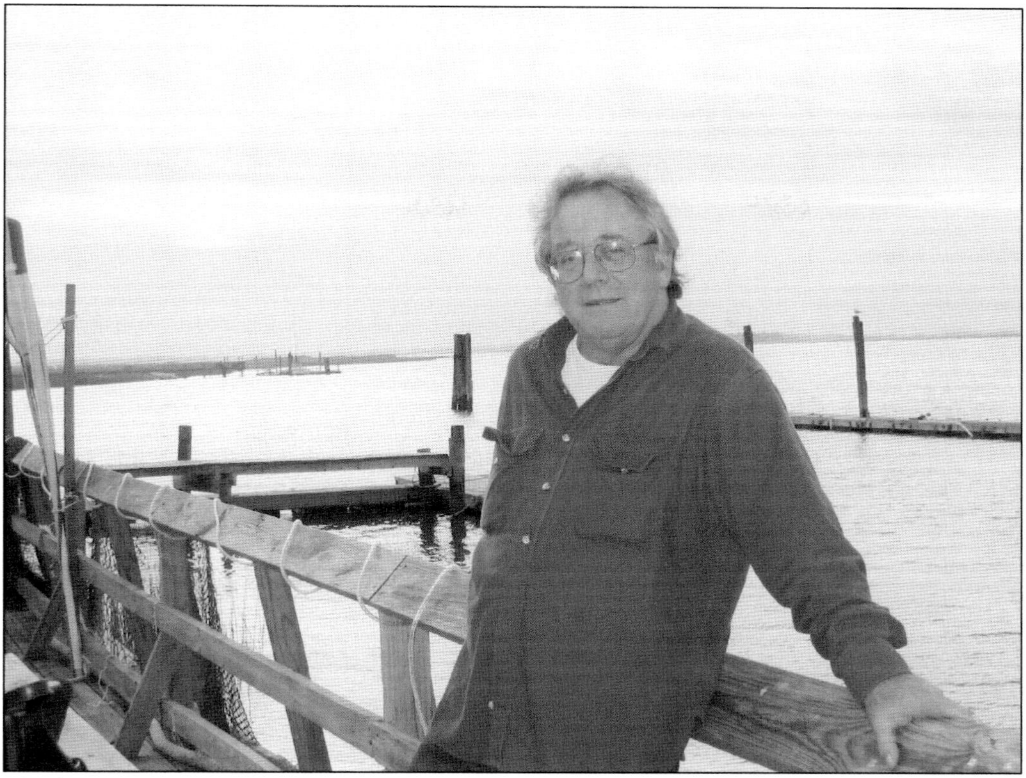

The late singer-songwriter Rick Huff is fondly remembered each year on February 23, officially regarded by the city as Rick Huff Day. In celebration of "the poet laureate of Folly Beach," friends remember Huff through his songs, including "Folly Beach Weather Report" (below). (Courtesy of the Huff family.)

Jimi Hendrix on the jukebox, Rush Limbaugh on TV
And everything that's in between is pretty much anarchy.
It's boozers and it's users and a few religious rights.
Sometimes they all mix it up and sometimes there's a fight.
But mostly they all get along and try to live together,
And talk about local politics and bitch about the weather.

Each time you pass by Crosby's, either way things change.
Comin' home feels better; leavin' feels so strange.
They're startin' to build condos; they're tearing houses down.
And some, who like it as it was, feel more lost than found.
If a man's home is his castle, then the river is our moat.
This song could be our battle cry if we all hit the note.
You can see those storm clouds brewin' like smoke along the ridge,
And will the last one comin' home tonight, please blow up the bridge.

'Cause she's wet, wild, warm and damp,
Hotter than a hooker in a Boy Scout camp.
I'm glad I got a piece of her before she got out of reach,
She's crazy but I love her, FOLLY BEACH.

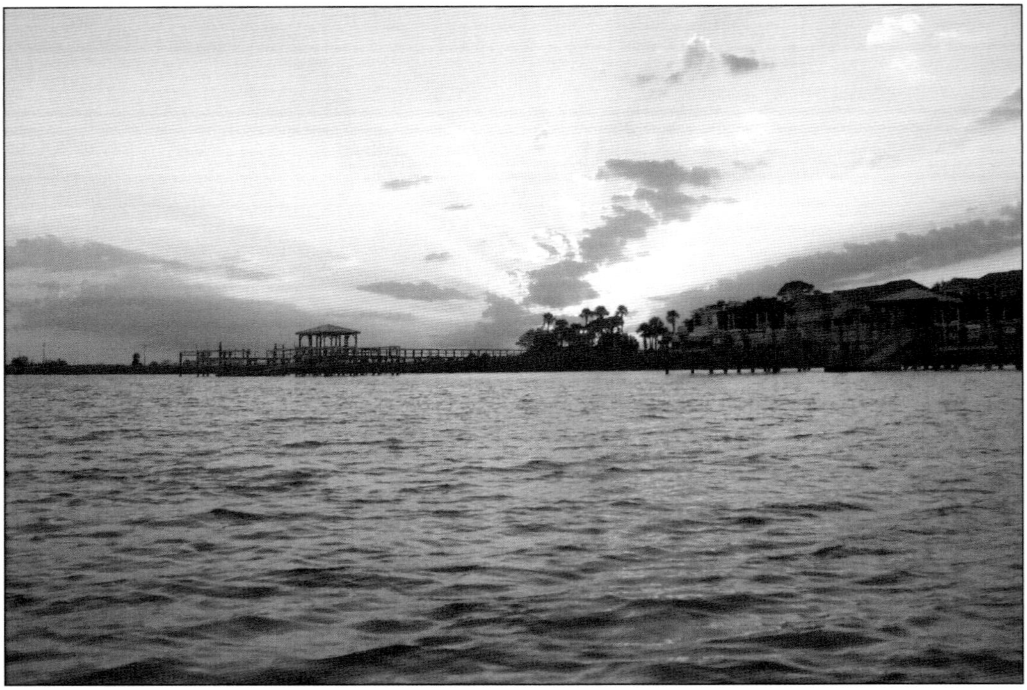

Whether you are in need of solitude or fellowship, Folly Beach can cure what ails you. (Above, photograph by the author; below, courtesy of Bonne Isenhour and the *Folly Current*.)

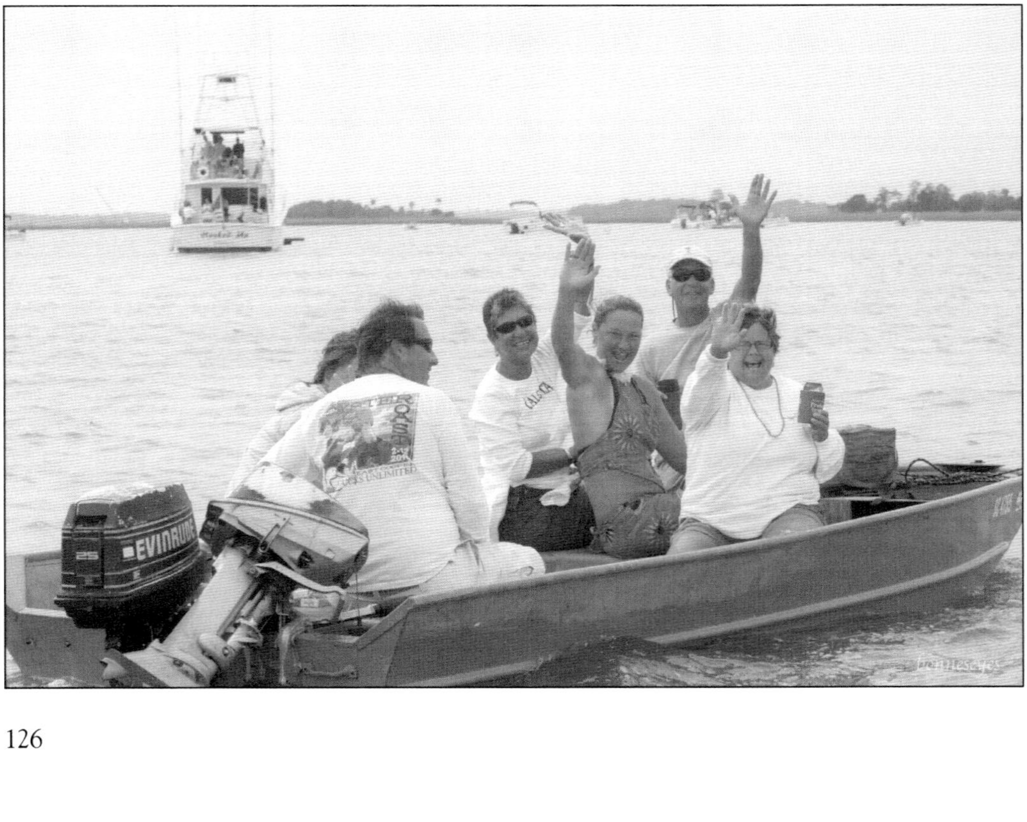

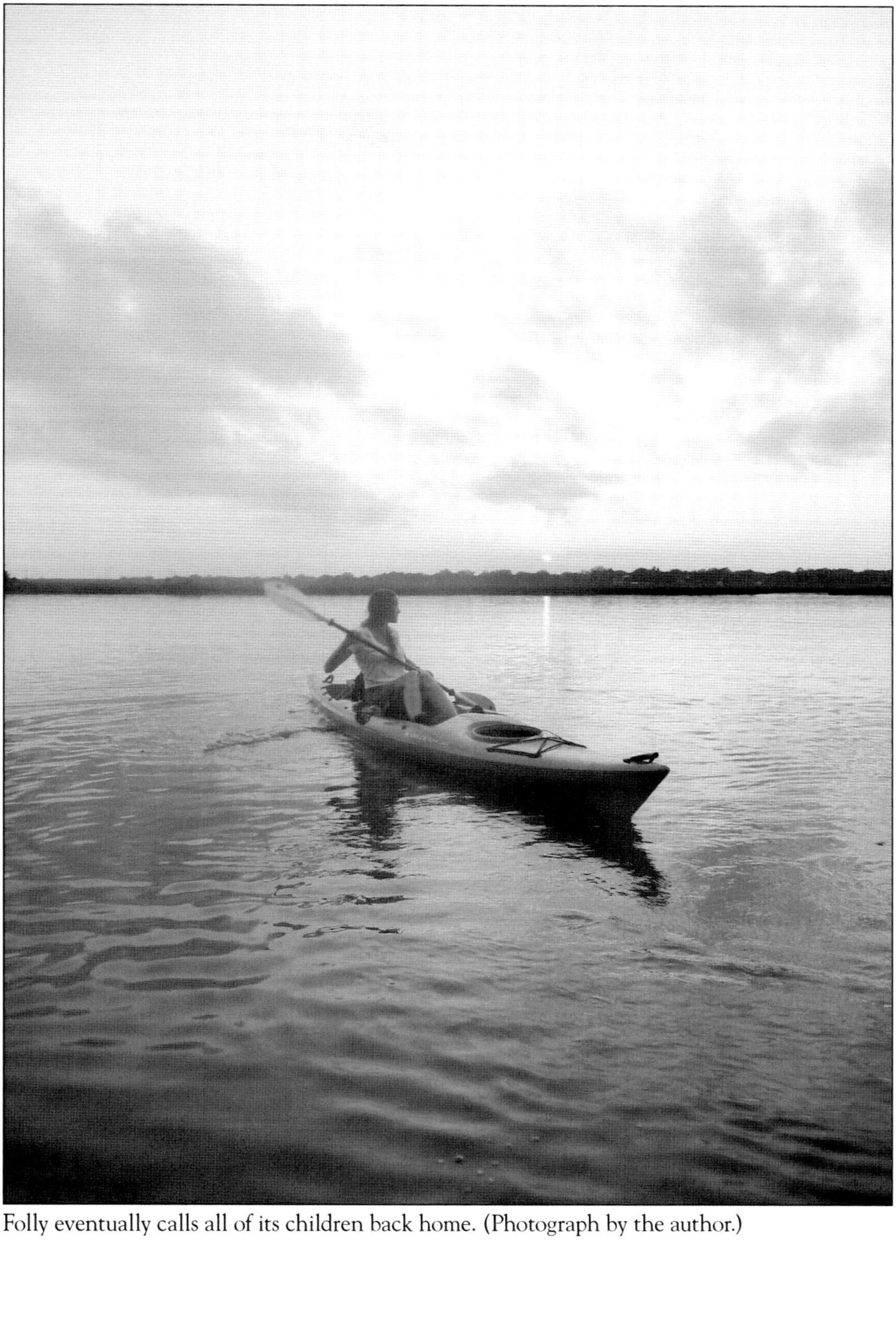

Folly eventually calls all of its children back home. (Photograph by the author.)

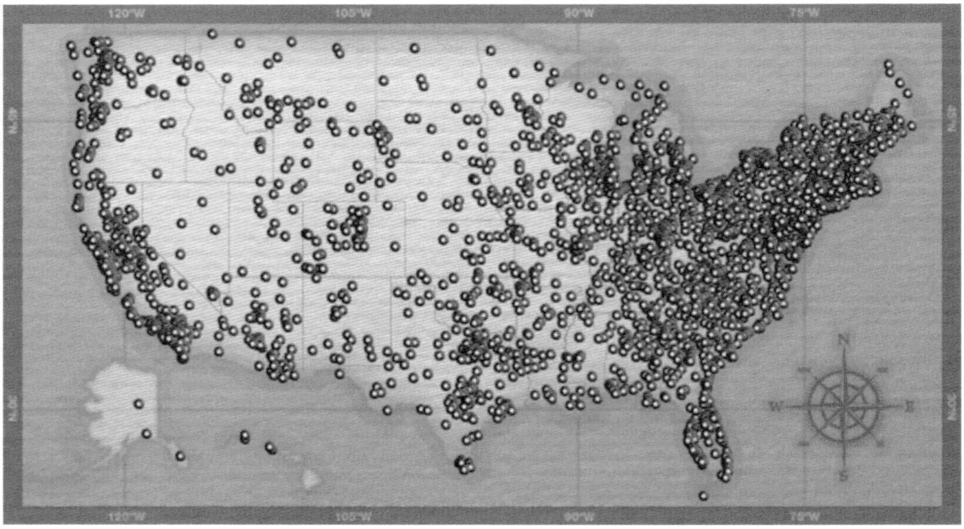